MW00338060

Guiding Mother Home

Guiding Mother Home

Understanding Alzheimer's Caregiving, The Law,
Sibling Struggles, Eviction And More Guns

Betty Alder

Hansville Press

Copyright c 2016 Betty Alder

All rights reserved, including the right to reproduce this book or portions thereof in any form whatsoever

For information
Hansville Press
info@oldparetnsandpurpletulips.com

Published 2016

ISBN-13: 9780986190827
ISBN: 0986190829
Library of Congress Control Number: 2016958623
Hansville Press, Hansville, Washington

Printed in the United States of America

Dedication

This book is dedicated to "Francine and Roger Malfait." Thank you for years of intense and sacrificial devotion to our family, years that would not let me shy away from the pain and unpleasantries involved in helping you through your declining years. I know my choices for you were not always appreciated, but I am ever hopeful that they were right choices, at least in the eyes of God. I remain optimistic that we will have opportunity to acknowledge that as we are reunited as a family in the presence of our precious almighty God in eternity.

The author's mother and father, Francine Malfait
7/6/1914 to 1/23/1995 and Roger 9/8/1910 to 2/2/1991

Note to Reader: At the end of this book are a number of questions to think about as you read this book

Life Before Alzheimer's

Mother encouraging
a snowball fight, c1950s

Mother instructing the author and her brother Rolf at one of our
many stops on a Cross Country Road trip, Early 1950s

The author, her dad, and brother Rolf at another roadside point of interest

Family outing to Spirit Lake and Mt. St. Helens, the author
and Rolf, Dad, Mother, and her mother's father

The author's dad and friends enjoying
digging razor clams at Long beach, WA

The author standing by a pie cherry tree

The author, an enthusiastic fisher-person, landed a
derby prize-winner, Columbia River, c1955

Gardening is a high priority at 516, partly necessity, partly enjoyment – the author among the corn rows

The author and her mother enjoy a trip to a local rose garden

Malfaits' abundant vegetable crop

The author's husband, the author and her mother
before Alzheimer's

The author's son in USMC dress blues

CHAPTER 1

Get On With The Fight!

DAD DIED FEBRUARY 2, 1991, maybe of complications of the stroke he had in 1990—maybe of Alzheimer's. His death certificate states under "Cause of Death: Pneumonia, 5 days; Alzheimer's Dementia, 5 years."

I'll never know for sure, as Mother is adamant in expressing, "No, we're not having anyone take Dad's brain out and drop it in some old metal pan and poke around in it. Over my dead body, that's just not going to happen!"

It doesn't matter. The cost quoted to me is $900.00. There's no money to fix a hole in the roof and a thousand other things. There for sure is no money for such a scientific investigation.

After Dad's funeral, the cemetery service of internment is a brief routine ritual. The rest of the day passes in its own mundane fashion. Don and the kids leave on their return trips for work and for school. Aunt Mavis and I return to 516 with Mother.

Aunt Mavis has been a pillar of strength, support, and wisdom for me these past ten years—ever since the irrational behaviors that fractured our family ties and alienated us from one another. I appreciate her more than I can ever say, but at the same time my guts are rolling as I recall events earlier today. Rolf's speech during Dad's funeral did not help in any way to make amends.

I amble through the living room, pitching my coat on the couch. It lands on top of a pile of laundry that needs to be done. I ignore that task as others have and continue through the dining room to the kitchen.

The whole kitchen—the counter, the table, the refrigerator, and every other surface—is over-loaded with casseroles-plus! I'm glad Aunt Mavis is here, and I have someone reliable to talk to about what to do next—and there's plenty to do around Malfairs' home besides eat casseroles.

Despite all that crowds in on me, the house that Daddy built for Mother has a new emptiness.

Aunt Mavis is short in stature, but she's *tall* in energy, brains, and organization. She's nine years younger than Mother and fifteen years older than I, and she's had more life/death experiences than I, both among friends and family. She's a problem-solver, and she's not afraid to roll up her sleeves and work.

I feel like the weak link in our partnership. I am tired and overwhelmed, and I have been for some time. Actually, overwhelmed feels normal, but I know I can't continue the pace and regularity of my trips to Ridgeview and do all that needs to be done by myself. Mavis and I both feel Mother is not doing well. Her disorientation has progressed since the previous summer when Mavis visited, and it's not all due to her current grief in losing her beloved mate of fifty-nine years. Mom and Dad's latter years were filled with a stormy kind of bantering and bickering but constantly girded by unquestionable devotion and caring. Mother now focuses that intense devotion on whoever is with her at the moment, expressing an obsessive drive to control and manipulate that person. Since Dad died Mavis has been the prime target as Mother repeatedly tries to force her to yield to her desire to go home with her. The house, the clutter, the filth, the cats, the dog--all factors which stress, depress, and totally discombobulate the rest of us--hang in oblivion to Mother as she constantly pesters Mavis.

Late in the afternoon after Aunt Mavis and I have worked to create some semblance of order to the kitchen, Mother chooses to launch one of her attacks. Whether consciously or subconsciously, it starts predictably, "Oh, Mavis, I just don't know what I'm going to--"

Mavis' patience is gone. "Francine, you need to go in your bedroom and close the door and take a nice long rest. Betty and I have some things to do. Now! Go!"

Mother turns toward the bedroom, "I just don't know what I'm going to do. I never thought Dad would go first."

"Betty, come on. Let's get out of here."

I follow Mavis out the front door, and we walk around the house to the back porch. "I have to get away from her, even if it's just for a few minutes. We've had an awful lot of garbage these last few days, and I thought the two of us could carry the cans out to the alley. I think tomorrow's garbage day. Besides, maybe Francine will feel better if she gets some rest."

As Mavis and I round the corner of the house, I see the two metal garbage cans on the back porch, filled past capacity, lids balanced precariously on top. "Geez, Aunt Mavis, I can smell the garbage from here!" Up on the back porch I drop one of the lids on the concrete step. "Oh, man, someone forgot to use can liners, and these are way too heavy for us to carry to the alley. Let me run in the garage and get some tools."

I return with a shovel and a pitchfork. We tip the cans over one at a time and tilt them down the back steps. While Mavis holds the can on the steps, I arrange a heavy duty garbage bag below and dig out the tightly packed debris with the pitchfork: rotting meat bones, wet fruit peelings, kitty litter and poop, and old soppy Depends, melded in togetherness with rotting casserole remains from sympathizers of Dad's passing.

"My God, Aunt Mavis, I just put out the garbage last week. If garbage accumulates like this when I'm not around to check, it may necessitate in the future another appointment for me with Mr. Manilow at Adult Protective Services--and with Judge Fox! Both of them will want to challenge my effectiveness as a garbage administrator, as well as a guardian. They may even refer me to someone in the County Health Department to discuss total condemnation of 516. Who cares? I can't even keep up with the household garbage here, and there's so much more garbage in my whole family--it's criminal!"

"Oh, hush, Betty! I've listened to enough complaining from Francine. I don't need to listen to that from you. Now let's hurry up and get these out to the alley and get on to that kitchen."

By evening Mavis and I are beyond exhaustion, but we feel satisfied with our cleaning work on the downstairs part of the house. We collapse on the couch for a cup of tea. Mother had a long afternoon nap, and we hear her stir.

Mother comes into the living room and instantly wants a cup of tea with us, but we persuade her to join us in finishing yet another casserole dinner. Mother is oblivious to the similarity of our dinner menu, as she dips from one dish and then another. Afterwards, she returns to the living room and stretches out on the couch and almost immediately dozes off under several sheets of crinkled newspaper.

Mavis asks, "Betty, what's upstairs? I wonder how much cleaning needs to be done up there."

"I don't know, Aunt Mavis. I haven't been up there since before I filed for the guardianship. At that time there were a lot of guns and Rolf's stuff all over his bedroom. Actually there were a hundred and forty-seven guns around the stairwell and in his bedroom. I don't want to even think of doing any cleaning up there. I really don't think all those guns should be in this house, but the upstairs was always Rolf's area, and I guess he thinks it still is.

"Well, Betty, he doesn't live here now. Aren't there two bedrooms up there? Francine could never get up those stairs. We better get as much cleaning done as we can while we're both here. You never know when she may want to--or have to--sell this house. Besides, I want to see for myself if all those guns are still there. Come on, Betty, and give me a hand with this plywood that's blocking the stairs."

Mavis and I tug the two sheets of plywood which are used to block the stairway away from the stairs and proceed up the steps to the area which was Rolf's bedroom in growing up years--and, of course, where he is *not* living now.

In the original floor plan of this house there is a guest room at the head of the stairs. Then an open hallway wraps around the enclosed chimney and leads into a longer hallway running the length of the house to Rolf's room. Storage areas and canning shelves are built in under the slanted roofline, closed off by shortened walls but with entrances on either side of the guest room. The rest of the hallway is lined with a double closet and more built-in storage cupboards. Rolf's bedroom on the north end of the house is the largest room in the house, the spaciousness having been created by enclosing three dressers and a large closet into the space under the slanted roof area where the ceiling would otherwise have been too low for a person to stand. When Mom and Dad built the house in the post-WWII years, they were very thoughtful about the needs for storage, growing children with various interests, and potential guests.

Mavis and I proceed up the stairs, where guns and fishing poles still line the stairwell, but at the top of the stairs we have only enough room for the two of us to take a couple of steps into the hallway. The guest room is a bloated Fibber McGhee's closet ready to regurgitate at any moment. Butts of rifles and clusters of bows and arrows stick out from under piles of clothing still on hangers and draped across boxes on the bed. I can read some of the ammo box labels: Winchester, Remington, Smith & Wesson. Atop the clothing piles on the bed nestled like baby birds is a cluster of hand guns, some in holsters, some bared steel. More boxes occupy the middle of the room, and a prized stuffed deer head bearing a 4-point rack rests in its own nest on top of more draped clothing and old quilts.

Mavis gasps, "Oh, my God, what is all this?"

"I'm not sure, Aunt Mavis, but this stuff is definitely not Mom and Dad's, and it wasn't like this the last time I was up here." I move to the right, stepping over a pile of rifles strewn in the floor and criss-crossed like a game of Pick Up Sticks. I wiggle my feet in between the rifle stocks, planting them on the hard linoleum surface, and begin counting weapons. I wonder if any of the weapons are loaded, but I don't take time to check.

Aunt Mavis is poking around the flotsam and jetsam of the guest room when I stop counting, "That's two hundred I can see and count from where I'm standing. That's fifty-three more than before--and that doesn't include the ones I can see in there on the bed in the guest room. It looks like a bombed out munitions dump up here." I stoop over and rearrange some of the guns, so Mavis has a place to walk. She edges past me into a narrow path around the chimney and into the hallway leading to Rolf's room.

Aunt Mavis expels another gasping repetition, "Oh, God, what's this?"

I share her amazement, "Wow! What happened to the closet?"

The closet doors are gone, and the closet space has morphed into an ammunition depot, housing buckets of spent shells, more than fifty boxes of live ammunition of various calibers, loading tools, and several containers about the size of three-pound coffee cans marked Gun Powder.

Aunt Mavis picks up some empty shell casings from the floor and drops them on the work table. "What *is* this? I've never seen anything like this."

"I think it's a work area for loading ammunition. I'm sure Rolf knows how to do that. I wouldn't touch any of that stuff. Some of it may be dangerous."

Aunt Mavis brushes imaginary dirt from her hands, and the two of us squeeze around boxes which appear to have been intentionally piled like alternating rows of bricks to form a barricade to the open doorway of Rolf's room. We follow a zig-zag pathway through the piles of boxes. Spaciousness of years past has been consumed by assorted clutter extending almost floor to ceiling. The pathway terminates beside a sagging twin bed.

I step toward the head of the bed, "I guess this is where Rolf sleeps when he *doesn't live here.* These olive colored sheets and pillow cases are kind of a modern color. I wonder if he bought them that color or if it's natural color-processing from his oily work clothing. I don't recall sheets like this in any washings I've done in all the years I've been coming here." I lift the pillow gingerly as if I might contract some deadly disease. "Whoa, look at this! The big square handle and protruding clip make me think it's a 45. I'm not sure, but I know it's loaded. Let's get out of here, Aunt Mavis. For all we know Rolf could have this place booby-trapped."

Mavis is already weaving her way to the exit. Any ideas of cleaning in this area have blown away.

I catch up to Mavis at the stairwell. "Wow, someone's been awfully busy. This is where most of that lumber Mother is having to pay for is being used--gun-racks and the loading table in the hallway. I didn't see the two saws Dad supposedly purchased. But as I recall, Rolf locked them up to protect them--well, he said it more colorfully--but he locked them up."

"You're right, Betty, someone's been awfully busy here, and I'm sure your dad didn't do this kind of work."

At the bottom of the stairs Mavis and I replace the sheets of plywood. "You know, Aunt Mavis, there's something I missed seeing up there. There used to be an old black trunk that sat over there in the corner under the little window across from the chimney. I remember it from my childhood. On rainy days Mother used to go through it with Rolf and me and tell us stories and show us mementos of family history. There was a family Bible and an old picture album and a lot of other neat stuff. I didn't see it today."

"I remember that trunk. Francine showed me some of that stuff on my visits out here. In fact, that may have been the same old trunk she moved out here with from West Virginia when she came to meet Roger. I think she had everything she owned in that one old trunk. You know, she was only about nineteen or twenty years old when she made that long trip on the train by herself."

"Yeah, I sure wouldn't have done anything like that when I was nineteen. I wouldn't have done that when I was my twenty-nine--probably not even now! But, Aunt Mavis, there was one particular item of special interest to me in that trunk."

"What's that?"

"It was a small round gold watch on a chain. It was kept in a black crocheted handbag that had tassels all over it and was closed by a draw-string at the top. The handbag was stored in that trunk. Do you know anything about it?"

"Of course, I remember that. It's a pendant watch which was an engagement present from my dad to my mother--that would be your Grandpa Ben and Grandma Lilly. He gave that to Mother sometime in the early 1900s. I remember seeing it on Mother when I was a little girl. When they went to church or some place special, she wore it around her neck. She carried that crocheted handbag, too. My mother died when your mother was only thirteen. I was about six years old then, but I remember seeing the watch especially then, because Daddy gathered all of us kids together back at the house after Mother's funeral, and he gave Francine the pendant watch and told the rest of us that she was in charge now that our mother was gone. And he was giving her Mother's watch because she was all grown up now. And someday when Francine was married and had a family she should pass it on to the oldest girl in her family. I think Dad wanted Francine to have it then as a symbol that she was the oldest, and he wanted her to take that responsibility seriously and to help him with the rest of us three younger kids. It really was your mother who raised us, you know. We were all pretty well grown when Dad married again.... Yes, I knew your mother had that watch, and she was supposed to give it to you when you were thirteen, or when you got married."

"Aunt Mavis, that's the story she always told us, but when I was thirteen, she said, "Betty, you're just not responsible enough to have this now. It will be waiting for you in this old trunk when you get married--or when you have a daughter. Then I want you to pass it on to her."

"So how come you didn't get it when you got married?"

"Oh, I don't know. Mother should have given it to me then, I guess, and maybe I should have ask about it. But it was one of those little details that got lost in the wedding plans. We both remembered it later and lamented that it would have been a wonderful piece of jewelry to wear for "something old" in my wedding. We talked about it once or twice after that, but eventually Mother said, 'Oh, I'll just wait till El is older and give it to her for her wedding. You'd probably lose it anyway, and El would never get it.' Well, more years have passed, and here we are today--I guess one could say I lost it! We can't find the trunk, much less the watch!"

A couple days later Rolf stops by and joins Mother, Mavis, and me for the evening news. In conversation Mavis asks, "Say, Rolf, what ever happened to that old trunk with the family Bible and some other heirloom things in it? I remember it was upstairs over there in the corner by the little window."

"That old trunk hasn't been in the upstairs corner for twenty years or more. I don't think there was anything of much value in it. I don't know what happened to it."

I could not restrain myself. "Rolf, I'm interested in that trunk, too. I'd like to know where it is."

"Yeah, why's that?"

"There's an old pendant watch in it, and it's supposed to be mine."

Rolf lurches up from his relaxed slouched position on the couch, "I don't know anything about an old pendant watch." He jabs a finger in my direction and shakes it in rhythm with his words, "But I can tell *you* one thing for certain--if it's there, it's there! And, my dear sister, you can have whatever it is you want when Mom, here, is dead!"

I pull myself up to a more alert position. "You know, Rolf, we've heard enough about death lately, and it's not your place to be making those kinds of decisions. This is not your house."

"Well, it's not *yours* either!"

Mother lowers her newspaper, licks her finger, and turns to a new page. "Now, Rolf, that watch has been Betty's for years, and she really ought to give it to El now that El is about to get married."

"See, Rolf, even Mother remembers I was supposed to have the watch before now. It has nothing to do with Dad's or Mother's death, or whose house this is."

Rolf turns to Mother, "Well, Betty don't need it right now."

My anger surges, as this object I haven't thought about for years becomes a priority. "No, Rolf, I don't *need* it right now, but I don't suppose you'd like it if I had some people come and move all those guns and stuff out of the way--or out into the front yard--so I could at least find a black trunk upstairs!"

Rolf's finger again jabs in my direction, "You let anyone move anything up there, and I'll just have to blow them away! Now, I'm not going to sit here and be involved in any more of this kind of discussion. I'm gonna get on my way, and *you* can sit here and get all worked up and have a heart attack!" He jerks himself the rest of the way off the couch and stomps to the front door.

I can't help myself. I laugh. "Oh, Rolf, that's too funny! Who's talking about heart attacks?"

Rolf disappears into the darkness as the front door slams.

Mother doesn't even look up from her newspaper.

Aunt Mavis gives a silent, hopeless shrug.

In a way, I feel sorry for Rolf. He is such a big over-powering oaf and paradoxically a cowardly little wimp. I may not feel that way if I'm the one who gets *blown away*, but anyone who has as much weaponry as he does in this house, on his person, and under his pillow, must be more than somewhat insecure.

Rolf's behavior tonight disturbs me, as did his speech at Dad's funeral earlier in the week. My stomach and my brain are roiling. I don't know about my heart; it may be roiling, too. Mother is relaxing in her oblivion. Aunt Mavis is caught between Rolf and me.

I need to talk to someone else.

It's not quite 8:30 PM when I call Pastor Ted, the minister who conducted Dad's funeral service. I need to thank him again anyway, and maybe he can help me see Rolf in a better perspective.

Pastor Ted himself answers the phone and tells me he and his wife would be delighted to see me in their home. They are not busy at the moment, and it's not too late. I should come on over.

I leave Mother and Aunt Mavis and do that.

Pastor Ted and his wife, Ester, are happy I have come to visit them. He tells me, "We both sort of expected you to come by with Rolf the other day before the funeral, but we're very happy you've come tonight. We remember you all so well when your whole family attended our church. Your mom and dad continued to attend for a number of years after you and Rolf were off to college and then out on your own.

"You know, it was about that time your dad even went with our adult Bible study group when we went to the Holy Land. I don't know why your mom didn't come with him. He wanted her to, but he said she just didn't want to leave home and fly on an airplane. He was so much fun on that trip. Some time after that, we lost contact with the Malfaits. The years just flew by.

"I noticed you had your beautiful family with you at your Dad's service. That was lovely to see."

"Yes, thank you, I'm very proud of my husband and my children. Don is back home now, and Nick and El both are back at college. They all left immediately after the cemetery service, but I'm staying on for a few more days with my mom and my Aunt Mavis. There's an awful lot to do around Malfaits' place, and as you may have guessed Rolf and I do not work too well together."

"Well, after talking to Rolf about the funeral service and hearing of his desire to be a speaker and *get some things said that needed to be said*, I sort of understood why you didn't come. We both remember Rolf when he was much younger. He was such a bright, enthusiastic lad. When we met him again a few days ago, we found him to be quite different. I had some real fears regarding Rolf's demeanor and his assertiveness in expressing his need to speak at your dad's funeral. I wasn't sure the thoughts he wanted to share about family history were all positive. I told him I expected anything he had to say at such a time should not be adding to any family member's personal grief. If he did that, I would have to see that he stopped, even if he wasn't through presenting. Also I emphasized that I would allow him only ten minutes to speak. If he took any longer than that, I would be coming out on the platform and kindly shutting him down. I really worried he might be planning to do some *grand-standing*.

"You know, Betty, I was sort of caught playing both the role of pastor and counselor—and that's okay. Rolf is very forceful, opinionated, and dominating."

"Well, Pastor Ted, I wasn't as domineering as Rolf about what should be covered in Dad's funeral service. I didn't have a need to chastise anyone publicly nor to set the record straight in any manner. I would have appreciated saying a few words to honor my father at that time, but it wasn't really that important. I'm sure Rolf wouldn't have approved of my speaking, and that would have just been another fight.

"However, after the service and some things that occurred this afternoon and this evening, I felt a strong silent urge to reconnect with you folks and provide some updating on our family from the *other* Mafait sibling's viewpoint."

For Pastor Ted and his wife, I recap some of our family saga, including explanation of the guardianship and the grounds on which it was sought. When I concluded my account, both Pastor Ted and his wife shake their heads in sadness or sympathy--or both.

"You know, Betty, I've been retired from the ministry for a number of years. I went back to school and became a certified counselor, and I've been running my private counseling service here in Ridgeview for twelve years now. I have dealt with a great number of troubled people--broken marriages, fractured families, and much more.

I sensed Rolf had some problems, and I was unsure about his intent in presenting at your father's memorial. Your account tonight helps me better understand Rolf's presentation. I would say his major hang-ups are most likely guilt, shame and jealousy. And, I must tell you the chances of Rolf ever changing are remote. He's been on his path too long. I don't think you should spend much time and effort worrying about him. You should keep your commitment to your mother. Get her out of that house and away from Rolf's negative influence and his deviant mental persuasion. If your mother is ever going to snap back, it has to be away from Rolf in a clean, healthy, positive surrounding."

"Pastor Ted, this is not new advice to me, I've been told by counselors, doctors, lawyers, social workers—well, you know---but I seem locked in my own paradigm. I can't possibly do it now. There's too much turmoil right now, and I don't have a clear plan."

"It doesn't have to be right now, Betty. It *shouldn't* be right now. Give your mom a month or so after your aunt leaves. During that time, prepare your plan to move her. Be ready to put it in motion quickly.

"Also, prepare yourself for her to hate you. She will. It won't matter. It will be the right thing to do. But, she *will* hate you, and probably as never before!"

"Oh, man, I don't know if I can face all that will be required to move her and to endure her wrath, too."

"Betty, you need to also be prepared to use law enforcement if necessary and proceed to evict Rolf. It is *not* his house, as your legal investigation has verified, and he will have to worry about himself and his guns by himself."

"Pastor, you're not the first person who has told me that either."

"Betty, from my perspective as a pastor in that Ridgeview church for twenty-eight years and more recently in these past twelve years as a counselor, I am quite confident in telling you that I think it's evident to anyone who has personal dealings with Rolf that he has mental problems. I'm going to say definitely sociopathic and maybe psychopathic. He may not be dangerous now--but potentially he may be.

"And, Betty, more from my pastoral view, you're going to have to truly trust God to see you through this.

"You *are* doing what's right and you must not stop now!"

I depart the pastor's home feeling my hazy idea has taken another step forward, being validated by someone with far more family, legal, religious, psychological, counseling and love experience than I have. At the same time I feel weaker than ever before, and the queasiness in my stomach does not cease.

Dear God, I'm not really up to moving Mother from the house that Dad built for her--her home of fifty-plus years--and evicting my brother. I've said all along I don't want to get dead trying to do what's right, legal, and honorable. But, God, I am duly impressed with the similarity of advice from all the professionals I have consulted: two lawyers, two ministers, two personal family counselors, two county guardianship counselors, and various senior citizen personnel. These are all professionals who have dealt frequently with family adversity. God, if it's You speaking through others, then I have heard You several times. But, God, I'm so scared.

A voice within me challenges, You've already accomplished what you set out to do--to prevent further physical abuse. Your family is on file with Adult Protection Service. You gained control of the major amount of income. You've paid up all of the small bills. You've prevented constant petty thievery. You've transferred property to your mother's name, and Rolf can't force her to sign property or anything else over to him. What more is there? Let the State take over this guardianship. It will be safer and saner for you, especially if Rolf does become dangerous.

An equally persuasive inner voice counters, Betty, you're just tired. Your work is not finished. Neither of you was brought up living in filth nor would it have been acceptable for you to tolerate loved ones sitting about in their own urine and feces amidst antiques, dog hair, junk drawer debris, original art works, crystal and cut-glass treasures, bath tubs full of used Depends, and piles of rocks collected by a senile family member. Betty, you are not going to join the ranks of dementia nor wear it as a facade of uniqueness as Rolf does. You are *not* finished!
GET ON WITH THE FIGHT!"

CHAPTER 2

It's Still Hard With Only One

AUNT MAVIS STAYS two months after Dad's funeral, and that is comforting to Mother and gives me some emotional and physical relief. For a woman who rarely cried during the past fifty years, Mother more than makes up for any missed tears in the time after Dad's passing. Her sobbing episodes are probably more disconcerting for those who must listen than for Mother herself, but her sister's presence helps quell these emotional outbursts.

Aunt Mavis says she has figured out the routine. "Betty, I know when she starts with 'It's just me and Rolf's old dog, Taco, and these old cats in this big old empty house--' I know right then she's going to go into one of her sobbing sessions. Then when the tears slow down, she's going to light into me about why she can't come home with me. It doesn't matter whether I respond to her weeping or not, she keeps her sing-song repetitive chant going, 'Oh, my God, I don't know what I'm going to do without Dad. I guess I'll just have to go home with you.' If I don't answer at all--if I don't try to reason with her--if I just ignore her--she will eventually stop. And *eventually* is not always in a short while. I just let her go for however long it takes."

"But, Mavis, don't you think other than that she's some better?"

"Oh, yes, I think she's a lot better now than right after Roger died. But if I stay here much longer, *I'm* going to be crazy. I need to be getting home. I'll have more work on my own place than I can ever catch up with. As for Francine, I don't think you're going to be able to keep her in her house much longer, even though that's what she wants. Rolf is no help. She certainly can't do all that needs to be done around the place. And you shouldn't be expected to do everything. I think you better get on with some kind of plan to move her."

"Aunt Mavis, I know moving her from 516 has to be in her future, but no matter what kind of care facility I find for her, she needs to be seen by a doctor and have a complete physical before she moves anyplace. I made an appointment for her, but the earliest one I could get is a month away. It will probably take me that long to persuade her to go to the doctor. I hate to even think about trying to persuade her to move from her home."

"Betty, I'm not so confident you'll ever persuade her to leave here. Maybe that lady you talked to before would take Francine at her place on Whidbey Island now that your dad is gone and Francine is by herself. Maybe it wouldn't be as much work now as when there were two of them."

"I'll check on that."

After Mavis departs for her home in West Virginia, I try to pick up the strands of my own family life, and I concentrate on my teaching efforts. At the same time, I dig out my journals and leaf back to the entries I made in interviewing nursing homes and foster homes when I was contemplating moving the two of them to a facility where they could live together. I make my list and begin phone calls with my questions.

I also continue regular trips to Ridgeview. Most of the time things are calm, even somewhat enjoyable. Mother and I discuss Dad's death certificate and the stated cause, which indicates pneumonia and Alzheimer's Dementia. I emphasize only the pneumonia part. We also talk of his insurance, the funeral costs, and her possible trip next summer. She is pleased Dad's insurance money covered the funeral and a headstone, and there will be some money left for her. We talk of *her* eventual death, and she understands her own life insurance is inadequate to cover her eventual funeral costs. She jokes that she can't afford to die.

We visit the cemetery and take pencil rubbings of kinds of things on other people's headstones which she likes. She wants flowers on her side of their stone. She likes dogwood and tells me it's really the North Carolina State Flower, but North Carolina is pretty close to West Virginia. Both she and Dad probably had people from there. She likes the idea of a tall fir tree and a deer on Dad's side of the stone. Dad would like that. She wants their last name to be in really big letters, so she can find it when she visits the cemetery.

Most of our conversations center around how she is to live and her possible eventual trip to visit Mavis. I carefully bring up the subject of living where she could have more personal care, but each time she is emphatic about staying as long as possible in the house that Dad built. She is calm but adamant regarding this.

On one of our enjoyable evenings as she and I finish a pleasant dinner at a local restaurant, without any provocation and unrelated to anything we had been talking about during dinner, Mother suddenly blurts out, "I don't know why Mavis got up on her high-horse so. She up and ran off without a word. She didn't even say good bye. If that wasn't bad enough, she didn't ask me to go home with her. She just gave me the shitty end of the stick!"

Diners at adjoining tables glance our way. Such an outburst has not happened for quite some time, and I am embarrassed and flustered. Knowing Mavis has gone way beyond the bonds of sisterhood to be helpful and comforting to all of us, I lean across the table toward Mother, make eye contact, and pat her hand. "Mother, Mavis did say goodbye to you. She sat right next to you on your couch in your living room. She hugged you and gave you a kiss on the cheek. Then she said she'd come back if you ever needed her, or you could come to West Virginia to visit her. She did invite you to visit, but she asked you to come next summer when it would be warmer and there would be more to do."

Mother jerks her hand back, maintains the eye contact, and raises her volume well above what is acceptable in the restaurant, "Why, she did no such thing! She just lit out of here!"

I lower my voice. "No, Mother, you're forgetting what really happened that last evening in your living room."

Mother wads up her napkin and tosses it onto the plate, maintaining high volume. "I do remember that last evening. She didn't need to act so shitty. She just got all pissy. She thinks she knows everything. She just whirled off without even a goodbye."

"Mother, no, *please*--Mavis didn't do that. She did say goodbye. Now, if you're mad at Aunt Mavis, that's fine--you call her and yell at her, but don't take your anger out on me here in this restaurant."

My firmness has no influence on Mother's volume. "I didn't take anything out on you! You need to tend to your own business and leave mine alone!"

"Yes, I can do that, if that's what you want. I can leave all your business up to you." I wad up my own napkin and toss it across the table near Mother's. "You don't seem to appreciate anything I've done anyway."

Mother's volume goes down slightly. "I do appreciate what you've done. I just think I can do things myself now."

"Maybe you can."

"I want to sell the house."

"Go ahead and list it."

"Well, I will."

We both sit for several minutes staring at the soiled napkins. I do not allow myself to speak. Mother breaks the silence, "Let's get out of here and go someplace where they have some decent pie and coffee."

I pay the check and leave a generous tip hoping to make up for any embarrassment we may have caused. Mother rises and takes my arm and we move toward the exit under the scrutiny of curious diners' eyes. Before we are out of the dining area, our waitress and the busboy descend upon our table and clear and scrub with vigorous motions, eradicating all evidence of our ever having been there.

In the car Mother says she doesn't want any pie and she's all coffee-ed out. We ride to 516 in silence. I walk her to the door and kiss her cheek. "Goodnight, Mom."

"Goodnight, Betty. Thank you for a nice dinner."

Mother gets her key in the correct position on the first try. When I hear the deadbolt release, I back off the steps into the darkness. From the porch erupts a raspy rattling sob and then a loud wail. "It's just me and Taco and these old cats in this big empty house..."

I stand in silence on the walkway.

Mother fumbles with the key trying to pull it out. Finally the door opens and she moves through the crack of light. She closes the door, oblivious to me still standing on the walkway at the bottom of the steps. I wait a few minutes, telling myself the desire to get past this part of her grief must somehow come from within her. I step back up on the front porch and place my ear against the cold metal of the wicket and listen. All is quiet within. A light comes on in the front bedroom. I step off the porch into the darkness.

I feel like chopped meat.

I am no match for my Mother!

The next morning when I go by the house to pick Mother up, her greeting is warm and friendly. She's all dressed except for her shoes and I follow her to her bedroom to help her with them. Bits and pieces of last evening's discussion of a potential trip to West Virginia have stuck in her mind. I assure her, "Mother, I know Mavis really would enjoy a visit from you next summer. She honestly wants you to come and stay with her for a while. I have to tell you though last night in the restaurant was embarrassing and hurtful. I was upset by the awful things you said about Mavis and how loud you were. You need to stop and think about when Dad died and you called Mavis and wanted her to come and be with you and help you. She did that. She came immediately and at her own expense, and she stayed for two months. You need to look at the positive things and not just that you didn't get your way about going home with her. You have to be in better control of yourself before you go on any trips anyplace."

Mother is quiet. "I do appreciate Mavis coming to be with me."

"I hope so, Mother, because no one else could have done that for you."

"I'd like her to come back next summer."

"Well, she's been here twice, and it really would be nice if we could work out a way for you to go visit her. You still have a lot of relatives in West Virginia, and I think it would be good for you. I may have to check you onto an airplane like a piece of luggage, though."

Mother chuckles, "Oh, Betty, do you think that would work? Do they do that on airplanes? Maybe it would be cheaper for me to go like baggage. I wouldn't mind. Could you go with me then?"

I shake my head and laugh at the strangely *realistic absurdity* of her reasoning. "No, Mom, I can't take any trips like that as long as we have two kids in college at the same time. It's too expensive. And, the airlines aren't going to let either one of us fly like baggage. But, if you're going to travel anyplace, you're going to have to be in good shape physically. The airline will want to know that you're in good enough shape physically to do that. That means you need to go to the doctor for a thorough physical check-up and have gotten a written confirmation from the doctor. Will you go to the doctor and have a physical?"

"Well, I certainly don't need one."

"I know you don't, since you haven't had one for twenty years or more. However, you can't fly unless you are physically fit, and that has to be verified by a doctor, not you."

I don't know if airlines have any such requirements, but I hope Mother will buy into my reasoning as I continue, "Besides, a doctor needs to check your incontinence problem."

"What problem do I have?"

"Incontinence--your problem with urinating."

"Well, I don't have that problem all the time."

"Mother, at this moment we're sitting here on bed sheets that are badly stained, and it couldn't have all come from your emaciated little cats."

"I know that, but my water problem only happens sometimes in the night."

"Yes, Mother, but if there's any chance it could be corrected, or at least lessened, wouldn't you like to try?"

"Of course I would."

"Does that mean you'll go to see a doctor then and have a physical?"

"Yes."

"Now, Mother, I'm not going to twist your arm, but I did make an appointment for you next month."

"With who?"

"With a Dr. Jared Jones."

"Well, he's that old fool who chases after women and has been married three or four times!"

"No, no--that's your old doctor of more than twenty-five years ago. He's no longer in town."

"Well, I'll go to my own family doctor."

"But, Mother, you don't have one."

"Yes, I do."

"Who?"

"Well, I can't think of his name, but I've been to him."

"Are you thinking of Dr. Kettle?"

"God Almighty, No!"

"Dr. Putnam?"

"Maybe. Yes, it might be Putnam."

I decide not to remind her that her friend Dr. Putnam died several years ago. "Well, if you decide not to go, I've done my best to help. And I am not going to hog-tie you to get the job done. I collected names from people we have dealt with for Dad--Barbara at the hospital--and the staff at the nursing home. I narrowed it to three names, and then I just picked the one that was mentioned most often. This Dr. Jones has a reputation for liking and working well with older patients, and he doesn't mind doing Medicare work. His name came up most frequently."

"Well, okay."

"Does that mean you'll cooperate, even when they ask you to step up on the scales or give blood?"

"Yes, but I don't like it."

"I know, but I'll take you in and stay with you, if you like."

I head for the kitchen and what I'm sure will be a sink full of dirty dishes.

Right now we're both feeling comfortable with the doctor appointment, but deep inside I know anything can happen in a month.

Anything can happen in an instant around here.

CHAPTER 3

~∞~

Mother's Appointment With Dr. Jones

ON MY NEXT trip down I'm impressed that Mother has not forgotten our previous conversation about the doctor's appointment for a physical, and she seems much improved in alertness generally. She is eating well, at least at Sally's, the little corner cafe just a block down the street.

When she and I stop there for coffee, Sally gives me a quick update as she puts our cups down on the counter and smiles at Mother. "Your Mom's one of my best customers. She's in every morning about nine o'clock. She's doing real well on her own." She pats Mother's hand.

One of the regular patrons seated at the back booth with a couple of friends calls out a hello and asks, "Francine, are you going to be moving up near Betty now that Papa's gone?"

Mother is loud and clear, "'Lord, no, Betty and I can't live that close to each other."

The three in the booth laugh and shake their heads.

After coffee, as Mother and I walk back down the block to 516, I ask, "Is Rolf still working?"

"Oh, yes, but he's in and out."

"Since Mavis left, I've noticed Rolf seems to be around more. He's answered the phone the last couple of times I've called. Are you okay with that?"

"Oh, he's back to his usual cantankerous self."

"Are the two of you getting along?"

"Sort of. I just ignore him when he gets like that, which is most of the time. But, you know, he's better company than no company at all. I guess I'd say he hasn't really been bothering me or screaming at me--and he doesn't ask me for money anymore."

"Well, that's good, because you sure don't have any to give him, especially not if you're going to save for a trip."

Mother and I go about doing our errands and grocery shopping. When we return, Rolf is at the house sprawled out on the couch. We both have our arms full of groceries, but he makes no effort to help us. We struggle through the living room to the kitchen and unpack the bags. I curse quietly to myself, 'Damn, this seems like the old Rolf to me.' Mother heads for the bathroom, but she doesn't quite make it, and I can hear her grumbling in the living room about 'They don't make these Depend things like they used to.' At least she knows she needs to go. That's an improvement. Also she is wearing the Depends, and she no longer saves the used ones in the bathtub for my next work day.

Mother is busy in the bathroom, and I pass through the living room on my way to get the last of the groceries. I try to be cordial to Rolf. "How do you think Mother is doing?"

"I guess okay. I really haven't been around. I've been working in Morton the last three days." Rolf crosses his arms over his chest.

"What are those horrible looking sores on your hands? Did you hurt yourself driving the log truck?"

"Ah, Mom was fussing at me yesterday about my hands and wanting me to go to the hospital. I poured some alcohol on them."

"What *is* that? The wounds are open and look full of puss."

"I don't know. I guess I bumped myself, and then it got infected."

"Want me to go back to the store and get some hydrogen peroxide?"

"No, that stuff don't do no good. I been pouring PineSol on them."

"You're putting PineSol on open cuts?"

"Well, it don't feel so good, but it must be doing somethin' about the infection."

I wince. "I don't think that's a good thing. I'd be happy to get the disinfectant for you, but if you want to inflict self-pain, that's fine, too. They're your hands." I figure Rolf has inflicted enough pain on other people that I don't really care very much what he does to himself. But I offer the third time, "I'll gladly go get the peroxide."

Rolf growls something unintelligible, and I go on about my business.

For all the warm fuzzy feelings and the sense of encouragement for Mother's improvement, it is only a few days after this trip that my telephone rings about 2:30 AM. Mother is stressing, "I don't know what those insurance papers were I signed with you the other day. I tried to tell Rolf, and I couldn't get it straight."

"You signed a claimant form for surrendering Dad's two policies."

"You're going to have to get down here right away and explain that to Rolf."

"Mother, I'm not coming down there to explain anything to Rolf. It's the middle of the night!"

"Well, you're going to have to help me explain it. He's all angry about it."

"Mother, those were very legitimate papers. You have to surrender the policies to collect on the insurance."

"Well, I don't want any crooked business going on behind my back."

"When have I ever done any crooked business behind your back?"

"You haven't, but I don't want that kind of thing happening!"

"What is it Rolf wants to know that has upset you so? Is he suggesting that crooked business is going on?"

"You'll have to ask him."

"Mom, you're the one calling in the middle of the night. You tell me."

"No, I'm not going to carry any tales. You're going to have to come down and have a long talk with him."

"Mother, I was just there, and I tried to talk to Rolf. All he would do is pout and sulk. I am not going to play his stupid game. I've been doing your business stuff just fine, and I work very hard at it. He hasn't been any help at all. You have to remember, he was the one who took the insurance policies and *forgetting* he had them just delayed the process. He probably did the same thing with the wills."

Oh, Betty, they're around here somewhere. We'll both look some more next time you're down."

"Mom, that's the kind of stuff I have to put up with. Rolf can't manage himself nor his own personal finances! I pay your bills on time. I'm trying to get you out of debt. I'm trying to help you save for a trip next summer.

Mother, I'm not going to let you ever again accuse me of stealing or any other kind of crooked dealings. I *haven't*, and I *don't!*"

"Well, I didn't say you did."

"No, but it sounds as if Rolf is doing exactly what you and I talked about. You were fine as long as Mavis was there. Now Mavis is gone home and Rolf's back hanging around, getting inside your head and creating doubts about what's going on with your business. You told me you were going to ignore that stuff."

"I just want everything to be honest and not behind my back."

"Mother, I have to take your checkbook and your budget book to the judge in the Superior Court. In the court process I have to account for everything I do. The judge must be convinced I'm being honorable in carrying out your business. If that same judge analyzed what Rolf has done to you financially, I'm rather sure it would be less than honorable. Now, it's late and I'm going back to sleep, if I can. I have to teach tomorrow, and you need to go to bed."

"Well, you explain all this to Rolf."

"Mother, if Rolf needs to know something he is welcome to call me. If it's not urgent, I will see him next time I'm down there. Now, let's both go back to bed where we belong. Goodnight!" I put the receiver down without waiting for her goodbye.

Damn, I hate Rolf's insecure little tantrums. He's a fifty-five year old man. I hate what he does to her emotionally. A time or two I've thought it's all her dementia, and she works herself into spells of emotional turmoil. But it's not like this when I'm there, and despite the sobbing spells, it didn't happen when Mavis was there. Rolf goes out of his way to cast doubts and fears in her. He's sicker than she is.

Dear God, help me to be the vessel to carry out your will for justice and honor for Mother. I pray also that even though Rolf seems totally irredeemable to me, that in your divine power you might shake him to his very soul with an awareness that the whole earth was not created just to somehow screw him over. I can't deal with him, God. I hate what he does to her, and most of all, I hate what the notes and financial records of Malfaits have shown he has done to them over the years. At the same time that I hate what he's done, please help me not to hate him. I need your constant guidance with my own shortcomings, and especially my un-forgiveness. Please lighten the load for all of us who are having to deal with the related stresses and strains of this family tragedy. Please comfort Mother and help her to regain her strength and interest in living and making her own life useful, and allow this progress despite the hatefulness and petty jealousies that are constantly pushed upon her by Rolf. Dear God, as I have often referred to your blessings in this family ordeal as being the purple tulips of my life, please continue your purple tulips now--for me and for all whom I love and care for!

In the following days and weeks my prayers frequently decry my lack of ability to work with Rolf. I accept that Rolf's redemption is between Rolf and God, and my lack of forgiveness is my problem. I find myself asking God to be with Rolf, to bless Rolf, to help him find himself and happiness and to be able to recognize God's will for his own life. I would really like my brother back, but if that cannot be, I will continue to pray for this stranger named Rolf. I will consciously separate Rolf's behavior from Rolf, the person.

Spring drags on. Communication from Social Security informs Mother that she will not receive any portion of Dad's previous amount, because hers was the larger check, but they are pleased to inform her that in about three weeks she will receive the once-in-a-lifetime death benefit of $255.00. The same mail delivery brings an overdue notice from the city for a $500.00 assessment for a mandatory city sewer hook-up. Also, Fibex Credit Union has an overdue notice for Rolf's mortgage payment of $468.90, a bill due to an agreement made between Rolf and Dad several years ago. The loan was made to consolidate Rolf's debts when Mt. St. Helens blew up and he lost his logging job and his truck. Mom and Dad co-signed for the loan with a verbal agreement that Rolf would satisfy the debt when he got back to work. Rolf has been back to work, but he has never paid anything. Dad's deceased and Mother's income is reduced.

Rolf's mortgage takes almost half her monthly money, and she has only about $550 to pay for the sewer hook-up and back taxes, fix a leaky roof, have food to eat and other necessities--and save for her trip? Ha! She owns acreage on Whidbey Island, but I can't sell that property, because there's no road access, although I have negotiated with property owners on the other side of her land for this purpose. I was told by the property owner there that the law would eventually force him to give me a way in to her land, but he would make me jump through every possible legal loop available to avoid giving her access. I would have to sue him to get even that, and when we were finished he would give the bare minimum required by law—he thought that to be eleven feet in width.

I feel dumb, numb, defeated. This whole scene is so fecalistic the new bigger sewer hook-up couldn't even begin to clear the lines.

I strive for any shred of positiveness. I do not discuss the serious details of Mother's financial situation with her. Instead she and I visit the cemetery with an armload of beautiful spring flowers from the yard. The visit goes well, and we extend our afternoon with a drive down the river to Clarkston Point. The setting sun casts dramatic orange and magenta streaks across little islands scattered down the middle of the river and on the hills in the distance. Mother and I have a pleasant dinner in a restaurant at the Point. As the sun concludes its spring kaleidoscope, I am momentarily lulled by my escape from her financial worries and a sense of improvement in her well-being. At the same time she is lost in nostalgia intermingled with her grief.

On the way home she tells me, "Poor old Dad--he won't be able to go to the beach and dig razor clams this year."

"No, he won't," I sympathize.

A couple of minutes later, "It's too bad Dad won't be able to go to the beach and dig razor clams this year."

I feel funny about her repetition, but I again agree, "No, I guess he won't be doing that. Of course, he really hasn't dug clams for five or six years anyway."

"I'd like to go down to Clarkston Point again some time and take Dad's hunting partner, Henry, to dinner. He's been so lonesome since Norma died."

"That would be nice, Mom. We'll do that the next time I'm down."

There is a long quiet period as I drive on toward home. Suddenly Mother jerks forward in her seat, "Betty, Betty, where do we turn?"

"Turn for what?"

"Where do we turn to get to that nursing home? We have to hurry and get down there and visit Dad."

"Remember, Mom, he's not there. He died, and earlier today we visited his grave site. We put cut rhododendrons and tulips and daffodils on his grave."

"Oh, yes, he died the 25th of April, didn't he?"

"No, Mom, he died February 2nd. It's been over three months now."

An awkward, choking quietness engulfs us both for several minutes, then Mother asks, "Is Dad really dead?"

"Yes, Mother, he died February 2nd. Remember we took flowers from your yard today and left them on his grave this afternoon."

"Yes, of course, I know that."

"Mother, this drive along the river and dinner at Clarkston Point have brought back lots of happy memories of fishing, hunting, clamming and such. That's kind of confusing when you're tired and full of a good dinner and full of a good day. You've been thinking a lot about Dad today. I know you miss him. And some of the memories are almost like he's right with us. That's okay. Our brains play funny tricks on us like that sometimes."

"I know. I feel confused all the time. I miss him so much. I put out my hand in the bed last night, and he wasn't there. Then I remembered he's gone. It's so confusing."

Mother doesn't cry, but she seems tired from the struggle of trying to figure it out. She is quiet and sad. A few minutes later she breaks the silence, "Is Dad dead?"

"Yes, Mom. He's been dead a little over three months. We all miss him. This confusion will continue to come over all of us. It's part of grieving for him. It's okay."

A little later when Mother is secure at home and ready for bed, and just before I depart for The Sterling Motel, I remind her, "You don't lie in here reading magazines tonight, Mom. You need a good night's sleep, because your doctor's appointment is tomorrow morning at 10:00 AM. I'll be here early."

"I don't need to go to any doctor."

"Mother, this is the appointment for the physical."

"I don't need any physical, and I don't want to go."

"Oh well, I'll still be by early to pick you up. If you decide you're not going, then you're not going. I told you before I wasn't going to twist your arm."

The next morning I arrive at the house an hour early.

Mother tells me, "I'm ready for my physical, and I've had my bath."

I look around the bathroom and see a pile of laundry in the tub mixed with a couple of used Depends, but there are several towels hanging out to dry on the rod above the tub, and her hair is pretty and fluffy. Who knows--maybe she did take a bath. "Mom, are you going to change those slacks and that shirt?"

"No, this is what I wore to dinner the other day, and I'm not getting all gussied up for some physical. This outfit is fine."

"They are indeed the same black slacks and purple turtleneck you wore when we went to dinner at Clarkston Point yesterday." Under my breath I mutter, "And you wore them all weekend. I haven't been able to get you to change, and I'm sure I won't be able to get you to do that this morning. I'll be lucky to get you to the doctor's office. I guess your clothes and your level of cleanliness will just have to be part of the doctor's observation."

When we arrive at the medical center, we are less than a dynamic duo. Mother is shuffling and seems especially wobbly this morning. She's hanging hard onto my arm. We locate the correct office, and as soon as we enter she plops down in the nearest chair. I get the paper-work and begin to read the questions with her. She is cooperative about letting me help her with this chore, and she's fairly clear with her answers.

Shortly a nurse opens the door and calls, "Mrs. Malfait? Please come in."

I ask, "Mother, do you want me to go with you?"

"Of course not. I can see the doctor by myself."

She disappears through the door. A few minutes later the nurse returns and asks, "Would you mind keeping your mother company? It may be a few minutes before the doctor can see her."

"Oh, sure." Noting mild desperation in the nurse's face, I jump up quickly and follow her to the patient room.

Mother is dressed in a cotton gown and seated on the end of the examination table with a paper sheet over her legs. "They sure don't have much for warmth around here. This flimsy little shirt doesn't even close up over a body, and there's no warmth at all to this little paper sheet."

Mother and I find plenty of other little things to chat about, especially since she hasn't been in a doctor's office for a while. Dr. Jones doesn't keep us waiting very long. He has a friendly greeting for both of us when he comes in.

Then he turns to Mother, "Now, Mrs. Malfait, let me see your paperwork here. Hmmm. Francine--that's a pretty name."

"Thank you."

"May I call you Francine?"

"Yes, that'll be fine."

"You know, Francine, I was working at the little desk in the hallway when you walked by with Sheila, my nurse, after she weighed you. I heard the two of you chatting, and I noticed that you slur your speech a little bit and you've got a shuffling gait as you walk. How long has that been going on?"

"I don't slur, and I get around the best these old legs will carry me."

"Well, you keep getting around as best you can. Getting around is good for you. When is your birth date, Francine?"

"July 6, 1914."

"Very good. Do you know who the Vice President of the United States is?"

"I have no idea, but that Sadam Hussein is creating havoc in the whole Middle East. We should just go in there and wipe him away."

"What year is this?"

"1989."

I shake my head and glance at the doctor. He continues staring at the papers on his clipboard. Mother is unaware that it's 1991, but at least she got her birthday right.

The doctor continues, "What's today's date?"

"Let's see, this is July 25th."

Dr. Jones makes a note on his paper. It's really April 25th.

"Say, Francine, I don't want to be too personal, but what is your age?"

"I'm 74. I was born in 1914."

Dr. Jones scratches some figures on his note pad. "Well, if you were born in 1914, you must really be 76 right now, and this next July 6th, you'll be 77. Is that right?"

"No, that is not right. I'm 74 right now."

"Oh, okay." Dr. Jones begins talking to Mother about Occult Hydrocephalism, explaining that it's a correctable condition in which persons cannot hold their urine. I'm sure he's going through this explanation for me, but he continues at every opportunity to make eye contact with Mother as he checks her nose, throat, and ears, and listens to her heart. "I'd like to know if that's a problem you have, but I can't tell until I send you for a CAT scan. Then I can accurately diagnose. Francine, have you ever had a CAT scan?"

"No, I don't think so."

"Do you think you have an incontinence problem?"

"What is that?"

"Do you ever have trouble holding your urine?"

"No. Never."

"When you sneeze, do you ever have trouble holding it?"

"No."

I struggle to keep my mouth shut. Lately *I'd* have to answer yes to that last one.

"Do you wear Depends, Attends or anything like that?"

"Yes, but I should be getting over this "old time of the month" soon."

Next Dr. Jones goes through a lengthy list of "Have-you-ever-had-questions."

Surprisingly Mother's answers are quite accurate.

"Do you take any medications?"

"No."

"Aspirin?"

"No."

"Well, Francine, you're remarkably healthy for your age, probably due to not taking any medications nor going to a doctor, huh?"

Mother chuckles and answers, "Absolutely."

"So why did you come to see a doctor today?"

"My children made me come."

"Yes, children do get kind of bossy, especially when they're older."

Mother chuckles and rolls her eyes toward me.

"Now, Francine, will you allow my nurse to help you and you give us a urine sample?"

"No, I don't have any urine right now."

"Oh--okay, you lie back and rest. We'll have you try again a little bit later."

The nurse helps Mother lie back on the table, and covers her with a warmed sheet. Mother expresses her appreciation to the nurse, as Dr. Jones signals me to follow him to his office.

We talk of the general situation, the fact that I have recently received a legal guardianship, Mother's forgetfulness, disorientation, cleanliness issues, and Rolf's presence in the house not being constructive emotionally, physically or financially. The doctor is very encouraging and feels that right now it's especially important to not be too demanding with Mother.

"After all, Betty, she is remarkably healthy, despite a little dirt. I think you're going to have to accept that you cannot be responsible for solutions to all the problems inherent in your family situation, and a little dirt isn't going to hurt anyone."

I'm sure Dr. Jones doesn't realize how *little* dirt there is in the Malfait house. I continue to listen as he gives me his perspective of faith and the Christian obligation to parents. Though I didn't ask for his sermonette, and I think much of what he is saying goes beyond normal medical doctoring, it does fit reasonably well with my personal philosophy and beliefs.

Dr. Jones leans toward me and gently taps his pen on his clipboard emphasizing, "I'm sure you're working overtime fulfilling your Christian obligation. And, as far as your description of your brother Rolf is concerned, his condition is probably not a disease. Rolf makes choices, and he chooses to be how he is. He has been at it so long he is not likely to change. I would encourage you to continue to be faithful and prayerful, and to be listening for direction. Betty, you need to let go and let God do *his* own work on *his* own time schedule."

Dr. Jones and I go back into the examination room where Mother is still lying back. The nurse joins us and assists her to sit up. The doctor again asks, "Francine, can we get that urine sample now?"

"I don't need to go. I told you I don't have any urine for you." At that very moment Mother releases all the urine she doesn't have all over the examination table and the floor. She doesn't even notice. "I'm sorry, Doctor, I just don't have to go right now."

Despite all the doctor's good counseling about faith and letting go, I feel a ball of anger, hurt, pain, shame and frustration in the pit of my stomach. My cheeks are aflame. The nurse busies herself with towels cleaning up. The only one who has *let go* is Mother.

Dr. Jones concludes, "Well, Francine, if you can't give us a sample, that's okay. Let's get you cleaned up a little bit and dressed."

Shortly Mother and I leave Dr. Jones's office and go for the CAT scan appointment, which had already been scheduled.

Later in the month I receive a call from Dr. Jones's office requesting me to come for a follow-up appointment without Mother. At that appointment he shares that the CAT scan shows several infarctions or lesions in the brain, some fairly recent. Mother definitely does not have Occult Hydrocephalism, the correctable condition we all had hoped for. She has had several mini-strokes, and her condition is irreversible. One cannot say how long she might stay at her current semi-functional level of public behavior. In Dr. Jones's opinion, the filth and the household conditions should not be a major concern since it is possible for a person to be comfortable, and to some degree happy, in such surroundings.

Dr. Jones spends a long time counseling me in regard to my feelings and my stress. He urges me to involve my husband, as head of the household, to confront Rolf from a masculine perspective regarding the practical business and legal decisions that must be made in order to "look out for the widows," according to the Bible's teachings. I have a hard time with his message to involve Don, as the head of the household, in this Malfait family mess. I feel as if anything I have done in the last four years has been after much thought, professional consultation and always much prayer. I claim no great accomplishments, no intellectual plan, nor any personal wisdom. I believe God has answered my prayers, and he has been available in every instance when I seek him. And he has been available when I'm *not* actively seeking. I have learned that faith is not an intellectual experience one goes through while sitting on some church pew in a hallowed building listening to beautiful music and gazing off through gorgeous stained glass windows. I admit I have shielded Don from the irrationality, pain and maybe even potential physical confrontations with any of my family, and in particular with Rolf. The doctor is saying, let that idea go--let the confrontation happen--let your faith truly be from your heart. Dr. Jones willingly offers to sit in and guide such a confrontation at a future next appointment with me, Don, Rolf and himself as the participants.

"Betty, you need to bring all of the forces affecting your mother's life together. Things will not change until then. You also need to get back to your lawyer as soon as possible and get a fully clarified *Durable Power of Attorney*. A *Guardianship* will not be power enough to put your mother in a care facility."

"Should Mother be in a care facility now?"

"Yes, Betty, she is totally incompetent! She's not going to ever be any better. She will become worse. You have some very heavy decisions to make, and you cannot be running to a court hearing for each separate issue relevant to your mother. You need to have a full Durable Power of Attorney. Let me say again, Francine is permanently incompetent and totally so--she doesn't know correct dates and times; she cannot solve small problems; she is incontinent; she forgets her husband is dead; she *cannot* function competently independently in her own home. She needs to be in a care facility *now!*"

Dr. Jones sits with me silently for several minutes before he asks, "Betty, are you going to continue to let Rolf live in *his* home?"

I am instantly alert, "It's not *his* home. All of Mother's assets are hers for as long as she is alive, whether she is competent or not."

"Rolf seems to think it's his home, so what are you going to do about that?"

"If it's necessary to evict him to gain financial support for Mother's care, so be it."

"And that's where I feel your husband, as head of the household, would be better equipped from a masculine perspective to take care of this type of business."

"Dr. Jones, you make me feel unable, or somehow incompetent, myself. I agree Don has the ability of which you speak, physical or emotional, masculine or whatever. It is he who often helps *me* see the whole picture and encourages me by focusing on what has been accomplished. He makes me believe there will be a satisfactory end to all of this turmoil. *But* I will have to wrestle long and hard with myself before abdicating *all* power and authority to him as the "male head of the household" and expect him to step in and solve Malfaits' problems. One of our strengths has always been equability. In my own upbringing I believe I was liberated long before liberation was a bra-burning exercise for women. That may be one of the reasons Mother says, "They, God no, Betty and I can't live together." She knows even in her mental condition that we are both strong-willed women. Maybe it's one of the reasons she is so empowered now in her senility. However, I will think about doing the confrontation conference with Rolf, Don and me, *if* it's guided by *you*."

"That's good. I hope you will give it serious thought, because it really needs to be done."

On my way out I make the appointment for a confrontational conference, but I leave the office disappointed at Mother's diagnosis and lack of hope for recovery, especially in light of what I had perceived as recent improvement. A part of me is frustrated and, in fact, pissed at Dr. Jones preaching to me on submission.

That was one strange doctor's appointment! I'm thinking, Whose appointment was it, Mother's or mine? Did I choose wisely for a doctor for her? Dr. Jones' name was on every one of my lists when I asked for recommendations for a good doctor for her--Dad's nurses at the hospital, the nurses at the nursing home, my lawyer, people in senior services, and a couple of Mother's friends who frequent Sally's cafe. Well, the one counselor at senior services did say Dr. Jones was an excellent doctor, medically speaking. He worked well with older patients and didn't mind taking Medicare and Medicaid patients. But he was a *little different*.

I think he was a lot different!

When I reach my truck in the parking lot, I jerk open the door with more force than is necessary, toss my purse onto the seat with the same degree of energy, and pull myself up onto the seat. Gripping the steering wheel hard, I pump the gas pedal and turn the key. The roar of the engine seems to stimulate my voice. "That was one crazy medical appointment! I wonder if Dr. Jones doesn't have as big a problem as Mother. Why didn't I speak up? Why didn't I question his using the medical appointment to lecture me?

"Lecture? I think I was grossly disrespected. I don't think his comments to me were at all kosher. I think I was so flabbergasted that I was stunned into silence. He seemed so professional and so perceptive of Mother's problems. What made him try to analyze my problems? That was weird! Unprofessional? I think so. And yet, is there some bit of truth in his perceptions? If I put aside my frustration and anger it seemed everything he said was strictly Biblical. Or was it? That submission stuff happens to be a Biblical part that always triggers personal rebellion in me.

"I don't know if I can keep that appointment or not. I don't know who is crazier--Mother, Dr. Jones, or *me*!"

Dear God, I need another purple tulip. If this was your man, your messenger, please help me to understand, to discern your will.

My stomach is churning. My head is thumping. Is Dr. Jones some kind of Biblical nut case? I can't say he's a quack. He seemed to do the right medical procedures. His senior citizen manner is more than positive and soothing.

My hands hurt from gripping the steering wheel. I don't know how long I've been sitting here in the truck with the motor running in front of the doctor's office muttering my lamentations and prayers. I don't know whether I am doing the "letting go" part or rebelling against being "submissive to the husband."

I suck in a deep breath and put the truck in gear. I don't bother to go to The Sterling Motel nor to 516 for a working weekend, though I had packed for and planned to do that. I turn the truck northward and go home--to my home, my family, my security.

CHAPTER 4

---∞∞∞---

Rational and Prudent Choices

SPRING BECOMES SUMMER with the usual amount of bizarreness in Mother's home, plus an added feature of the telephone often being left off the hook. When it's time for one of my weekend trips to Ridgeview, I get a busy signal for two days in a row. I can't remind Mother I'm coming, so I just get on my way.

The three-hour-fifteen minute trip is consumed with my mumbling. She can't be talking on the phone that much. Yeah, sometimes she doesn't get the phone replaced in its cradle correctly. Yeah, sometimes the cats knock the phone off the hook--but not as often as lately. Rolf seems to be around there more. He may be *taking* the phone off so he can sleep. Or-- would he take the phone off the hook so she and I can't talk?

This interruption in my ability to communicate with Mother is a blatant reminder that a rational and prudent person *must* move her out of that house. If Rolf were cooperative, this would already have been done. Based on his behavior, I wouldn't doubt that Rolf may be intentionally taking the phone off the hook. Repeatedly he is neither rational nor prudent--it may be that neither one of us is--but I have been charged by a court of law to be so.

When I reach 516, it is Rolf who opens the front door for me. No hello, just, "Yeah, hey, I was wondering about how that doctor's appointment went for Mom."

"Her tests are completed, and I made a family appointment for all of us--you, me, and Don--with the doctor. We're going to discuss Mother's overall condition and how to deal with it."

I rummage through my purse for the appointment card. "Here--the doctor's name is Dr. Jared Jones. His office is in that big medical complex

39

between the library and the hotel. The address and the time are all on the card. It was he who suggested we all attend, since we are all affected by her future."

"Yeah, well what did all those tests show?"

"That's what Dr. Jones is going to share with all of us, and if you need to know more details than that before you go, you'll have to call the doctor. You were supposed to go with me when Mother had her physical, but as usual you didn't show."

Rolf shakes the card at me and crams it in his shirt pocket. "Yeah, yeah, well, I might just go see this doc this time."

"You always say you'll go, but will you?"

"Yeah, this time I think I should."

I'm not at all sure he will go, but I change the subject. "Say, while you're here, is the phone being left off the cradle for a reason?"

"Yeah, as a matter of fact, it is. I had to take it off to avoid a bunch of calls from weirdos."

"What kind of weirdos?"

"Oh, sometimes we get early morning calls--some guy blubbering in a drunken stupor and breathing heavily. There's been a kind of a steady stream of 'em lately."

I glance about the living room and pick up a stack of bills from the coffee table and thumb through them. From the yellow slips indicating registered mail to Rolf, I suspect he is avoiding answering the phone for other reasons. "Rolf, it's worrisome when I can't reach Mother. The other day I had to call a neighbor and have him go over and ask Mom to put the phone back on the hook. Also, Aunt Mavis says she has been unable to reach Mom and has gotten a busy signal numerous times for days in a row. I tried to call her last night and again this morning before I came down, and I got a busy signal both times. That's ridiculous. It has to stop. Could you please keep the phone accessible to all of us?"

"Yeah, yeah, sure."

I am desperate for Rolf's cooperation about the phone being left off the hook. I don't dare broach the details of Mother's monthly budget and his mortgage, but I can't stop my immediate reaction when I open her phone bill, "God Almighty, Mom's phone bill is again over $100.00. She isn't making *any* long distance calls. She only talks to Mavis when Mavis calls her. Rolf, if any of these calls are yours, it's got to stop."

I drop the stack of bills back on the coffee table.

"Yeah, yeah. You know, I've had pretty hard times here lately, but things are pickin' up. I think I'll be able to make that mortgage payment myself this next check. That oughta help."

"I'm sure Mother would appreciate that." To myself I'm thinking, I'll have to see that to believe it. I think Rolf's only interest in 516 is to have a place to occasionally crash, a dry place to store his junk and his gun collection.

I glance out through the blinds in the living room window, "I see Mother in the next block walking this way. She's probably coming back from breakfast at Sally's. I need to do a couple of errands before I pick her up for bill-paying today. I just stopped by here to check on the phone first. Would you tell her I'll be back about noon?"

I depart for The Sterling muttering to myself about the phone and all the new piles of mail scattered about the living room, much of which appears to be registered mail to Rolf.

The motel manager greets me at the desk as I register, "Hey, how are you?"

"Oh, not bad. I'm here for another big work weekend. That's about all."

"How's your mom doing without Papa?"

"She's awfully lonely."

"I been thinking about you all, because I've been hearing your Mom's name on the police scanner lately. It sounds like she goes down to the nursing home there behind the hospital trying to visit your dad. I guess when they tell her he's gone, she won't take no for an answer. The cops have had to go down there a couple of times. In fact, I think the same thing happened yesterday afternoon, and the cops drove her home. I really gotta admire her spunk though, you know?"

My hands quiver over the registry, and I look up at the manager through blurred eyes, "At this point I have a little more trouble admiring her spunk than you do."

"Oh, God, I'm sorry. I didn't mean no harm. It's just you could tell she really cared about him, and she wanted to see him. And--she just forgot he was dead."

"I know she forgets. She's becoming more and more removed from reality. Whenever I leave, she'll say, 'Now, Betty, you be sure and visit Dad on your way out of town,' and she repeatedly asks, 'Is Dad really dead?' I hadn't heard about the nursing home trips and the cops taking her home though. I'll stop by there and check on the situation. Thank you."

When I stop at the nursing home, Michelle, a nurse whom we all got to know during Dad's stay, is on duty. "Oh, yes, Betty, your mom has been by several times lately, but I'm not so sure it's a problem. I talked to her the first time. That was about two weeks ago. I just re-explained that Mr. Malfait had died and she should go on home and not be troubled about her mistake. She left quietly."

"Yeah, but the manager at the motel where I stay said he's heard her name on the police scanner more than once this week--most recently yesterday. Has she been coming down here often?"

"Well...yes, she has come several times, but I don't know that it's really a problem. Usually one of us tells her again, and she says she's sorry and turns around and goes back home. I guess it was a little more of a problem yesterday though. I wasn't on duty when she came in. One of the new girls talked to her and thought your mom had wandered in off the street and was someone with a drinking problem, because of her slurred speech and how wobbly she walks. When your mom realized the girl thought she was inebriated, that compounded the problem. Your mom was highly insulted that someone thought she was drunk, and she became very angry. She was quite persistent that she had never had a drop to drink in her entire life and anyone with such notions was not going to keep her from visiting Roger. Some of the other staff tried to defuse the situation and reason with her, but she was just too angry and irrational by then. She wouldn't listen at all to anyone. And, you know, she can be quite forceful when she wants to."

"Tell me about it.... It is true though she doesn't drink and never has. Not a drop."

"Betty, I'm really sorry, but the staff didn't have any other choice yesterday. They had to call the police to take her home. It's just how we have to handle angry, irrational people who might interfere with our work here. Then she came again later in the evening, and I guess she was still angry with us because of the morning episode. She was once again being pretty loud and insistent that she was going to see Roger and no one was going to stop her, so the staff felt they had to call the police again to take her home."

"Michelle, I know how much she appreciated you and your staff here. I'm sorry this happened. I have a plan to move her, but I don't know how fast I can get it done."

"Betty, you have a big job to do, and you shouldn't worry about the police. They are very skilled in dealing with these folks. I'm still not sure it's a serious problem just yet. At least now we're all aware of it. These things happen more often than you might think. Your mom was really a sweet person to deal with when your dad was here, and she generally has been very responsive to directions. You may want to get her in for a physical though because of her unsteadiness. I have noticed that's a lot worse."

"I just had her in for a physical. The wobbliness and slurred speech is due to mini-strokes which have occurred--or may be occurring. I *know* what the next step is, Michelle, and I'll continue with my plan for moving her. Thanks for understanding."

"Well, like I said, your mom and dad were both sweet people to work with before, and I do wish you well with the next steps of your plan."

When I return to 516 to pick Mother up, Rolf is no place to be seen and the registered mail letters have disappeared. I comment casually, "I hear you've been visiting at the nursing home."

Mother doesn't ask how I know. "Oh, yes, I went down there the other day to visit Dad, but the nurse told me he died and was buried. I came right home then. I guess I just forgot."

I decide not to mention her ride in the police car. "Mother, we all may forget like that when we're lonely or sad or highly stressed. Remember when I asked you about visiting Janice's place for a while? That's the place on Whidbey Island I had hoped both you and Dad might go, so you could be nearer to me and I could see you more often. It might be a place now where you could rest and relax, at least for a while. What do you think?"

"I think I need a rest."

"Does that mean you'd like to go to Janice's?"

"Yes, but I'll have to talk to Dad about it."

"Mom, Dad is dead, remember? We had his funeral, and last time I was down you and I picked out the headstone. We got dogwood flowers on your side, and we--"

"He is *not dead!*"

"Mother, we all want him to be here with us, but you want it so badly you can't accept that he's gone. It's okay to want him back like that. It's okay."

There is no response. I continue by verbalizing the whole funeral service for her: flowers, music, preacher, cemetery. "He really is dead, Mother, and he's buried, and you and I have visited his grave several times."

"That's what the girl at the nursing home said when I went to visit today."

Today? Did she go today? Did she go there before she went to Sally's cafe, or did she go there after I saw her coming back from Sally's. She had a brown bag in her hand when I saw her. I wonder if she bought a treat for Dad? How long does this denial stage of grief last? Is her situation denial in grief or denial in dementia? What kind of loneliness is it to be without someone after being with them for more than fifty years?

"Mother, sometimes our brain plays tricks on us. That happens especially when we're very unhappy and lonely. Are you lonely, Mother?"

"Yes, I'm awful lonesome."

"Will you think a little more about visiting at Janice's?"

"Okay."

I feel that's all I can say at the moment, and Mother and I leave to do our usual errands. When we return to the house and are unloading our groceries, Rolf drives up. As usual, he doesn't offer to help, but he does hurry to unlock the door for us. "I'm glad I caught you two. I need to explain a couple things before you get in the house and start wonderin' about 'em."

As I enter the living room I can see five new guns scattered about on top of the piles of junk on the sofa and on the coffee table where the registered letters had been earlier. "What the hell is all this?"

"Yeah, yeah, I knew you'd want to know. I went to a gun show in Portland with Lars, and I traded a bunch of guns for the ones you see here."

I turn and go to the kitchen to put the grocery bags down--before I squeeze the eggs into pre-scramble status. Returning to the living room I study the first gun propped up against the couch. It's an antique--the kind one has to ram the load down the barrel.

"Yeah, that was a really great find. I already have one pretty much like it, but this one is an earlier model and it's in almost perfect shape."

A second gun looks like a high-powered 22 pistol with an extended barrel, and there's a couple of larger caliber bolt action-rifles. The rifle propped against the coffee table has a white tag hanging from the trigger guard. I lean over and finger the tag reading aloud, "Model 270--$725.00. That's a pretty expensive piece."

"Like I said, I *traded* for all of 'em. No cash was exchanged."

Maybe they are trades. I sure can't get any cash out of Rolf. Probably fellow gun bunnies can't either. I don't have time nor energy to argue. Instead I tell Rolf about Mother's recent wanderings and trips to the nursing home. "She's really sad and lonesome right now. I think it would be good for her to get away, and she and I have talked about her going to Janice's on Whidbey for a while."

Rolf is less than enthusiastic about that idea. "I don't know that she ought to do that. She seems fine right here, where she's used to everything and has friends. It would be a lot better to have someone come in here to help her with the work, and maybe even be a little bit of company for her."

"I've tried that several times, Rolf. She always agrees, and then when they come she won't let them in the house."

"Well, if her and Dad's Whidbey acreage could be sold, she could live pretty well on that for quite some time."

"I've tried to do that, too, but as you know, it's currently land-locked. No realty company will list it that way."

"Well, it seems like she could get along on what she has coming in."

"Damn it, Rolf, don't you realize when Dad was alive your mortgage took one fourth of their income? Now that he's gone, Mother's income is $1019 per month, and your mortgage is $468.70, almost *half* of her income. The ownership of that Whidbey property keeps her from qualifying for any kind of assistance. She has no money to pay for help, and your debt is making it more than difficult to make ends meet around here. Yes, she could get along fine if she could have all of her income for *herself*."

"Well, like I told you, things are looking up a bit. I think I'll be able to contribute here at the end of the month."

"Rolf, what do *you* want for Mother? What are *your* suggestions?"

"I don't know. I just don't know."

"You don't know about that, but you know you need more guns. What are you going to do with all these? It's not right for you to be acquiring more guns while she pays your bills. It's not right for all this stuff to be scattered all over her house. It's dangerous. When can you get all these guns out of here?"

"I just don't know, and I told you these guns today were trades." Rolf lurches up from the couch. "Hey, run me over to Oregon."

"Run yourself over to Oregon! Use your own gas! I have a couple more errands to do and a phone call to make. I need to know if Don is coming down tomorrow for Mother's medical follow-up appointment with Dr. Jones. And don't forget that appointment yourself. It's for all of us, and you did say you'd attend, right?"

"Yeah, yeah, I won't forget."

"Well, I need to get my errands done. I'll be back in an hour. If you're still here, maybe I can take you then."

"Okay. I'll wait." Rolf flops back down on the couch.

I get my errands done, and an hour later I return. Rolf's car is gone. Good! I didn't want to take him anyway. As I get out of my truck I wave at Ruthie, a neighbor two houses down the block, and she motions for me to come down. As she chatters away while making us a fresh pot of coffee, I can't help but notice her shaky hands and some of the same irrelevancy and paranoia in her conversation as I encounter regularly with Mother. To myself I question, *Oh, Ruthie, is it happening to you, too?*

A few minutes into our first cup of coffee, like a bird-dog on a trail, Rolf arrives on Ruthie's doorstep. I guess I should be glad he's not a gun-toting hunter. He opens the screen door and lets himself in, "Hi, Ruth. How's it goin'?" He jerks his head in my direction, "Yeah, I just ran down and cashed my unemployment check. I saw your truck here on my way back."

Ruthie is gracious as usual. "Let me get you a cup of coffee, Rolf."

Rolf comes into the living room and sits down. "Oh, no thanks. That stuff'll kill ya. I never touch it."

"Well, Rolf, I don't believe it's hurt me much in eighty years." Ruthie brings the pot and warms my cup.

I sip the hot steaming liquid. "Rolf, I thought you needed to go to Oregon?"

"Oh, well, that was just to get some lotto tickets."

Ruthie returns to the living room and casts chastising eyes on Rolf. "Now, Rolf, those lotto tickets will be the downfall of you. Look there at your shirt pocket. It's stuffed full of those old tickets."

Rolf pats his pocket. "Oh you never know when you'll be a big winner. Of course, I may not live long enough to collect all of mine when I win. I got this nasty blister on my foot, and it's all infected. My leg seems like it's swollen, too, but I went to work with it like that two days this week anyway. I hauled fifteen loads one of them days, sore foot and all."

I silently question, *How could you be getting an unemployment check if you're working? Could a driver really haul fifteen loads in one working day? I doubt it.*

Ruthie's words caution him, "You better be checking on that leg and foot. That doesn't sound good."

"Oh, I don't have the kind of money it takes to go to the doctor. I may be able to get on Kaiser Medical here pretty soon though. Until then I'll take care of it myself."

Ruthie asks, "And how do you do that?"

Rolf takes out a large Buck pocket knife. "This here is my instrument of care. I used this little number on it the other night, and then I went to the health club downtown at the mall and sat in the steam room for an hour and then in the Jacuzzi for another hour. That ought to have done something for it."

I can no longer be silent. "Geez, Rolf, I'm glad I don't go to your health club."

"Ah, that chlorine would kill anything I left in the water. They use that stuff so strong there's no way the water wouldn't be fine for other people." Rolf gets up to leave. "Hell, whatever it is will probably kill *me* before it hurts anyone at the health club. Well, I gotta get down to the house and check on Mom and Taco. I bought Mom one of them hot roasted chickens for dinner. I better get down there and get it in to her."

I would like to throw up on Ruthie's floor in reaction to Rolf's benevolent expression of care and concern for both his foot and his mother. My coffee cup is empty and cold--and so am I.

Later at the house when Mother and I are by ourselves, and she is pleasant and chatty, I bring up the subject of Whidbey Island again. "You know, Mom, I was thinking some more about your going to Janice's place. She does a lot of canning and freezing, and she's got a garden. You might even enjoy helping her. You've been wanting to have another garden. There's all that wonderful home-cooking, too. I know you like Sally's Cafe, but being at Janice's might give you a change. That could be good. There's two other ladies there now. I really like little Fern. She's cute and funny. There's a lot of activity, and you might enjoy some of the things they're involved in. Do you think you would like to visit for two or three weeks to just sort of see and decide for yourself?"

"Of course I would. How much does it cost?"

I am shocked at her immediate reply. I'm not sure I even heard her right. "Did you say yes, you'd like to try it?"

"Yes, but I want to know how much it costs."

"Uh--well, let's see, I think it would only be about $100.00 more per month than your monthly income. But right now you have some insurance

48

money from Dad. You could afford that amount for a while. If you don't like it, then we'll have to think again. I really think you'd enjoy more company and have more things of interest to do."

Mother never asks what her monthly income is, how much her bills are, nor how much insurance money she has. She simply says, "Yes, I think I'd like to go to Janice's."

This is too simple, but I stop while I'm ahead. "Mother, I need to say good-night now." I lean over to kiss her. She usually turns her cheek for me to give her a goodnight peck. Tonight she drops her newspaper and places a hand on either side of my face and kisses me square on the mouth. This is an evening of shocks.

Mother snaps her paper back into reading position. "Thank you for all the work you've done today. You drive carefully now. I think I'll like Janice's."

I close the front door and step into the darkness. Tears stream down my face.

Dear God, I know I'm going to move Mother from the 'house that Dad built' to go to Janice's place--but not for just a while. This move-- or a similar such move--will eventually be permanent. I haven't gotten this far without your help. Please continue to be with me.

CHAPTER 5

Dr. Jones' Second Sermon

THE NEXT DAY I meet Don, who has driven down especially for the family appointment with Dr. Jones. Rolf is a no-show. Dr. Jones meets with the two of us anyway.

After introductions, Dr. Jones glances at his notes and begins. "My first point to both of you is that Rolf is trying to yank Betty's chain. Forget it. Rolf makes choices, and he will have to live with his choices. Forget him.

"Secondly, Don, you need to exercise your *head of the household* position. Besides telling Betty *no*, you need to confront that brother-in-law of yours. Let him know he's not being forthright with his mother nor his sister. The Bible teaches us to honor our fathers and mothers--and his behavior is not honorable."

Don is staring at the doctor, shaking his head slowly up and down but squinting his eyes--his way of silently saying *Huh?* It wouldn't matter if he had a comment or a question. Dr. Jones continues to bull-doze through his sermon for several more minutes. I clinch my teeth as tightly as I do when trying to reason with Rolf. In fact, I think I have some of the same anger at the doctor and his domineering presentation as I do when talking with Rolf. Before I can unclench my teeth and speak, I am brought back to awareness when I hear Dr. Jones use my name.

"Is Betty's work in Ridgeview causing any worry or strain on your personal relationship?"

Don and I answer simultaneously, yes.

I add, "But Don is wonderful. He's very understanding and perceptive. I think we are managing the stress issues pretty well."

Before I can expound any further on our stress reduction techniques, Dr. Jones ignores me and looks at Don as he says, "Just tell her *No*! Give God a chance to work out this whole family issue on *His* time-line."

Don and I look at each other in wide-eyed disbelief. Shock? Numbness?

The self-anointed voice drones on. "And let me make a third point. Don't worry about Mother's safety and cleanliness. Turn that over to God, too. God will take care of Mother, and he will do that in his own time. Betty, you have done everything that could be expected of you, and more. Let go. Listen to God. Look for his signs and answers in the Scripture. Don't worry about your mother being on the police scanner because she's trying to visit her dead husband at the nursing home. Let the nursing home staff deal with that. And Ridgeview Police are excellent at taking care of such problems."

How does Dr. Jones know about Mother's visits to the nursing home and her being on the police scanner? Does he do his doctoring, his preaching, and listen to the local police scanner as well?

"And a fourth point I want to emphasize is that if Mom is happy sitting in her dirty house with the dog and cat and Rolf and the smell of cat feces, let her be happy that way. You know, sometimes when you move these folks, the change is too much and they get worse."

I ignore my meandering thoughts and tune in to this last point. "But, Dr. Jones, I've already made the arrangements for a move to a foster care home on Whidbey Island. That's what you recommended when we spoke at the appointment after Mother's CAT scan. You specifically said, 'She can't function competently independently in her own home. She is incompetent. She needs to be in a care facility *now*!'"

"Be that as it may, Betty, you've been terribly hurt, and rightfully so, by Rolf, and also by your mother and dad. No matter what I said at the last appointment, it's obvious your mom and dad did not treat Rolf and you equally. You need to acknowledge your anger toward them, and then forgive them all."

"I really think I have forgiven my parents, but I'm not as confident I have forgiven Rolf. About the time I think I have, I get angry at him all over again about something else. It's all I can manage not to hate him."

"Yes, I recognize you have a lot of anger toward him, and that's not healthy for you. Now, Don, you and Betty should share decision-making in regard to Mother. But you--Don--you should be confrontational with Rolf. You should be the one to tell him how things are going to be."

Don has said almost nothing up to now, but he tells the doctor, "I would be willing to do that. I'm not afraid of Rolf. I've stayed out of this mess so far because Betty asked me to. I try to be understanding and supportive of her and her family members. You know, over the years we have shared a lot of good times with her family."

Dr. Jones persists, "That's all well and good. And you should continue to be supportive--supportive by being confrontational with Rolf and laying down the law."

"I don't have a problem with that."

I am frozen. I have multiple problems with most of this conference, but I can't unclench my teeth and make my mouth form any words.

Dr. Jones must sense my increasing silent frustration and think I need a second dose of evangelical preaching. "Betty, just let it go. Let nature take its course. Let God work in His own time. Don't try to control the progress. Don't be disappointed in the results. God can use you better if you let him carry all the burden and solve the problems. Use the Scriptures for signs and answers. Forgive Mother and Dad for setting up such a trap for Rolf. Forgive Rolf for falling into it. Forgive yourself for trying too hard and for blaming yourself when it doesn't work out to what you think is satisfactory."

My brain is on overload. Now what am I going to do about Mother going to Janice's? About the only Biblical confidence I have is that I feel like Noah building an ark when there isn't a raindrop in sight.

The doctor isn't through preaching. He seems oblivious to time as he continues by giving his personal testimony of struggling to *do right* within his own will in his medical practice. "I used to feel an urgency to help each patient to the fullest, to give all the service each one demanded, to fight the staff at the local hospital on the patient's behalf--and on and on and on. Ultimately I learned to turn my whole life over to God--the good, the bad, the patients, everything. Then I could just be God's man, and I had only one master and one will to obey. Life was so much better.

"Last year this office generated $780,000 gross in patient business, but my earnings were only $78,000. People don't pay their bills. So what? I feel greatly at peace because I am doing God's will. The almighty dollar is not my master."

We all sit in silence, heads bowed--but not in prayer.

Dr. Jones closes his sermon. "Betty, the Bible says, 'Do not reprove a scoffer, or he will hate you; reprove a wise man, and he will love you.' That's Proverbs 9:7-8. I want you to hold that Scripture in your mind and heart every day."

The doctor stands.

We stand. I think Don thanks Dr. Jones for his time and concern. I don't feel thankful.

I don't know if I can hold Dr. Jones' closing verse--or anything else he said--in my head for the amount of time it takes me to get from this office through the darkened waiting room and out into the parking lot, much less hold it in my heart every day. I don't wait for *the head of the household*. I open the door for myself and step into the cool evening air without look-ing back.

I am drained.

Dear God, what in the world was all that about? I've never had a doc-tor's appointment like that! Now I am really confused and overwhelmed!

Don joins me in the front seat of the truck. We sit quietly debriefing, commiserating, trying to make some sense of the past hour and a half. Finally Don moves to the center of the truck seat and takes my hand. He reassures me. "Betty, he doesn't see all the details of these last several years. He is not the Almighty, even if he sort of comes across that way. Let's both just think about what he said. I'd say you should use things he suggests that you can relate to, and don't worry about the rest. He was mostly telling you how it was for him. In fact, a lot of the time today was about him and his problems and not about your family and its problems. That doesn't mean you have to do things the same way he does, and that doesn't mean you and I have to live our lives like he does. I think you've done an incredible job with your parents. I do have to agree with him that you work too hard, and I want you to try harder to take care of yourself. But I think together we've managed fine."

"But the things he said today are not the same as what he said previously."

"Maybe not--maybe he's having as much trouble thinking about your family situation as you are. Betty, just keep plugging along. We'll both keep moving along, working together. I know you'll make right choices. You have so far."

Don embraces me and kisses me. "You are going to be fine, and so am I. We both are depending on God to get us though this ordeal, and we know he will do that. Dr. Jones' opinion is just one man's opinion--he's just a man--sort of an angry man at that. Maybe even a frustrated preacher man. Right?"

"That's for sure--one of those backwoods, Bible-beating, evangelical, John-the-Baptist types. He's probably home now chowing down on some locusts and honey!

"I'll think about what he had to say some more. Right now, I'm pooped, and I know you are, too. Thanks for coming down today."

"Yeah, I better get going." Don gets out of the truck and comes around to the driver's window and leans in and kisses me again. "You've done it right so far. You'll be fine. We'll both be fine."

Don gets into his car for his three-hour and fifteen minute return drive to our home. I start the truck engine and go to my home-away-from-home, The Sterling.

In my room I rummage around in the nightstand drawer for the Gideon Bible.

Dear God, Dr. Jones said to look for signs in the Bible. I'm looking. Help me to understand your will. And if Dr. Jones is your man, help me to understand his message. He said Proverbs 9:7-8.

Verse 7: He who corrects a scoffer gets shame for himself, and he who rebukes a wicked man only harms himself. Verse 8: Do not correct a scoffer, lest he hate you, rebuke a wise man, and he will love you.

Okay, God, so the guy has a great memory for Bible verses. He obviously has no Alzheimer's genes in his family history. Please, are you speaking to me, or is Dr. Jones doing the speaking?

God, that was the strangest doctor's appointment ever!

I toss the Gideon Bible back into the drawer, turn out the light, and fall asleep.

The next morning, despite yesterday's appointment with Dr. Jones, I feel rested. I go to Mother's house and work calmly with her most of the day. We both feel pleased with our accomplishments.

In the afternoon Rolf drives up and greets me, "Yeah, what's up?"

"Mother and I are just finishing our chores. Where were you for the follow-up appointment with Dr. Jones yesterday?"

Rolf throws his head back, squints painfully, and slaps his forehead in a mighty gesture of forgetfulness. "Ahhh--So what did I miss?"

"Well, it was very informational, and I guess if you want to know details firsthand, you will need to make your own appointment and go talk to Dr. Jones."

Rolf shrugs and walks away, leaving me to wonder if he already did that. Is that why Dr. Jones seemed to change his recommendations about Mother?

God, who's guiding whom here? You? Dr. Jones? Rolf? Me?

I don't know whether Rolf went to see the doctor or not. I don't have time to figure who's the wise man and who's the scoffer. I don't need to be rebuking anyone. I have plenty to do just to manage what I do know, and that is that there's a ton of work to be done in this house in preparation to move Mother to Janice's. I complete my work weekend and go home feeling assured my plan is moving forward.

At my own home Sunday evening I catch up on her budget book and balance her check book. I attack a messy pile of uncorrected schoolwork on the dining room table. Tucked in with the school papers I find a copy of *Family Devotions*. I don't even remember the last time I attended church nor the last time I read any of the devotions. I absently thumb through the pages to the current date. The recommended supportive Bible verses listed at the top of the page are Proverbs 9:7-8 and Matthew 5:4, 5:6, 5:10-12.

I snag a Bible from the nearby bookcase and turn to the ninth chapter of Proverbs. The black print squirms before my eyes, 'Do not reprove a scoffer....' The rest of the verse blurs as I slam the Bible shut and toss both books onto the piles of school papers on the floor.

God, I don't believe this. That's two in a row! This is more than coincidental--more than purple tulips. This is spooky! I can't deal with this.

I leave the table and survey my own kitchen. If things continue to be unattended around here, it won't be long until my house looks like 516. I start with the dishes, then gather a load of laundry. Next I attack any other tangible task that presents itself. Hours later I return to the table to straighten the stack of uncorrected school papers and put things in order for my Monday morning rush to get to school. I open the Bible again, this time to the recommended verses in the book of Matthew.

Blessed are those who are persecuted for righteousness' sake, for theirs is the kingdom of heaven.
Blessed are you when they revile and persecute you, and say all kinds of evil against you falsely for my sake.

Rejoice and be exceedingly glad, for great is your reward in heaven, for so they persecuted the prophets who were before you.

Okay, God, I sort of get the picture. This is the third time I think you've spoken. I don't need to be beaten over the head with the purple tulip! I'm not a prophet by any means, but I am comforted by your word. Forgive me, and thank you.

CHAPTER 6

Rational And Prudent Choices At A Faster Pace

DESPITE ALL THE professional feedback, spiritual and scriptural delving, my mind is boggled. Mother deteriorates a bit more each time I see her. Dr. Jones may be able to leave such worries to police, nursing home staff, or others and feel that is God's will, but I haven't been able to do that. I am not as vocal as Dr. Jones in overtly and confidently professing to be within God's will. When I am quiet and prayerful and listen to my inner being, I sense when I'm doing things right and when I'm wrong, but is it really within God's will? I feel terribly insecure.

Right now, leaving Mother to her loneliness and aimless wandering desperately seeking to visit my deceased father at the nursing home is not right. This cannot continue. In my heart of hearts I've known for some time she shouldn't be living by herself. I *am* going to move her. Part of me doesn't want to do the deed, because I know she doesn't want to go--at least not permanently--but it's the *right* thing to do!

Is it God's will? I don't know.

When I next check in at The Sterling, a message awaits me at the desk. It's from Mary, a counselor in Community Senior Services, asking me to come see her as soon as I get into town. The note is brief, but there is an urgency about it. Before I go to 516 and my usual work routine, I visit Mary as requested.

She is happy I responded so promptly. "Betty, our volunteers have tried several times to reach your Mom by phone after you asked us to put her on the CAP's Daily-Dial Phone Check Service. No matter who calls or at what time of day the phone continues to give a busy signal. I personally have tried at different times, including in the evening. Her phone can't be that busy. The phone must be off the hook."

"Yes, my brother seems to be staying at the house more now that Aunt Mavis has gone home. He says he's been taking the phone off the hook, so he won't have to listen to weirdo phone calls from breathy, drunk voices and such. I don't believe that, but I've not been able to get him to stop. I've spoken to him about it several times, but he claims he often just forgets to put it back."

Mary continues, "Well, I even went out to the house. Your Mom answered the door, but she wouldn't let me in. She said she would put the phone back on the hook right away, and she was very appreciative that I had told her it wasn't working. I left and went to a nearby phone and called her. She answered, and things seemed fine. She was very friendly and chatty and thanked me again and promised she'd try to keep the phone on the hook. Wouldn't you know, the next day when our people made their daily phone call they couldn't get through. Now, if it's your brother who is leaving the phone off intentionally and preventing people from contacting your mom, then I have to report that action to APS."

"Oh, God, Mary, here we go again. I'm trying to get my plan to move Mother put into action, but I can't keep up with all that is demanded for her--for you, for the court, and now for APS. Next I suppose Mr. Manilow from APS will leave me an urgent message to come and explain about the telephone to him. I already know how inadequate I am. I don't need him reminding me that he may have to ask the court to appoint another guardian. He's already told me that option."

"You know, Betty, you need to not worry about all the details. We're each doing our jobs--and so are you. You're making progress. This will all come together."

"I don't know about that.

"One good note though, I finally got Mother in to see a doctor--I chose Dr. Jared Jones, because his name came up on everyone's recommendation list from the hospital staff, the nursing home staff, my lawyer, and even the people here in your office. But I have to tell you, that was one weird experience! I don't know what to think about him. What is your opinion professionally?"

"I'm not sure how to answer that. Over all, he's a very good doctor. People either love him or they hate him. We have had some negative feed-back regarding Dr. Jones' religious tactics. However, as far as his skills--he's excellent. As far as his caring attitude with seniors--he's marvelous."

"Well, Mother had to have a physical before I can move her to Janice's foster care home, and I hope his findings are accurate."

"Oh, I'm very sure you don't have to worry about Dr. Jones' profes-sional findings. He has been known to be a little preachy, but otherwise I wouldn't worry about his skill and findings.

"Betty, be of courage and just do it--move your mother to Janice's on Whidbey Island. Use what money you have until you run out. Then sell her house and use those funds to pay for her care. Your mother is at the stage where she is not going to get better. That's just how it is--trust me--I have worked with these folks for over fifteen years now. The bright side is your mom will be cleaner and safer. She won't be so lonely. She will prob-ably make new friends, and possibly actually be happier."

I leave the counselor's office considering the things I have to do to move Mother and at the same time worrying about how I will get her to co-operate. When I arrive at 516, I find Mother in the kitchen eating Pork 'n Beans out of a can. She doesn't even hear the doorbell, and she doesn't show much surprise when I use my key and let myself in. Taco is howling frantically, and the floor looks as if he has howled a few other times and has been ignored. The bedroom is equally disastrous, reeking of urine from piles of used Depends, some with feces rolled up in them. There are flies blitzing the place, and they look very well fed!

I warm some soup in the microwave for Mother, and make her a couple of slices of toast.

"Oh, this is so much tastier than those old cold beans."

While Mother eats, I attack the kitchen like the wife of "Mr. Clean." I swirl about on a mission of vengeance against every particle of dirt and grime, every unseen germ, and every nasty spot missed by lesser able prod-ucts. I'll never make it to earn a role in a television ad, but the scrubbing is good for me and the kitchen.

"Oh, Betty, you work too hard. Couldn't you leave some of that until later?"

"You're right, Mom. I don't think I can breathe much more of these cleaning fumes. I need a break. Your lawn needs to be mowed, and I'm too pooped right now to even think about doing it. I saw the neighbor kid mowing his lawn a little bit ago. I'm going to run across the street and see if I can get him to mow yours."

Ryan is an industrious teenager saving money to pay the fee to take his driver's test and for his car insurance. He's eager to accept my job offer. Ryan's mother comes out to join our conversation and to affirm what a good lawn-care worker he is. I've already noticed the nice job he did on his own lawn, how perfectly he edged along the sidewalk, and how he is cleaning up his lawn mower and edger before putting them away. I explain to Ryan and his mom that I may soon be moving Mother, maybe for a while, maybe permanently. I offer him the job on a regular basis whether anyone is home at Malfait's house or not, explaining that Rolf does seem to be in and out of the place. Both Ryan and his mom assure me the work will be done regularly. Ryan will keep track of the numbers of times he mows, and I will pay him whenever I am down to Ridgeview again.

I glance across the street and see Mother emerge onto the front steps looking up and down the street. "Uh oh, I don't want her to cross the street, so I'll just run. We have a deal, right?"

Ryan wipes his hand on his jeans and reaches out to shake with me.

"Thank you, Ryan. Thank you both. That's one big worry gone!"

I run back across the street. It doesn't take much persuasion to get Mother to walk to Sally's Cafe for lunch. The walking and the fresh air are good for both of us. When we return, Rolf is at the house, sprawled out on one end of the couch surrounded by yellow legal pads, two or three worn pocket books with leafy page markers sticking out, and a small black leather suitcase propped open on his lap.

"I wondered where you guys were."

"Well, Rolf, it was pretty much of a mess around here. Mother and I worked all morning to clear the decks just in her bedroom and the kitchen. We needed a break, and we went down to Sally's for lunch."

"Yeah, the house has been pretty bad here lately."

"Rolf, it seems like you could help control some of this a little bit--like maybe just dumping the garbage once in a while."

"Well, like I said before--I worked my ass off, and it didn't really do any good. I don't intend to do any more around here than I absolutely have to. I intend to *be* around here as little as possible, and I intend to *do* as little as possible!"

Rolf snaps the little black suitcase shut, slides it down on the floor between his feet, crosses his arms, and scowls up at me awaiting my response.

"Okay, if that's how you want it."

Rolf releases his arms and picks up a large manila envelope he has left out on top of a stack of newspapers on the couch. "Now, let me show you this. I've been busy with a lot more important things. You oughta be interested in this, too. Here, let me show you these photos and see what you think." He produces a sheaf of blown-up photos, a worn paperback book on the Green River killer, and several newspaper articles about the various victims of the Green River killer. "I've been investigating this guy who lives in Lacy. He's a real good suspect. He was stationed at Newcastle with the Coast Guard. Ingrid--you know, Mom and Dad's friend down at Newcastle--well, she actually knows him. He's been a friend of theirs clear back to when her boys were still in school. This guy's a real roller. He supposedly made a trip to Florida here a while back to pick up some six hundred thousand dollars from some kind of Federal settlement. Actually, I think what he finally got was some smaller amount like twenty or thirty thousand."

"Rolf, where do you get all this information? Where did you get these pictures? What is all this stuff?"

"I get a lot of little tidbits of info from Ingrid. She don't suspect me of having any investigative intentions."

"But, Rolf, this guy's a friend of theirs. These are pictures of his family wedding. That's just a proud dad and his daughter at the wedding reception. They always do special shots of the daughter and the dad."

"Yeah, but what you don't know is this guy don't want anyone takin' his picture, even at his own daughter's wedding. Ingrid says he really made a fuss about it, both with the photographer and other wedding guests who were taking pictures. It almost turned into a fight. She says that ain't anything new though. The guy's been paranoid about picture-taking for years. That ain't all--the most impressive thing is this guy's been in all the areas where the killer was knockin' these women off. I've followed the time lines pretty well, and he's been in proximity to each of the killings right at the time. These pictures add another important bit of evidence--his face isn't known to anyone for any other crimes. He's never been on no wanted posters."

"And how did you get his picture?"

"Oh, you know, Ingrid don't bother none to count her pictures when I give 'em back, so I just *borrowed* a couple of 'em."

"What are these weird drawings?"

"I ain't no artist, but I had the pictures blown up, and then I drew those features on top of the photo in the way I figure this guy disguised himself."

"God, Rolf, I don't even see a relationship between the man's photograph in the wedding picture and your drawings. I don't see how you get your ideas."

"Well, the Green River Task Force seems interested and that's what counts. They see a connection in my thinking. Here a while back I spent some three hours with them guys. In fact, I've seen 'em on three or four different occasions now."

"The *real* Green River Task Force?"

"Yeah, *the* Green River Task Force."

"Where do you do all this kind of reporting to them?"

"I go up to Seattle. They've reduced the staff drastically, but they still got a couple of guys working on the case."

"Yeah, and you go running around with your blown-up pictures stolen from Ingrid and shooting off your mouth, and they'll be investigating *you*."

Rolf laughs, "Funny you should say that. I was talkin' to a friend of mine in the County Sheriff's Office, and that's what he said. 'The first thing you know, Rolf, the Task Force will be investigating you'."

"Oh, bullshit, Rolf! Who are you trying to impress?"

"Say whatever you like, but I think I'm onto something--and the Task Force *is* paying attention. They must think I'm onto something, too."

"Good luck to you and the Task Force!"

I leave Rolf sharing his pictures with Mother and go to the kitchen. I need some fresh air. I open the back door and step outside, continuing across the back lawn to the grape arbor where it's cool and the air is heavy with the pungency of purple clusters of Concords. I pass by the cherry trees and through the garden gate along a row of raspberries muttering to myself, "Geez, Rolf is nuts! Is this Green River stuff a hobby with him? Is it an obsession? Is it intimidation? He at one time was majoring in criminology in college, but he switched his major to history. Did he get just enough criminology learning to be dangerous? Be logical, Betty. Rolf is a liar, a cheat, and a thief. In fact, he's an obsessive liar, an obsessive cheat, an obsessive thief. Is he now an obsessive Green River killer detective?"

I rest my head against one of four-by-four garden posts.

Dear God, I hope Rolf is not dangerous to Mother, to me, or to anyone else. He has such distorted viewpoints. If there ever is to be a healing, God, it just has to be up to you. He's impossible for me to deal with. He never sees any errors in anything he does. I get so sick and tired of his flapping mouth, his expertise on everything, and his arrogant authority over everyone. Regardless of the situation or the story, Rolf always sees someone else at fault, and he has no hesitation to place blame on others.

God, I can't help but wonder if someplace back through these traumatic years since the big family hiatus if, in fact, it was Rolf who stole the money--and then--when he was unable to admit his error, he just got deeper and deeper into a pit of guilt because he feared people wouldn't like him or love him ever again. In my own personal agonizing, I would relish a truthful answer to the destructive lies of the past. I believe his lies and other behaviors were an influence in the deterioration of both Mother and Dad. God, if the culprit in the money theft was Rolf, I could forgive and forget. I would rather have the brother back. Sometimes, God, I want to scream out at him--Give it up. Tell! Let's forgive each other the anger and hurt of these past years. Let's make amends and be a family.

God, if guilt and shame over the initial missing money from Dad's bedroom is not the root of Rolf's problem, then I am even more at a loss. I don't pretend to understand complex psychological deviation. From the years of our childhood on into our adult years I was honestly never aware that Mother and Dad treated us differently. I felt a comfort and pride in Rolf's uniqueness, his sense of adventure, and his attitude toward work and his work ethic. I rarely felt parental favoritism. And if I did, it was over Rolf being older and getting to do things like ride horses or drive before I could. I am unaware of what changed the positive nature of our relationship over the years. I just know that now for whatever reason, Rolf's actions are mean and maybe dangerous, and I don't know what the cause is. I do not see much hope for change. God, I sense how futile and wasted is my hope that Rolf will miraculously become what he never has been. I see him as some kind of sociopath with no feelings, no guilt, no care for others--someone who needs no help or other person in his life, and yet who charms many people. God, someone like this can never get well unless you do a miracle. Oh, God, I would welcome that miracle, but meantime I ask you to prevent me from being judgmental toward Rolf. I truly leave him in your hands. I implore you to help me and to direct me to make choices which are right for Mother.

And, God, I really can't fathom this Green River Killer investigation kick Rolf is on. It's way too bizarre--so bizarre I have wondered myself if he is a player or an investigator. God, please protect me from any harm from Rolf, real or imagined. I give him to you totally from this day on.

I do not go back into the house. I leave the garden and circle the house, letting myself out through the side gate. I go to The Sterling where I make a brief phone call to Janice on Whidbey Island, updating her and asking if she may have Mother come up sooner than we previously had agreed upon. Then I write Rolf a letter concerning my plan for Mother.

Guiding Mother Home

May 26, 1991

Dear Rolf,

Basically I know in my head and in my heart that you won't approve of what I am going to do today, but because I need to be in contact with Mother by phone regularly and because her trips to the nursing home have become daily and sometimes twice daily, I can't continue my school year being disrupted by phone calls from nursing home staff or the police. Mother has been eating at Sally's store and tells them she has no money to pay, and yet she has $50 in her little purse. If I had been able to talk to her on the phone I could have reminded her of that, and you are no help with phone communication.

Also Mother has become more persistent that Dad is not dead. The mess and the unhealthiness of the house is worse than ever. Our mother *can* live better than this. She deserves better. In her right mind she would never have allowed either of us to exist as she is living.

Rolf, I'm really sorry for all the hurts and frustrations I have caused you over the last few years. I know neither Mom nor Dad have been easy to deal with, and in your own way you have tried to help, although I have been critical of your techniques. Also some of their financial decisions actually set up a kind of trap that you fell into. I know you feel caught now and you would like things to be different.

Rolf, I love you and I care very much about what happens to you. And if in any way there can be reconciliation between us, I will always want my brother more than any material thing, and I will remain open to dialogue on that subject. However, for right now, Mother needs to be in a better living situation, and I need to be separated from your obstructionist habits and viewpoint. I am enclosing Janice's name and phone number where Mother will be on Whidbey Island.

Mother says please feed the dog and the cat, and she's leaving you this twenty dollar bill to help with that. It's most likely not enough, but after all, Taco is your dog.
Love,
Betty

I seal the letter in a large unmistakable manila envelope and write his name in bold print across the front.

Tomorrow's mail to 516 will be earlier than usual.

CHAPTER 7

—∞∞∞—

Leaving The House That Daddy Built

I FEEL RESTLESS and unsettled as I prepare for bed. Once the lights are off, I toss and turn, repeatedly squinting at the bright red numerals on the digital clock by the bedside. Sometime after 10:00 PM I fall asleep.

The next time my eyes squeeze the numerals into focus, it's 4:00 AM. I'm a flaccid sweaty clump, curled into a prenatal position grasping my stomach to quell massive stabbing cramps. I think I have a fever. I'm shaking uncontrollably. I force myself to make a wobbly trip to the bathroom where I suffer repeated bouts of diarrhea. I don't know if I'm stressing over my letter to Rolf, Rolf's Green River killer investigation, or moving Mother today knowing she'll never be back to 516. Or do I have food poisoning? When the bathroom sieges let up, it's almost 6:00 AM. I return to bed and fall into an exhausted sleep.

I wanted to get an early morning start, but it's almost 9:00 AM before I am able to drag myself out of bed and get to 516. Rolf is not about, and since I never know if that means for a couple of hours or all day, I leave the letter in an obvious spot on the kitchen table.

Mother has just returned from having breakfast at Sally's. I have not talked to her about leaving for Janice's place today. I didn't want her to change her mind, but time has run out and I have to bring up the subject now. "Well, Mom, are you ready for a trip to Whidbey Island?"

"Oh, yes. Are we going today?"

"We can if you want to."

"Okay, let's go."

"Well, if we're going to do that we better get busy right away. You don't have anything packed."

The House that Daddy Built

Mother immediately helps me pack a couple of bags, and she carries each one to the car. Everything seems so automatic. She's so willing to go, but her attitude is about the same as if we are going on a bill-paying trip or a walk to Sally's cafe. I know she can't possibly understand where we're going or why or for how long. I feel bad--sick--and not just from my horrendous night. I feel sick, because I know I'm at least in part being deceitful, because I know she will never be coming back to live in the house that Daddy built for her to live in for the rest of her life.

Once we're on the freeway with miles racking up, Mother is an enjoyable traveling companion. She is in good spirits and interested in almost everything that passes in our view. I am especially thankful for her attitude, because I continue to feel horrible. I stop at every roadside rest-stop and make a dash for the facilities. Each time Mother says she doesn't have to go.

Finally in the early afternoon, we pull into a drive-in. "Mother, we've got to get something to eat, but we're not going to eat until we *both* have a bathroom break. You've got to change that Depend."

"Well, maybe I could go a little bit."

She makes no objection as I go into the handicapped stall with her, and we both chuckle at our vigorous urine streams. "Mother, I don't know how you lasted so long. I thought you would be drenched, but you're almost totally dry."

"Well, I don't have that problem all the time, you know. I'll be awful glad when this old time of the month is over. It seems like it's going on forever."

We finally get into the restaurant, and Mother eats heartily--a burger, fries, and a milkshake. She enjoys everything and remarks about how tasty the food is. I continue to be terribly nauseous, and I fall asleep with my head in my hand and my elbow propped on the table.

"Betty, Betty, you better wake up and eat something. We still have a long drive, and I've never driven your car."

"Oh, that's okay, Mom. I can drive."

"Well, you've hardly touched your food. You need to eat something."

"Oh, Mom, I just don't feel hungry."

"Well, I'll just help you out a little bit."

Mother reaches across the table and drags my food to her side. As she finishes my lunch, I let my head slip back down against my hand and sleep a few more minutes.

Back in the car we continue north, passing small towns and beautiful countryside, each receiving lavish appreciation from Mother. A bit further on, the Seattle skyline and freeway traffic are not so much appreciated. Her recitations of admiration for whatever kind of scenery we are passing begin to be punctuated with, "I just don't know when Dad and I will ever be able to take this trip again. There are so many cars and buses and great big old trucks. I don't think Dad could drive in all this traffic mess." She begins to stare blankly straight ahead, and her conversation becomes repetitive, slurred, and irrational. I know she's tired.

I'm on my own sort of automatic pilot in our conversation, each time telling her in a flat, non-emotional tone, "Dad can't drive this trip, Mother. He's dead. He died February 2nd. Remember? That was the day before El's birthday."

After several repetitions, she raises her voice, "Dad is *not* dead!"

I lower my voice and maintain a monotone. "Yes, he is, Mom. We buried him at Ridgeview Memorial Park. You picked out the headstone with the dogwood for your side and a deer with mountains and trees for Dad's side."

It's quiet for a moment. "Well I don't know why I can't get that through my head. Is he buried yet?"

"Yes, Mother. Pastor Ted preached his funeral service and Rolf spoke."

"Oh, yes, Pastor Ted talked about all the nice things Dad and I had done for them over the years."

"Good. You're remembering now."

"Now who's place are we going to on Whidbey?"

71

"Her name is Janice."

"Oh, yes, she's a friend of your friend, Doris Musieleski."

"Right. You're absolutely right."

"Now how long am I going to stay there?"

"I don't know exactly--at least until school's out."

"How long is that?"

I hedge a moment. "I don't know the exact date, because I don't know how many days we have to make up because of snow and the teacher strike. You'll be fine though."

"Well, she won't want me to stay up there a month or more."

"Oh, Mother, she'll want you to stay that long or longer. She's looking forward to meeting you, and I think you'll enjoy meeting some new people. Don't you think so?"

"Well, yes, I like meeting new people." There's a brief pause, and she adds, "I think I'll just go home with you today though. I can stay with you and Don."

"No, Mother, I need to have you be with Janice."

"Why?"

"Well, it's because you and I both think you need a rest and to be with other people. I need to be able to talk to you, and Rolf has made that pretty much impossible by constantly leaving the phone off the hook."

"I know he does that, but sometimes the cats knock the phone off the hook."

"Yes, the cats do that, but the last couple of times it was the upstairs phone that was off. You can say it was your cats if you like, but the cats can't get upstairs because Rolf has the stairs blocked off with those big sheets of plywood."

"Yes, I know. He doesn't need to have those big old wood pieces there like that. The kitties wouldn't go up there anyway. This morning the phone was off the hook in the kitchen, and I put it back because I thought Mavis might try to call me and she wouldn't be able to get through."

"Well, she has tried to call and not been able to get through. That's why a couple of times I've asked your neighbor to come over and have you put the phone back, so she could try again."

"Now where are we going on Whidbey Island?"

"We're going to Doris' friend Janice's place."

"I've never met Doris, have I?"

"No, I don't think so."

"You took me to her house once a long time ago."

"I did?"

"Yes, she lives right on the beach there by the ferry, but she wasn't home."

"My God, Mother, your memory is better than mine. I had forgotten that."

"Will I meet Doris this trip?"

"I don't know. She travels quite a bit. I think she's in Africa now. I'm sure when she's home and knows you're at Janice's she'll stop by and introduce herself. She has often remarked she would like to meet you."

"How long am I going to stay at Janice's?"

"At least until school is out."

"Couldn't I just stay with you and Don?"

"You can visit us after school is out, but before that there isn't anyone home at my house during the work day."

"I don't mind being by myself."

"I know you don't, but I would worry. What if you left the house to try to find the nursing home?"

"Well, I wouldn't do that. I'll visit Dad when I go home."

"No, Mother. Dad is dead."

"Why, he is not dead. No one informed me of that."

On and on--miles and miles! Now where am I going? Who's Janice? Why can't I just stay with you and Don? When are you going to move to Whidbey? When are Don and you going to retire? How much will your retirement be? I don't know if Dad will be able to cut down all those trees that are growing on our property and build us a house. How long am I going to stay? How much does it cost to stay at Janice's? Dad is *not* dead. Is he buried yet? Have you already made arrangements with Janice? How do you know Janice?

We finally arrive at the Mukilteo ferry landing and fortunately are loaded promptly onto the boat. Once we're parked safely, I try to get Mother to go with me to take a bathroom break. She says she doesn't need to go. I really don't either, but I have to get out of this car for at least a few minutes.

Cold wind laced with salt air gusts through the car deck. It feels good as it lashes against my face, validating that I am alive and capable of feeling cold. After a short walk around the car deck, I shiver and climb back into the car. Mother hasn't missed me, as she is staring out the windshield at the white caps on the water. I lean the seat back and fall asleep.

"Betty, Betty, wake up. That man in the red vest is motioning to us. I can't drive this car off the ferry. Wake up!"

I jerk to alertness, hurriedly start the car, and lurch forward exiting the boat. Our drive up South Whidbey is gorgeous. Mother chatters pleasantly recalling details of the island as she recognizes occasional familiar landmarks.

"Look Betty, there's that old log store. They sell fresh salmon there. I'd like to get some. If you'll stop, I'll buy it."

We don't stop, and she doesn't seem to miss the fact that we don't.

A short way further, Mother recalls, "Oh, yes, I remember this Y in the road just ahead. That's the vineyard, right? If we take that right-hand fork, we'll end up right where our property goes in. Let's not miss our turn."

"You're right, Mother, but we're going to take the other fork in the road today. We'll visit your property another day. How do you remember things like that? It's been years since we've been up here."

"Oh, I remember visiting our property and driving up through there on a bumpy old logging road. Dad and I had a picnic with you and Don and Nick and El--way up on top of the mountain."

"You're right."

"Dad will never be able to find that old logging road though. It's probably all grown up. Now where are we going?"

I tell her the plan once again as we drive on through a forested area and eventually the wheat fields and corn fields in the center part of the island. We turn off several side roads and finally pull onto a gravel driveway under a big log entry arch. Burned lettering indicates "Whispering Firs." I ease around the wooded circular driveway and stop in front of the steps to the house.

I turn off the engine and lean my head against the steering wheel.

Thank God, we're home! Oh, God, I dare not utter the word home aloud, as even the possibility of this place becoming home will start Mother with a million more repetitions of some kind. Anyway, thank you, God, for our safe trip. Please guide us both.

CHAPTER 8

Janice's Place

I JUMP OUT and go up the steps and ring the bell. Janice answers almost immediately and greets me with a warm hug. She then goes down to the car to welcome Mother. She opens the car door and introduces herself. She tells Mother how much she's heard about her and how wonderful it is to meet her. She helps Mother rise from the car seat and embraces her warmly. Mother likes her immediately. Janice and I both help Mother negotiate the front steps and find our way into the house.

"Have you had dinner, Francine?"

"Yes, we had a big lunch. I'm not hungry. I think I need to go to the bathroom though."

As I recall I didn't have lunch, but I'm not really hungry either. I do need to join Mother in the bathroom trip though.

"Well, we're just having dessert. So you both join us in the dining room when you're ready." Janice runs off toward the kitchen, and Mother and I find the nearest bathroom.

When we emerge, Janice calls out, "We're all out here in the dining room. Come join us. We're having dessert with strawberries from the garden."

Mother moves ahead of me into the dining room, where she surveys the generous helpings shortcake

Francine enjoying her "vacation" at Janice's place after Dad's death, spring 1991

piled high with strawberries and real whip cream. She immediately pulls out a chair at the dining room table and makes herself at home.

Janice introduces Sadie, who is seated at the far end of the table. She glances up momentarily from her plate, a woman with a sharp, angular face, punctuated with heavy, bushy eyebrows and shocks of white wiry hair sticking out from her face in irregular clumps of uncontrolled kinky curls. Sadie resumes her intense study of the remaining strawberries on her plate. Without looking up again and directed to no one in particular, in a very soft voice Sadie grumbles something unintelligible, "Last thing we need--another woman--men are--I like better--men work...."

I'm sure Mother can't hear these remarks, and that's probably a good thing.

Janice ignores Sadie's remarks as she goes on to introduce her ex-husband, Joe, who is also seated at the table enjoying dessert. Joe has been working on the property today, and he and Mother begin a conversation about Janice's garden and the home-grown strawberries in the dessert and which species of strawberries grow best on Whidbey Island.

Little Fern, a sort of anorexic eighty-ish looking lady, is having her dessert in her special chair in the living room, but she comes through the dining room and stops to welcome Mother and stays to chat. She's friendly and quick witted. Pretty in a delicate way. She laughs easily and adds a happy note to the dessert group. Mother and I both like her.

As the table is cleared Joe makes his departure. Mother leans toward me and says in a shouted whisper, "We're not staying here tonight, are we?"

"Yes, Mother, we are staying here."

"Well, we need to get on out of here and get to your house for the night."

"No, Mother, I'm sleeping here tonight. And you're going to be staying here with Janice for a while."

"Well, how long is that?"

"At least until school is out."

Mother and I move to the living room, and she renews her vocal routine from our earlier five hours in the automobile, but now it's more of a tired song-like ritual without much emotion to it. Shortly Janice comes down stairs dressed in her nightgown. As she and Mother converse, I run out to my car and get our bags. I leave Mother's things in the room Janice has designated, and I dress in my nightclothes there. Then I come back to the living room and spread my sleeping bag out on one of the couches. Janice, Mother, and I continue to visit, and the minutes tick by until 9:00 PM. Janice goes to help one of the ladies with her pills, and a few minutes later returns to the landing, which is three steps up from the level of the living room. She calls down, "Come on up, Francine, I have your bed all ready for you, and I have your night clothes laid out."

Mother pulls herself out of the big chair where she has been sitting and shuffles over to the couch where I am stretched out in my sleeping bag, "Why can't I sleep right here with you on that other couch?"

"Mother, you can't do that. Janice has prepared a bed for you and it's waiting. It's nice and fresh and clean just for you--and you are going to sleep in the bed she has prepared." I close my eyes, wait a moment, then roll over away from her. Moments later I know she is still standing near me in the dimmed light of the living room, and I can see Janice still standing on the landing. I make myself remain with my back to Mother. Finally I hear her shuffle around to the other side of my couch-bed and go up the steps to where Janice is waiting.

"You certainly have a beautiful home here, Janice."

"Thank you, Francine. Come on this way and let me help you. The bathroom is right down here."

At 1:30 AM I awaken. It's Janice involved in a quiet scramble near the outside deck door trying to get Sadie to close the door and not go outside. Sadie has gotten up, completely dressed herself, and is ready to start the day. She wants to go outside to look for Joe, whom she likes to visit with while he's working around the place. Janice persuades her it's a bit early for Joe to arrive to work today. I kick off the afghan which is covering my sleeping bag as the house seems warm to me. I fall back to sleep.

At 5:00 AM I hear Fern in the kitchen preparing a cup of tea and a banana for herself. She proceeds quietly but verbalizes each step of her routine, including coming into the living room where I am "sleeping" and having her snack in her special chair. She doesn't speak to me nor seem aware of my presence. And when she is finished, she returns silently to her room.

A bit later I hear Janice in the kitchen preparing breakfast. Mother has gotten dressed and come downstairs. I don't see her, but I smell her. Although I laid out fresh clothes and Depends last night, she seems to have avoided them.

I get up sleepily and greet Mother and Janice. In reasonable quietness Mother and I get to the bathroom to do what's necessary to protect Janice's beautiful furniture.

When we return to the dining room Sadie is sitting at the table eating her breakfast. She pauses between quick jerky bites and commands, "Sit down, you two. I guess if we have to share with someone else, we have to share."

Mother and I seat ourselves, and Sadie gets up and leaves. Janice passes by her, gives her a hug, and tells her, "Sadie, I love you, but this lady needs a home, too."

Mother ignores the comment and dives into the orange juice, home-made buttermilk pancakes, bacon, and rich black coffee. Her concentration is focused on whether to have the home-made loganberry, blackberry or maple syrup. She selects the loganberry, pours a liberal amount over her pancakes, and begins to eat heartily.

A sad thought flits through my mind, as I recall years back when Mother told me Dad was so much better after his stroke. "Oh, Betty, Dad is eating like a logger. He's going to be well in no time."

Mother is eating like a *lady logger*. But I know she'll never be *well*.

After breakfast Sadie returns and helps clear the table. Mother leans over and says to me, "Have you settled up for all this?"

"Yes, I have."

"Well, good. We ought to do something nice for Janice for this. Now we better get on out of here and get on our way to your house."

"No, I'm going home a bit later today. You're staying here for a while."

"Well, how long do I have to stay?"

Mother's routine is kept in "shouted whispers," which Janice obviously hears from the kitchen. Janice coaches me from there in her own whispers as I direct Mother's attention to the property with its pleasant wooded setting, the garden spot, the beautiful breakfast and the comfortable bed.

Janice comes back into the dining room and announces, "Let's all take a little hike now. Exercise is good for all of us. Francine, I'd like to show you my whole place. It's about five acres. I heard you say you liked to garden. I have a garden, which Joe has been working on for me, but not nearly what I'd like it to be. Maybe you could give me some suggestions on that."

Mother's interest thankfully refocuses on gardening, and we follow Janice out of the house and onto a well kept path leading to a garden spot. Below the garden there's an orchard with cherry, apple, plum, and nut trees. Mother wants to continue through the orchard and the meadow beyond. "What's below this?"

"That's a path down to my road and the mail-box. Would you like to pick up the mail with me?"

"Oh, sure, as long as we're down this far."

We all cross the road to the mail-box, and Janice asks, "Francine, would you like to walk back through the woods?"

"Oh, that would be nice."

"It's a little bit rough. Joe hasn't quite finished the path through that part of the property, but I think we'd be okay."

"Janice, I followed Dad on so many deer hunting trails and fishing trails, I doubt any of your trails could be as bad."

With a helping hand she follows Janice down into the shallow road-side ditch. The other side of the ditch is steeper, and with me pushing and Janice pulling and all three of us giggling, Mother climbs up the bank into the wooded area, a wonderfully shaded section with huge second growth Douglas fir, grand fir, hemlock, cedar and thick clusters of ferns.

Mother looks upward and makes a complete turn about. "Oh, this is lovely. There ought to be a deer or two in here." She looks back down around her feet, "And look at all these beautiful wildflowers. I saw some wild strawberries back there in the ditch, and these pretty little things right here are wild violets. Oh, and here in the middle are some twin flowers, and I think that big drooping one behind the Salal is called False Solomon's Seal."

Janice is impressed. "You're quite a botanist, Francine."

"I've always loved flowers--wild flowers and the ones in the yard."

We all pause to watch two playful squirrels a few feet away as they do spiraling races up and down a tree, then jump from tree to tree and back down to the ground. They hide momentarily, then do it all over again. Just as we get back near the lush lawn behind Janice's house, a beautiful doe turns away from the rose bushes beside the house and slips into the woods coming face to face with us. She's gorgeous and we all three freeze in silent admiration, even though Janice knows she's been pruning her roses. Above our heads a red-headed woodpecker gives a sudden staccato drum roll. The doe bounds away in the opposite direction. Our tour is concluded.

As we go back into the house, it's near lunch time. I lie down on the couch out of view from the table where Mother has chosen to sit. Janice asks her to come to the kitchen and stir the soup. I hear them chatting about cooking, recipes, and other kitchen tasks. Janice sings bits and pieces of church hymns as she works. Mother recognizes and enjoys them, though she tells Janice she's not much of a singer herself. I hear the two of them in the pantry and Mother admiring all the home-canned fruits, jellies, and pickles. Janice asks her to stack the paper towels and napkins from a recent shopping trip on the shelf, while she goes back to put lunch on the table. Mother is not at all hesitant when she hears the lunch call. She immediately seats herself at the table and adjusts her napkin on her lap. She and Sadie both begin blowing and slurping their soup. Janice scurries in to her place at the table and asks us to join hands and say grace. Sadie is disgruntled about this interruption, but Mother is obedient and seems embarrassed at her faux pas. Lunch is split pea soup, tuna and cheese sandwiches, fruit compote, pickles and crackers. At the end of lunch Sadie promptly gets up to clear the table. Mother remains at the table and samples the contents of the serving dishes one bite at a time, licking her spoon after each bite and dipping it into the next dish. No one says anything regarding this.

I excuse myself and go about gathering my things and repacking my car. Janice and I complete some paper work. I leave some cash in Mother's little purse and some additional money with Janice, as a nurse's aide will be coming during the week to do toenails and manicures for the ladies. Mother wants to know how much to tip the girls, and we go over it several times. She seems to understand she can also have her hair done if she wants to. She has enough cash to pay for that, too.

"Okay, Mom, you have a good week. Bye."

Mother seems nonchalant as she gives me a peck on the cheek. "Good-bye. You be careful driving."

Janice leads me out through the kitchen and ducks into the pantry for a moment. "I'm really pleased so far, Betty. I feel it's right that your mom is here. Don't you worry. She will be just fine in her new home."

"Janice, I don't know about *new home*. I don't know if this is for the short run or if this is forever--but I agree, for now it feels right. Mother's fine, and I think I'm okay."

Francine's brother Malcom and her two sisters, Mavis and Mo, came to visit her at Janice's place

El also visits her grandma at Janice's place

CHAPTER 9

My Friend Doris

Is FOSTER CARE with Janice the answer to my prayers? Will it answer Mother's needs? Does a foster home substitute for the "home that Daddy built"? Will Mother be happy? Will my life be easier? Can Mother's financial woes be brought into balance? Will Rolf undergo some miraculous change?

A fusillade of questions hammers my brain as I leave Mother at Janice's and head for the ferry. Near the long stretch of beach about a mile before the ferry dock, I see my friend Doris' car in front of her house, and I pull into her driveway.

Doris and I walk on the beach and let the sun and the rhythm of salt water sloshing on pebbles refresh us. Doris has not been feeling well, and I sense her illness is taking a toll; but she keeps a busy schedule with family activities and planning for another trip to South Africa with a mission team from her church.

I appreciate today's opportunity to visit and to tell Doris about my mother. I also tell her what an important part of my life she has been. God's mission field does not have to be in South Africa; she has been a missionary to me right here both spiritually and practically in regard to my mother. Doris is a walking miracle, having lived far beyond her medically predicted years. In regard to her illness and everything else in her life, she reflects a simple child-like but intense faith in God's power to provide for the good spirit within an individual and strength to overcome evil. I feel so immature in this regard. I'm still not sure if that inner battle is my *yin and yang*, comedy and tragedy, black and white, or God and Satan.

We look out across the water and see the ferry approaching. I certainly can't solve my philosophical dilemma now. Ferries don't wait. I ask Doris to stop by Janice's and get acquainted with my mother. Then I rush for the boat.

CHAPTER 10

Adjusting To Janice's Place

I GIVE MOTHER two weeks to adjust without visits from me as per Janice's suggestion. During this time I get daily telephone reports from Janice. I don't speak to Mother directly, but I send her cards and notes. I make sure her sisters and brother know her new address, and they assure me they will write her frequently, and later after the introductory adjustment period they will call her regularly. I'm confident her sisters will do this. Her brother is a notorious promiser.

At the end of the two weeks, Don and I load the big Toro Horse Tiller into the back of the pickup for a trip to Janice's to prepare a garden spot,

a project which has developed via the notes to Mother and phone calls with Janice. Also, El is going to come down from college and spend the day with us at Janice's and help with the garden.

A Sunday dinner at Janice's Place:
Nick, Francine, the author, and El

When we arrive, El's little truck is already parked in the circular drive. I find everyone happily visiting in the kitchen.

"Well, my God, Betty, where'd you come from? Did you come with El?"

"No, Don and I just came over for the day."

"Well, where's Don?"

"He's unloading our big tiller. We're going to help Janice plow up some new garden space."

Everyone works to ready Janice's
garden, including the author

"Is he doing that right now?"
"Yes."
"Well, we better get down to that garden. He won't know where to plow?"

We each carry a folding chair and cold drinks down to a convenient spot under an apple tree. Nearby Don revs the tiller into a loud roar and the blades dig into the rich, black soil. Mother is excited and interested in the project and chats about the seeds she and Janice have bought already and the starter plants they will get after the plowing is done. We all watch the progress of each new row with the aptness of an Indy 500 audience, and Don and I and El take turns managing the big tiller.

El takes a turn at The Big Tiller

Francine overseeing The Garden

The author and her mother appreciate
the day's tilling work

When we are almost finished, Janice brings a picnic lunch to the orchard for all of us. The break for our strained muscles is as welcome as sating our hunger pangs.

As the afternoon wears on and Mother tires, she begins to speak with whomever is resting and keeping her company about not wanting to stay at Janice's any longer.

"Betty, when Don gets all this plowing done for Janice, I believe I'll go home with you. I'll stay a couple days, then I've got to get on to Ridgeview and check on Dad."

I decide not to re-teach Mother about Dad's death at this moment. "I know this is all kind of confusing, Mom, but going back to Ridgeview right now is not a choice. You've told me repeatedly you like it here."

"Oh, it's wonderful here. Janice is such a good cook. The food is great. She's a hard worker, too. She just cleans and cooks and works outside and go-go-goes! And she's always singing as she works."

"Well, why do you want to leave then?"

"I've got to go home and check on Dad."

El tries to help. "But, Grandma, I have plans to come see you again *here* in two weeks. This place is so much closer for me to come from the college. I can get here in less than an hour. If you were in Ridgeview, it's about five hours away, and that's too far for me to come for a day visit. Besides, I already told one of my friends she could come with me the next time I come to visit my grandma. Janice said it was okay. We could stay over in her basement apartment. Wouldn't that be fun?"

"El, you and your friend can come right on to Ridgeview and stay with Dad and me. We have plenty of room."

"But, Grandma, I can't do that, because Grandpa's..." El looks at me.

I am physically and emotionally tired, and it shows as I bark out the words. "Mom, Dad is dead! You have to stay put right here until school is out. We already agreed on that. Remember all those trips to the nursing home looking for Dad. The nursing home staff would tell you Dad was dead and buried and send you home. Then they would call me and interrupt my teaching day to tell me what had happened....

"No, Mother, you can't be in Ridgeview and wander around like that!"

"I can't be staying here. Janice won't want me to stay that long."

El joins the conversation again, "Oh, yes she would, Grandma. Janice likes you. She says you're interested in lots of things, and you talk a lot."

Mother laughs. "Well, Janice is interesting, too, but it's too expensive here."

El shoots back, "Janice told me that's all taken care of."

Mother looks at me perplexed. I look away, knowing nothing is paid for. Janice is waiting until I get court permission to spend Dad's life insurance money for this care.

Mother continues, "Well, I know this is expensive. I can't just sit around up here on vacation. I've got to get back home. Rolf and Dad need me."

I ignore the part about Dad. "You shouldn't be worrying about Rolf. He needs to get on with his life. He needs to get a regular steady job and pay his own way."

"I know that and I want him to do that, but he won't eat right. I need to fix meals for him and Dad. Rolf eats out all the time, and that's not healthy."

As the roar of the tiller approaches, I spring up from my chair and volunteer for an early turn, wresting the vibrating handlebars from Don and shouting into his face, "You need a break! El is going to the house for cold drinks. Please go with her!" As I maneuver the throbbing machine around the far corner of the garden, I see El and Don disappear on the garden path. Mother is sitting under the apple tree alone continuing her irrational diatribe to an empty pop can clutched in her lap.

Later in the evening Janice advises, "Betty, just be firm and tell your mother the doctor said she can no longer live safely by herself. This is the best place for her, and she may either choose to live at this home or she may choose to live in some other care facility--or a nursing home. The time has come, and the move must be made this summer while you are not in the classroom. Just tell her you can't go through another year like last year. Be very firm in your decision and in telling her."

Moments later I find occasion to employ Janice's recommendation. We are all back in the house, cleaned up from our garden work, and having a cup of coffee before Don and I leave for our home and El goes back to college. Mother attempts to resume command, "Betty, you need to help me get my things together now. I'm going home with you and Don today."

I lean toward Mother establishing direct eye contact, "No, Mother, you're not going home with Don and me today. You are not coming to our home until school is out. I will see you in two weeks."

I rise and separate myself from my unfinished cup of coffee. I gently kiss Mother's angry cheek, bid Janice goodbye and go out the front door followed closely by Don and El. Mother's protests are hanging in a silent, stabbing furor which I feel on my back as I pass through the doorway.

I have been *sort of firm*, but I didn't tell her she would no longer be living by herself. I couldn't. I feel rotten. Yeah, I'm a regular firm chicken!

Don and I bid El goodbye out front and we go our separate ways.

Dear God, it's time for another purple tulip. I shudder in trying to be firm in this decision about Mother's new home. I truly believe this move has been the right thing to do, and Janice's place is the best possible choice for right now. With your help I'll work out the finances. But it's the laying down the law to my mother that seems an impossible task. Maybe it's like Dr. Jones said that I myself slip in and out of the roles of daughter and guardian, and then I'm not firm enough in the guardian role. Please guide me and strengthen me in this whole process.

A couple of days later Mother calls. "Hello, Betty. Are you coming to get me today? I want to spend two days with you and Don. Then I want to get on home."

My firm guardian voice responds, "You're welcome to come over here to visit us when school is out, but you're a bit early right now. School isn't out yet."

"I want to come over there today, and then I want to get on home. I don't want to stay at Janice's any longer."

"Mom, I'm still in school, and I can't have you come right now."

"Then I'll just have to go home on the bus!"

"Mom, you can't do that."

"Why?"

"You can't be in Ridgeview by yourself."

"Well, Rolf and Dad need me."

"Mother, Dad is dead, and Rolf can fend for himself. He's older than I am, for Pete's sake. Besides, he's trying to get a job in Alaska; and if he does, there would be no one there to be with you."

I try to turn the conversation. "So, how is everything up on Whidbey?"

"Fine."

"Have you told Janice you're going to go home?"

"No."

"Do you like her place?"

"Yes, it's wonderful here. I like it fine. I like Janice, too. She's a wonderful person, and she is such a good cook. I just need to go home."

"No, Mother, you're not going to go to Ridgeview and be by yourself."

"Are you coming to Whidbey today?"

"No."

"Why not?"

"I'm preparing final exams for my students."

"Can Don come up here and get me and bring me over there?"

"No. Don is not coming up there today either."

"Well, when I see you, we'll talk more about this. I do just fine by myself. I never went to that nursing home to visit Dad, and I don't care what those people told you. They're lying. Are you coming up to pick me up tonight?"

"No."

"Well, I don't know why not. I'm going home on the bus if you're not coming."

"Mother, is Janice there?"

"Yes."

"May I speak to her?"

"Yes, just a minute. I'll get her for you."

I hear Mother calling pleasantly for Janice and Janice responding, "Yes, dear, what do you need?"

"Betty wants to speak with you."

"I'll be right there, Francine."

There's a clanking of pans and shuffling of feet in the background, and I hear Mother and Janice exchange the phone.

"Hello, Janice? Is everything okay up there?"

"Yes, we're all fine here."

"Has Mother told you she wants to leave--and if I don't come and get her today she's going to take a bus?"

"Oh my goodness, no. Francine hasn't said a thing about leaving or taking a bus. She's really doing fine. She may be feeling that, but she hasn't said a thing to me about leaving. In fact, she's very cooperative. She seems to enjoy doing little tasks in the kitchen and around the house, and all three ladies have been taking daily walks with me. Today we went on an outing to the garden shop and got some more seeds, and Francine picked out special kinds of tomatoes which she knew to do well in a Northwest garden. Francine and Fern have become fast friends. Fern doesn't care much for tomatoes, so Francine got some snow peas and carrots for her for the garden. Fern liked that, but she told your mom she didn't need to think she was going to rope her into doing garden work just because she got those snow peas and carrots. Your mom just laughed. Sadie just sort of tagged along and was grumpy to everyone. I don't think she's too interested in gardening."

"Well, Janice, I know mother likes Fern, but I don't think she likes Sadie very much."

"No, I don't think so. Fern doesn't like her much either. The two of them have had a few words for Sadie, but it's mostly because Sadie's so bossy and neither your mom nor Fern will mind Sadie, and that keeps Sadie kind of stirred up. I don't think it's a problem though. Sadie has been a person who has pretty well spent her whole life making other people miserable, and now that she doesn't function at total brain capacity, she has no idea how or why she should behave any differently. You know, if a person spends most of their life being ornery, they usually continue that behavior in their old age, senile or not.

"I have to watch Sadie pretty close. She has a tendency to wander off. Sometimes she gets up in the night and wants to go places, too. She's pretty determined to do whatever she wants to do whenever she wants to do it. If anyone was going to try to catch a bus, it would most likely be Sadie.

"Neither Francine nor Fern are like that. They are both very positive people and interested in lots of things. They are enjoying each other's company and developing a lovely friendship. Every afternoon they watch the news together, and Fern peels an apple and shares it with your mom. Some older folks keep on being nice people, even if they are senile. That's just how some folks are. Fern and Francine seem to be very happy being with each other. I'm quite surprised Francine wants to leave."

I feel a weariness, but I guess things are okay at Janice's place, or at least Janice can control the problems.

About 8:00 PM the same evening Mother calls again. "Janice has gone to dinner and to church with another lady, and I thought I would call you."

"Who's there with you and Fern?"

"Barbara. She's a friend of Janice's who comes in and works for her."

"Did you ask to make a long distance call?"

"No, I don't have to ask. Janice told me I could use the phone. I need to know if you're coming to pick me up tonight?"

"No, Mother, the answer is the same at eight o'clock tonight as it was when you called this afternoon."

Mother raises her voice signaling the predictable routine, "*When* are you--"

"Mother, you can't be making long distance calls like this without permission. We talked a long while this afternoon, and that's enough for today."

"Okay then, but I'll just have to go home on the bus. Good-bye."

"You do that, Mom. Good-bye."

Though my words are harsh, a part of me doesn't seem to care. Deep within my head a voice tells me, *Let it go; don't worry about it. Let God and Janice--or Barbara--or whomever manage --Mother right now.* My guts are rolling again. I feel shaky and nauseous.

A different voice taunts, *Chicken, Chicken--Your mom can still out-maneuver you with only a partially functioning brain. It's Francine who is managing the guardian! Ha!*

Dear God, help me let go. I know I can only do what's humanly possible. I believe I've done that in all the decisions I've made so far. I can only do what you direct and allow me to do. God, please help me find in you a safe and comforting refuge! Please help me do this right!

———∞∞∞———

CHAPTER 11

A Call From Auntie Mo

A SHORT WHILE later the telephone jars me to alertness. Aunt Maurine, Mother's younger sister who lives in Fort Worth, greets me in a soft, sweet Texas drawl. "Hey, Betty, I been thinkin' 'bout you today, and I just thought I'd give ya a call. How are y'all doin' up there?"

"Oh, Auntie Mo, the whole experience of moving Mother to Janice's was horrendous, and I feel it was right--but I don't know if it's going to work." I tearfully give Mo details of my phone conversation with Mother earlier today.

"Now, Betty Anne, you're fretting way too much. We all know your mama needs the kind of care being provided, and she seems plenty happy whenever I talk to her on the phone. I'm just glad you found someone as reliable as Janice."

My response is to fill Auntie Mo's ears with my long-distance sobs.

"Now, Betty Anne, you listen to me--listen up, girl. You've used good judgment so far. Older people generally suffer some mental confusion, some more than others. When it's time for them not to live alone, it's just time not to live alone. Nary a one of them will ever admit it themselves. I'm sorry you and Rolf can't agree on things, but I have confidence in what you have done and will do. You may have some even tougher decisions to make as time goes on. You keep doing what you feel is right down deep in your guts. Go ahead and sell that house. It probably should have been done long ago. Move Rolf out of there, and use Francine's assets for Francine. That's what should happen. If you can't sell the house, get Rolf's butt out of there and rent it."

"Mo, I'm not so confident either one of those actions will happen very easily. The house is not in any condition to sell, and Rolf seems to be pretty well embedded in the place. But I'm glad to know *you* think those are appropriate moves."

"Well, I know Mavis and Malcom think so, too. We've all been thinking about you and Don a whole lot lately.

"Now, Betty, I know you've been having a hard time, and I know Francine never has been an easy person to deal with when she makes up her mind about something. I'm sure that part about her is intensified now by her mental condition. You just be firm and do what you have to do!"

Dear God, is this how you answer prayers? If so, thank you. I really needed that phone call. I appreciate knowing that Mother's sisters and brother feel supportive of what I have done. I pray that you do use other people to deliver messages of your will, and that I have understood them correctly. Help me to continue to listen and discern, and please help me to be firm!

CHAPTER 12

Another Call, How's Mom?

BEFORE I CAN savor my renewed level of confidence, the telephone rings again. Rolf tells me all is quiet in Ridgeview. "I'm just checking up about Mom. I was gonna' call Aunt Mavis tomorrow, and I wanted to report to her how she is."

"Well, you can call Mother yourself and ask that, if you like--and so can Mavis. I've written to Aunt Mavis and Aunt Maurine--and Uncle Malcom, too. I've given all of them the telephone number and the address. I hope they will all communicate a little more often than they have in the past."

"Yeah, yeah. Say, I was thinkin' about givin' that little cat of Mom's to a kid down the street. Is that okay with you?"

"It's okay with me. I would be more concerned about what you are going to do with Taco."

"Oh, he's okay. I took him in the logging truck with me the three days I worked last week; and I took him for a good run down at the county line beach. He liked that."

"I meant what are you going to do with him for the long term? Likewise, what are you going to do with all those guns and other stuff you have crammed into that house--especially if you're going to go to Alaska?"

"Oh, I talked to Lars about going up there with me, but his father-in-law don't want him to go, and the old man offered him the same pay to stay put and help him with the oil route. I guess Lars figured that would be a good deal."

"If you're going to Alaska, Rolf, you need to tell me, because that house needs to be sold, probably sooner than either one of us may like to think."

"How much does it cost to keep Mom at Janice's?"

"Well, right now it's about $100 more per month than her income, but I'm taking that amount out of Dad's insurance money. When that runs out, then I'll either sell the house or the Whidbey property, whichever becomes salable first. The cost of keeping Mother at Janice's is about half as much as a nursing home, and right now she's got money to do that, but Dad's insurance money won't last forever."

"Well, from what I've talked to Janice about, Mom is doing pretty good. I hope she recuperates."

"Rolf, that's not likely. The doctors have all said she is not going to get better; and as the strokes continue, she *will* get worse. Yes, right now she's fine--in fact, improved and maybe even somewhat stable--but no one knows how long she will stay at this level. You need to have a plan in mind for you and your stuff. Rolf, I can't do anything about protecting the house or any other assets--especially yours. Mom and Dad just didn't do their legal preparations for aging and death. None of their assets can be protected in any way for you or for me. Whatever Mom and Dad owned is *hers* now, and I have to use her assets for her care. You and your stuff need to be out of *her* house. That's how it has to be. She will need assisted care of some sort indefinitely, and it will not be in 516."

"Well, I just don't know."

"Rolf, you're young enough to get a new job and begin anew. You have to believe in yourself and listen for God's direction. Neither Mom nor I can direct you."

"Yeah, yeah, I know God has had a hand in all this bad stuff that's happened to me, but I can't figure out what it was for. Sometimes I just don't want to try anymore."

"Rolf, you have lots of ability and you need to use your creative powers and listen. God doesn't do bad stuff *to* people. People make bad choices!"

"Well, I heard the son-of-a-bitch that had my truck locked up has it back out on the road again. I just wonder where the justice is in that. I just don't know."

"Rolf, you can't keep worrying about that repossessed logging truck. Can't you sell a part of that gun collection and take care of your financial obligations?"

"I don't know. I just don't know."

"You have more assets than a lot of people who go into business for themselves. You could run a gun shop. You could repair guns and load ammunition and who knows what else? I know you can't decide tonight, but you've got to have something in mind. I cannot emphasize strongly enough that I have to use Mother's assets for her and her keep, and I need to free her from your debt in order to do that. She can't pay her debts and yours, too. She has to have assisted care now--and for the rest of her life."

"I just don't know. I don't know."

"Well, you better *start knowing*! You better be getting a plan in mind, because when I have to sell the house, it's liable to happen very quickly."

"Well, I'm sure Mom's in good hands for now. Janice sounds like a fine person from what you say and from what I've talked to her on the phone. I'd like to get up there to visit Mom, but my old car probably ain't that reliable."

I don't bite on the poor-me line. "If your old car can make it to Vader, Ryderwood, and Seattle, it can make it to Whidbey Island. Then, of course, there's always a bus."

"Yeah, yeah. Say, I paid the paper girl here the other day. That was eight bucks."

"I think the best thing to do with the paper is to stop delivery."

"I don't think I want to stop it. *I* read it."

"Then do as you like. If *you* read it, then *you* pay for it. Mother will not be reading the paper. If she ever returns to Ridgeview, then she can start it again. So, if you continue it, it will be *for* you and paid for *by* you."

The phone is quiet. I feel the resistance, but he says nothing.

I continue, "The same thing is true for the cablevision and the long distance telephone service. Those two items are being canceled this week. Mother is not going to be needing them any longer.

"Yeah, yeah."

CHAPTER 13

───∞───

"Are You Here To Take Me Home?"

ON MY NEXT trip to Whidbey I find Mother and Fern sharing their apple in the living room. I overhear Mother saying, "I've already told that Sadie to stay out of my stuff. Now she's in yours, too. I'm telling you, Fern, I'm going to kick her ass."

"Now, Francine, let's have this apple first. Then we'll both be strong enough to kick her ass."

I enter amid their giggles. "Hi, ladies. It sounds as if all is going well here."

Mother doesn't get up but smiles, "Oh, hi, Betty. Here, have some apple with us." She holds out a moist chunk of apple. "We're doing fine. Are you here to take me home?"

"No, thanks, you ladies eat every bite of that apple. Mother, I think being here with people is good for you. It's nice to hear you laugh. I don't want you to be by yourself."

"Well, I think I could do pretty well by myself. I'm not afraid to be by myself."

"I know, Mother, you have rarely, if ever, been afraid of anything."

"I'm not afraid of that Sadie either."

"I suspect you're not, but there comes a time in a person's life when they need to be with others, and you are there now."

"Oh shit!"

"Besides, Mother, Janice enjoys having you here."

"I like Janice, too."

Fern gets up to depart, "I like Janice, too--and, Francine, I like you, too."

Mother looks at me decisively. "Betty, I can't just move in here."

"Yes, you can."

"I can't afford it."

"Yes, you can." Mother doesn't ask for details of how, and that's just as well as I hurry on to ask, "Is Janice treating you well?"

"Oh, yes, she treats everyone well. She treats each of us like we're the president or some such important person. Janice's a hard worker. She just works all the time."

"Mother, you've been a hard worker, too. You deserve a rest."

"Janice works too hard."

"Mother, I'd rather have you here in this situation where it's clean and beautiful than somewhere where the helpers don't have a personal concern. Would you say you are happy here?"

"Well, yes, but I just can't stay--Dad and Rolf need me."

"That's not true, Mother. You know that's not right. Dad is dead."

Mother hangs her head. "I don't know what's going on anymore. I never get any mail up here. No one knows I'm here."

"No, Mother, that's not true either. Janice says you get a card or a note every couple of days from Mavis or Mo. You've also had cards from friends and neighbors from Ridgeview--and from me and Nick and El. Those cards and notes are on the dresser beside your bed. I saw them when I put some things in your room just now."

"I don't know how those cards got there on that dresser. No one knows I'm here. When are you and Don going to retire?"

"In a couple more years."

"And you're going to be up here on Whidbey?"

"Yes, that's our plan."

"I'd like to be near the two of you, but I want my own place."

"Mother, I need you to be right here for now."

"Why?"

"Because your memory plays tricks on you."

"Why is that?" She leans forward looking at me with what seems to be a genuine show of interest and asks further, "What do you mean?" She sits staring at me, waiting.

I clear my throat and breathe deeply as I decide how to give a simple explanation. "Well, little blood vessels have broken in your head."

She nods as if understanding.

"And that sometimes makes your brain messages get mixed up."

Mother rubs her forehead and scrunches up her mouth and nose in a frown and begins wagging her head sideways in some kind of painful disbelief and frustration, or maybe denial. "It's so confusing. I don't know why I can't get things through my head any more."

"Well, the little vessels break, and that makes you forget things like Dad is dead. Mother, you need to have gentle people like Janice to remind you that's not correct."

"I don't know why I can't get it through my head that he's gone."

Mother becomes teary-eyed for the first time since coming to Janice's almost four months ago. "I just don't know what I'm going to do without Dad. I had him for fifty-seven years."

"Mother, it may have been longer than that. When were you married?"

She answers promptly, "We were married March 17, 1932."

It's my turn to be disbelieving, "You're right; that was your wedding date. See, your memory is wonderful with some things. It would have been fifty-nine years if Dad had lived one more month."

"Well, I have to go home next week. I want to go home to Ridgeview to live."

"Mother, for you to live in Ridgeview, I'd have to quit my job and move down there to live with you. Is that what you want?"

"Well, heavens no! I don't want you to quit your job, but I want to be in my own place--in the house at 516."

"I know you do, Mother, and I'm not sure how we're going to work that out."

"I can do my own wash; you don't need to come to Ridgeview to work. I'll hire someone to help me."

"Mother, I've tried so many different ways to hire help, and it hasn't worked out. Each time you sent them away--or you wouldn't let them in the house at all."

Mother juts her chin out and glares, "I'm leaving tomorrow, if I have to walk."

"I hope you won't really do that."

"I'm going to go to West Virginia and live in a trailer behind Malcom's."

"God, Mother, that's even further away. That's a more unreal choice!"

Mother continues to clobber me verbally with every breath, and I struggle to remain calm and consistent. "Mother, I care about you. I love you. You have always been there for me, and now you need help and I want to help you--but you have to *help me help*! Living in Ridgeview is *not* an option. If you insist on returning there, you will have to live in a care facility such as the nursing home down by the hospital or the one over by the river."

"I'm not living in that nursing home down by the hospital!"

"I don't really want you to either, but living by yourself is just not going to happen. I don't want to quit my job and come to live with you, because I'd like to help Nick and El financially complete their college educations. Besides, you don't want me to quit teaching anyway. And, Mother, as long as I'm teaching, you can't live with Don and me, because there's nobody home.

"Please, Mother, it's beautiful here, and we both like the place and Janice--and I like your friend Fern. At least for now, Mother, you *are* going to stay *right here*!"

"Shit!"

I leave Mother sitting in the living room and escape to the kitchen where I find Janice. "Geez, this is impossible!"

"Betty, I honestly think your mom is adjusting, despite her angry flare-up just now. She's pretty worked up. I couldn't help but hear her from out here in the kitchen."

"Is she like this all the time, or is it just with me?"

"Francine is generally very well-mannered and friendly, and she eats and sleeps well. She usually takes naps in the day time but sleeps through the night. She enjoys the woods, flowers and deer, and she is interested in just about everything. She does forget that your dad is dead, but I just remind her that he's gone."

"Is she calm about it when you tell her?"

"She always feels bad because she can't remember that. But she does re-member other details about things in the past--little things that one doesn't expect. Last week she told me Don was doing Gideon work for the high school baccalaureate services. She was very proud of him for that, and then she gave me all the details about what Gideons do throughout the world and who she knew personally who was a Gideon."

"Wow! That's quite accurate. I never cease to be amazed at the minute details from her past life that she remembers. It's amazing."

"Oh, yes, Doris Musieleski stopped by the other day and she stayed for dinner. She and your mom visited just like they were old friends.

"Oh, and the weekend before El and a girlfriend came down. They picked up some hamburgers and took Grandma to the beach for a picnic. Then the girls stayed overnight. Francine talked all this past week about her granddaughter. She is so proud of both Nick and El."

Despite Mother's outburst, I leave Janice's place with a wee bit more confidence that things are okay.

In the upcoming days Mother and I talk almost daily on the phone. She gives me few details, but she seems much calmer about being at Janice's.

As the school year draws to a close, I am well aware of my promise to her, but in our phone calls she doesn't mention coming to our home and I don't bring it up. I feel guilty about that, but I remain mum, and I let June pass into July and let myself enjoy a break from school--and Mother.

CHAPTER 14

—◦∞◦—

Happy Birthday To Me!

MY BIRTHDAY IS July 2nd and Mother's is July 6th. I'm sure we both could do with some partying in our lives, so I decide to celebrate my birthday by going to Whidbey and taking Mother for a day trip and a picnic to Deception Pass. I'll see how that goes and figure out another way to celebrate her birthday--maybe at our home.

When I arrive it's almost 11:30 AM, and she is just finishing breakfast. Her breakfast is so late I wonder if she will be hungry for our picnic. But she is pleased I'm there and she'd love to see Deception Pass again. She promptly gets ready to leave.

"Mother, how about you make a bathroom trip before we leave for our picnic?"

"I don't need to go."

"We'll be gone quite a while. We both ought to go before we leave."

"I don't need to go."

Janice speaks up, "She's been dry all morning and often lately for overnight." Then she turns to Mother, "Come on, Francine, let's get you ready for your trip."

Mother obediently follows Janice to the bathroom, and Janice lays out a fresh Depend and then hurries out. I wait a few moments and poke my head in. Mother continues her bathroom duties without looking up, but I note that she hasn't been wearing a Depend, and she is not putting on the one Janice left on counter for her.

I pick up the pad and offer it to her, "Come on, Mom, let's get this on."

Mother begins to pull up her clothing. "I don't want to wear that."

"I know, but I have the new car today with the cloth seats. I can't afford any mishaps, and we'll be gone a long time."

She pauses midway in pulling up her pants and glares at me. Then she slides back down onto the toilet seat. "Oh shit!"

Janice flits into the bathroom with us. "Francine, are you just antsy to get on your way for your picnic?"

Mother yields in obedience. "Yes."

Francine is determined to view the boats passing through Deception Pass. "I'm going out to the middle of the bridge whether you go or not!"

A short while later we are underway and Mother is in her good-natured travel mode. All is pleasant, and we soon arrive at Deception Pass. It's gorgeous and 80 degrees with a slight breeze. Mother wants to walk out on the bridge and watch the boats for a while.

"Mother, I don't know about that. You say you get dizzy and your head is swimming whenever you're up high. That bridge is several hundred feet up over the rushing water."

"Why, I've never been dizzy in my life. If you're dizzy, you wait in the car. I'm going whether you go or not."

We walk slowly, Mother with her arm looped through mine. I make sure she is on the side away from traffic. It's a very narrow walk-way and at least a long city block to the middle of the bridge.

Below us a steady parade of various sized boats passes under the bridge, some at top speed cutting sharp wake through the swirling emerald waters, others plying full throttle struggling laboriously against strong currents.

Mother stares off in the distance and asks, "Are those the San Juan Islands?"

"You're absolutely right. That's where we usually go on our family vacations. I think that smallest bump on the right is Decatur Island. Would you like to go there with us sometime?"

"Heavens no. I'm not going to get in any boat and go way out there."

"Are you hungry, Mom?"

"No, I'm not hungry." She turns and takes my arm and we return to the parking area. "When are we having that picnic you brought?"

I don't know if she's hungry or not, but I guess she's ready for a picnic. We drive down to the park which has a lovely covered picnic area almost right on the water, and we can see the boats at close range and look up at other people viewing from Deception Pass Bridge. I get Mother seated at one of the big cedar tables under the covered area out of the sun and spread out a checkered tablecloth. Before I can put out all the food, she finds herself a fried chicken wing and begins eating.

"You must be hungry, huh, Mom? I know wings are your favorite."

"No, I'm not hungry," she replies, as she strips off the last morsels of the first wing and rummages through the box for a second one.

"Well, I thought you were just finishing breakfast at Janice's when I got there this morning. I didn't think you'd be hungry this soon."

"Oh, I had a good breakfast of ham and eggs at Janice's this morning. I'm not really hungry." She rearranges the chicken wing bones on her plate and pulls the box of chicken over near her. She rummages through all the pieces, dropping legs and thighs back into the box, finally snagging a large breast portion. This is weird, as that was always her least favorite portion. It was, however, Dad's favorite. She often saved that piece especially for him. Along with the chicken breast, she helps herself to a generous portion of potato salad and a huge chunk of watermelon.

Francine dives into the picnic basket early at the Deception Pass birthday lunch

"Would you like something to drink with your lunch, Mom?"

"No, thank you."

"Remember you asked me to bring a thermos of coffee. Are you sure you wouldn't like some?"

"Oh no. Coffee goes right through me."

As I begin eating my chicken, Mother gets up and moves to the end of the table and opens the ice chest. She claws at the bag of ice and finally fishes out a plastic bakery box of strawberry shortcake and picks at the lid until it pops off. "Ohhh, this looks good."

"Yeah, that's what I chose for my birthday instead of a cake. Remember we're celebrating my birthday today. Do you want to wait for me for a minute? Let me finish my chicken, and then we could eat dessert to-gether. Today is July 2nd--that's my birthday. Yours is July 6th. Did you remember?"

Mother scoops her fingers through the cream and retrieves a large strawberry and begins eating it. "Did Don get you a present?"

"Yes, but he hasn't given it to me yet."

"Don should have come over here for this picnic with us." Mother licks her fingers. "Here, Betty, let me give you your birthday present." She pulls out her little black square purse, slowly unzips it, and takes out all her paper money. She licks the whip cream and grease residue from her fingers again and counts the bills out on the picnic table.

"No, Mom. That's your spending money for when Janice takes you all out to lunch or for ice cream or a stop at the gift shop."

"I'm just seeing what I've got. I couldn't get you a gift right now anyway. I only have sixty-five dollars. How about if I just give you money when I get paid, and you get yourself a nice blouse? You spend at least twenty dollars."

"Okay, that would be nice, Mother."

She crams the money back into her purse and fishes another strawberry from the mounds of whip cream.

"Mom, for today, why don't you just sing Happy Birthday to me? That would be a nice present. I'll sing with you."

"They, Lord God, Betty, we can't do that. I'm not going to scare all those people off from the next table. We'll sing later."

"Okay, but I'll remember you said that. How old am I, Mom?"

"Well, you were born July 2, 1938. You must be forty-one years old."

"No, it's worse than that. You're right, I *was* born July 2, 1938, but today I'm fifty-three years old!"

"Well, Lord God Almighty, you can't be that old, Betty."

We carry on bits and pieces of repetitious conversation. Mother is quite jovial and seems happy, enjoying the place, the boats, other people, and the food. I get cold sitting under the covered area and move a few feet out to a table in the sun. I call back to her, "It's nice and warm out here, Mom. Would you like to be out here, too?"

"No, I don't want out there. I'm getting cold."

I go to the car and bring her gray sweater back to her.

"That's not my sweater."

"Sure, it is; it's the one Mavis gave you for Christmas."

"That's not my sweater. I would certainly know my own sweater."

"But, Mother, this is your favorite one."

"That is *not* mine!"

"Okay, but slip it over your shoulders anyway. It's a warm one. Is that better?"

"Yes. Thank you." She reaches for another piece of chicken.

A lady from a nearby table stops for a visit, while her grandchildren play a short distance away. Mother is somewhat cordial but keeps eating. I pick up our garbage and go to the dumpster at the edge of the covered shelter.

The visitor calls to me, "Oh, lady, she's leaving. She's leaving. You'll have to hurry and catch her."

I glance up the beach and see Mother moving slowly up the path to the parking lot. She ignores calls from both the woman and me to stop and wait. I still have the plastic picnic cloth on the table and a few things to put in the cooler. I scramble while keeping one eye on her uphill progress. I am thankful for the part of the path where there are steps. She has to painstakingly labor with the handrail on each step to pull herself up. Then she resumes a steady pace on the gradual incline until she confronts the next set of steps. I catch up with her at the top of the path, thankful there is one last step a few inches higher than the others and with no handrail. She is unable to master it without my help.

We are both huffing and puffing, and I survey the parking area and spy a row of public restrooms off to the side. "Wow! That was a tough climb. But look--there's a great place for a potty break. Okay, Mom?"

"I'm not going to the bathroom in one of those shitty things. I don't need to go."

I avoid the argument and trust the Depend. Once in the car a burst of anger which must have been brewing during our lunch erupts. "Now, Betty, when we're through with all this celebrating, I'm going home with you."

"I am not going to take you with me today, Mother, but next weekend I'll come and get you. You can come over then for a whole week's visit with us, if you like. We'll celebrate *your* birthday then."

"I don't want to go next week. I want to go home with you *today!*"

I ignore the intensity of today, glance out the window, and try to change the subject. "It's so pretty on this part of the island. I had a really nice day today, Mom."

"Oh shit! Oak Harbor is a shitty little town. Why would you want a job here?"

"I don't want a job here, Mother. I just think it's pretty."

"Oh shit! Are you in trouble at your current job? Boy, if you are, you better watch out before you come up here to some place like Oak Harbor. You could be in a hell of a lot worse circumstance than you are currently in."

"But, Mom, I'm not in a bad circumstance. I love my job. I don't want to live in Oak Harbor."

"You couldn't pay me to live in Oak Harbor if they gave me the whole town, lock, stock, and barrel!"

As we drive on to Janice's, Mother continues to be disgruntled, ignoring me for the most part and quietly saying *oh shit* to punctuate anything I say. I guess I'm getting the brunt of her wrath because I'm not taking her home with me today--or that I'm not taking her *home to Ridgeview.* In some way she must know she's not going home to Ridgeview ever again.

Which one of those experts said she would hate me?

CHAPTER 15

—◦◦◦—

Mother Visits Our Home

THE NEXT WEEK arrives all too quickly. Although I feel as if I have not fully recuperated from Mother's last verbal assault at our picnic outing, I keep my word and go to Whidbey and pick her up for her promised visit to our home.

When I arrive at Janice's, Mother is pleased to see me and excited and happy about her trip. She packs and repacks her bag, asking me if she has everything she will need. At the bottom of the steps just before I help her get in the car, Janice and I sing Happy Birthday to her.

"Happy Birthday, Mom. This is July 6, 1991. It's your 77th birthday."

"Thank you for the birthday greeting. I think I'm only 74 though."

She hugs Janice goodbye and assures her, "Now don't you worry, Janice, I'll see you tomorrow. I'll be back tomorrow for sure."

Janice smiles. "I'll see you whenever you get back, Francine. You girls be careful now."

Having Mother at our house is not a burden, and yet it is a burden.

She is easily occupied and easily entertained. She enjoys sitting outside and watching Don paint the house. She pulls weeds around the roses. She helps set up the barbecue coals, and she enjoys cooking her birthday dinner steaks with Nick. Like a couple of mischievous children, they both snack on hot-dogs before the steaks get done. When the whole dinner is ready, she eats ravenously: a huge T-bone, second helpings of fruit salad, and repeated helpings of potato salad. She drinks apple-raspberry juice enthusiastically and enjoys birthday toasts, even though she recognizes Nick has been spoofing about her drink being real wine. She admires and enjoys the pink champagne birthday cake, and she joins in singing Happy Birthday to herself. Birthday cards and presents cap off the day.

As we're bagging up the paper garbage from the birthday presents and clearing off the picnic table, Mother asks, "Betty, will you call Dad and see if he had as nice a dinner as we had?"

"Yeah, sure."

Mother seems satisfied with my reply and is cooperative as I help her prepare for bed. Her goodnight kiss is as rubbery as her speech. I know she's tired, and she is already snoring as I close the bedroom door.

Mother awakens at 7:30 AM. Mandy, our friendly family dog of questionable Labrador/German Shorthair heritage, has bonded with Mother. I'm sure Mother would have slept longer, except Mandy barges right in at every opportunity, whether it's the bedroom or the bathroom. Mother doesn't seem to mind the interruptions. In fact, she'll stop whether she's pulling on her socks or changing her Depends and talk to Mandy and pet her and encourage her even more for the next time.

When I go downstairs to check, Mother has gotten herself dressed. Her bed is dry and her clothes are dry. "Wow, Mom, you had a great night!"

"Yes, it was a really good bed, and I slept like a log."

Mother leans down to fasten her shoes, and that is her downfall. She wets everything woefully--pants, chair cushion, rug, shoes and socks. There was no Depend to stem the destructive flood. We make a bathroom trip and do a change of clothes and still arrive at the breakfast table in good spirits--as if this is routine. It is.

We join hands forming our family circle, and Don says grace, thanking God for Mother being with us, and for her seventy-six years."

Mother turns to me, "Thank you, Betty, for helping me downstairs."

"Oh, Mother, I'd like to help you more--and I can when you're staying at Janice's. Mom, I want so much for you to continue there. I want to be near you. I know you want to be in Ridgeview, but I just can't do those trips anymore. I've enjoyed so much more time with you this past spring than we have had together in all the years since Dad's stroke. I wish you could see my point of view."

"I do see your point of view. I like Janice a lot, but I want to have a little bungalow of my own. I don't think I can afford to live at Janice's."

"Mother, I think we can work that out."

"Well, I'll have to talk to Dad about that."

I challenge her on this subject, "Now why can't we do that, Mom?"

It's a long wait, as we hold eye contact.

"Because--Dad--is dead."

I don't want to lose this shred of an almost coherent conversation, and I shift the subject. "Mother, you've relaxed and enjoyed Janice's so much, I think by next summer you'll be much more able to plan for your trip to West Virginia--and that just won't happen if you are in Ridgeview. You know, Auntie Mo told me the other day that she's going to go visit Mavis and Malcolm next year--maybe in September. That's such a beautiful time of year in Virginia with all the coloration of fall leaves. Mother, I promise if your land sells and your health holds up, I will take you for that visit then. Nick and El will both be out of school, and I think we could manage it financially. Maybe Don would go, too."

"Oh, that would be nice. Could we go by car? I'd like that better than going like baggage in an airplane. I've made that trip by car with Dad ten or twelve times."

"Well, we'll see, Mom. But I wouldn't want you to decide to live there. That's further away than Ridgeview."

"Oh, I couldn't do that and leave Rolf and Dad in Ridgeview anyway."

"Mother, Rolf needs to--"

"I know, Rolf needs to grow up. Dad and I can't keep paying his bills and ours, too. He won't listen to a thing I say though. Maybe you could talk to him."

I skip my usual review lesson about Dad. "Mother, we both love Rolf, but he doesn't care what other people think, and he isn't going to listen to me."

Mother's eyes come to rest on the telephone at the end of the couch as if she sees it for the first time. She leans over and struggles to pull the phone nearer to herself. "I think I'll call him."

She doesn't ask about long distance calling, whose phone, or what the number is. She is totally absorbed in struggling with the telephone. Her eyes squint, and her fingers fumble. I don't know if she's dialing correctly or not, but the phone is ringing. After innumerable rings no one answers, and she drops the receiver in its place.

"I don't know what he does with all his time. It doesn't matter what time of day I call, he seems never to be at the house. He just runs around all the time. I don't know why he won't answer the phone. He's always afraid the call will be from someone he doesn't want to talk to. He should answer it anyway. I might want to talk to them."

"Mother, maybe he's working today."

She ignores the plausible explanation. "Maybe I didn't let it ring enough." She again grapples with the phone and fumbles through the dialing routine. She stares at me while methodically counting the rings. After the fifteenth ring, she slams the receiver down. "Well, that's enough time for Rolf to walk down town and back and still answer the phone. He may be out looking for Dad, or he may be off having coffee. Shit!"

"Mother, I think it's better for you to be around other people with whom you can visit pleasantly and not get so angry about Rolf all the time."

"I like to be around people."

"I know. You've always been a people person. You certainly have this week. You've met all my neighbors, the postman, and even the refrigerator repairman.

"Listen, time has flown by here, and today we need to meet the garbage people. That's us--we *are* the garbage people. We haul our own garbage here, and you and I need to get it ready to go to the dump. We can't be lolly-gagging around here on the phone all day."

"Okay, I'll call Rolf and Dad later."

I ignore reality.

I load the garbage bags and Mother is a good helper carrying the recycling material to the truck. There have been some moments during this week when I have actually thought we could make some kind of living arrangement work right here in our home, despite the moments of unreality.

Mother has not been too demanding. Her conversation often doesn't make sense, but she seems satisfied to be around us as we carry out regular household chores. She likes being part of routine housework and is very pleasant going along for the ride whenever we do errands.

At the dump she tells me, "You know, Betty, they did a really nice job fixing this place up. It's very pretty with all the flowers. They did an especially good job with their landscaping and using those trees to sort of hide things. This is nice dump. They're not even burning anything. Are you sure we're at a dump?"

"Actually, Mother, it's a transfer station. We just call it a dump, because it's where the dump used to be. From this county they haul the garbage in those big rigs clear down to another county, and all the burning goes on there."

"Well, no wonder it's so much better than I remember it."

Mother has no realization that she has never been here before as she continues to banter. "All that garbage pollution is a terrible problem. I don't know where the next generations is going to haul their garbage to. Of course, people put an awful lot of things in their garbage that wouldn't really have to go to the dump. A lot of that could be recycled. Dad and I hardly ever have a full garbage can on pickup days. We recycle all our aluminum cans, and Dad is really good to pick up cans as we go along on walks.

"Boy, there's a lot of pretty homes along this road, but what's wrong with these people? Why would anyone want to live on a road where the main traffic is people hauling garbage to the dump?"

"Maybe the land is cheaper, Mom."

"I sure wouldn't want to live here, cheap land or not. They couldn't give me land like this for free."

I sense the mood switch and ask, "Mother, we've really been working hard this morning. How about if we go home and have a ham sandwich and some of that lush cantaloupe we have chilling in the refrigerator?"

"Oh, yes, that's the best cantaloupe I've had this season. That sounds good."

I follow the shortest route back to our house, and after a nice lunch on the picnic table in the backyard an occasion arises which confirms that I am unrealistic and wistful about any potential living arrangement for Mother with me and my family.

Mother scoots quickly off her end of the picnic bench and announces, "I have to go to the bathroom! I have to take a shit."

The fast scooting and urgency in her voice are followed by a flatulent rumble, as I rush to help her through the door into the house. We arrive at the bathroom to the sound of repeated ominous gurgling in Mother's slacks.

"Oh damn, Mother, I forgot to put Depends in this bathroom."

"I won't need any."

"I'll run downstairs and get them anyway. You stay right here."

I race downstairs, grab a Depend and run back up two stairs at a time, but I am brought up short as my nose smashes against the bathroom door. Mother has locked the door, and I perceive from the fumes escaping under the door that I am too late. I want to cry in her Depend!

I announce stupidly, "Mom, the door is locked."

"Of course, it's locked. I always lock the bathroom door."

I hear her get up from the toilet, flush, shuffle to the sink, and turn on the water.

"Mother, unlock the door."

"I'll get to you in just a minute. Do you need to go?"

"No, but--"

The door to the linen cupboard bangs shut. The water is turned off. It sounds as if she's wringing out a washcloth. Maybe she's washing her hands. She's definitely pulling and straining at her clothing. Finally I hear her shuffle over in my direction and fumble with the door lock. After several attempts, the door yields, and she smiles pleasantly. "There, I hope I didn't keep you waiting too long."

She has successfully removed her soiled Depend, rolled it up and left it on the counter--full of fecal material. She has a washcloth in her hand, and she moves back to the sink and begins washing her face with it. The stench is overwhelming. I gag as I check the toilet. It's flushed and clear. I strive to sound normal as I open the window and turn on the fan, "Wow, it's pretty potent in here!"

"Well, I'll have you know that's not *my* shit!"

"No, I'm sure it's not, but let me check your slacks and see if you got the Depend on correctly. The ones I have here at our house don't fasten quite the same as the ones at Janice's." I already know she's not wearing one, since I have in hand the one I got from the downstairs bathroom and have been dutifully clutching outside the bathroom door. "Oh, gosh, you don't have one on at all. Here, you need to put this on."

"Oh shit!"

She puts the washcloth down and returns to the toilet and allows me to help with her clothing. It is then I notice the brown stains on the washcloth, and it's my turn to say, "Oh shit! Mother, how could you be washing your face with that?"

"Now, Betty, don't be worrying about that. I rinsed it and turned it over!"

"Oh, my God. You can't do that!"

"Now, Betty that's one of life's little lessons--you just kick the shit out of the way or wash it off, and turn over to the clean side. You should have learned that by now."

I am aghast. I secure several clean washcloths, and Mother allows me to wash her bottom side and help her redo her face and hands. She is cooperative about putting on the new Depend. When we're finished, she stands in the hallway smiling pleasantly and making small talk as I spray everything in sight with disinfectant and wipe down the bathroom counters.

"My God, Betty, there's such a thing as being too clean. That old nasty spray is getting down in my lungs. I'm going back out in the backyard where Nick is."

"That's fine, Mom."

Oh, God, please. I'm still learning about humility, and I remain a willing learner. I know the only person hurting right now is me. Mother doesn't worry about germs. She doesn't worry this may happen on the carpet, on the couch, on the bed, or the big overstuffed chair-- or somewhere out in public. And she isn't aware that if she's becoming bowel incontinent Janice doesn't want to deal with that. Oh, God, please--

I gag my way through the rest of the bathroom cleanup, and when I return to the living room, Mother is engaged in grilling Nick about a phone call from a girl. "Why, that was a long distance call, Nick. That's a pretty serious affair if you're exchanging expensive phone calls all that regular. Are you going to be getting married here soon? You better tell me in plenty of time if you are, so I can save up for the big event. Won't your mom and dad be raising holy hell about that long distance stuff?"

I don't have time nor energy to worry about the long distance phone bill--nor a possible wedding for my son--nor raising holy hell. It's nearly the end of the week, and I am worrying about how to handle the battle I know is forthcoming when Mother understands we are going back to Janice's and not to Ridgeview.

It will never work to take care of her here in our home. I have petitioned the court for permission to sell her house, but I don't know how far the legal proceedings have gone. I myself am not anxious to confront Rolf directly at this point in the midst of all his guns and temper, but I am not going to put Mother back in that situation.

Mother is *not* going back to Ridgeview!

CHAPTER 16

꧁꧂

Back To Janice's Place

I AM RESCUED from my turmoil over how to peacefully return Mother to Janice's by a phone call from El, who is in summer school. She asks us to bring some furniture pieces to her and suggests Grandma come with us and see her new apartment.

An idea pops into mind. Janice's place on Whidbey is close-by to the Interstate which we must travel to get to El's apartment. We could take Grandma with us, visit El, and then drop her off at Janice's on our way back home. My dilemma is solved.

Mother is immediately receptive to the idea of a trip, and she is excited as we prepare the next day. She even helps Don and me load a few of El's things in the truck and secure the load cover. Her enthusiasm momentarily wanes when I say, "Okay, Mom, we're ready except for a last minute trip to the bathroom. You need to put on a fresh Depend before we start."

"I don't need to go to the bathroom, and I don't need any fresh Depend."

"Remember, Mom, we're riding in Don's truck."

There is a pause. "Well, okay, I'll wear that thing because of your truck seat, Don, but really I'm just about through with this old time of the month." Don stands silently, a vague smile curling at the corners of his mouth.

Mother follows me into the bathroom. "You know these old pads just get full of plain old flow water, Betty. It's not bloody anymore. I guess I'm lucky that way. The water comes from my female things, you know. I just can't seem to get completely over this old time of the month."

I try to be agreeable, "You sure do give a detailed medical analysis, Mom."

"Oh yes, I pick that information up from when doctors tell me things."

I place her soiled Depend in a plastic bag and dispose of it with no comment.

"Betty, you're just like Janice with those Depend things and a little plastic sack every time I turn around. Do you carry around a pocketful of those plastic sacks?"

"Not quite, but sometimes."

Once we're on the way, our travel time passes pleasantly.

At El's we get a quick tour of her apartment and then gather a picnic lunch to take to the beach. Grandma accepts an invitation to ride with El in her Chevie S-10 low-rider, a sleek black number with hot pink and magenta air-brushed graphics and tinted windows. It's El's pride and joy, a vehicle she has earned. Grandma almost gives it appropriate approval when she gets out of it at the picnic site. "This is quite a snazzy rig, El, but it rides rough as a cob. You must need shocks."

"The rough ride is because it's so low, Grandma."

"Well, I'd be getting new shocks all the same. I'll bet you get a lot of looks in that thing. That is a pretty loud paint job. You be careful who's giving you those looks."

Seeing El's summer apartment and catching up on all the news about her friends, the picnic at a local park, fishing boats, kids roller-blading, kite-flying, white-caps on the bay--it's been fun for all of us!

As we pick up the picnic things Mother tells me, "Betty, you call Dad now and ask him what he had for lunch today."

"Now, Mother, you know we can't do that."

She looks at me. "--because Dad is dead."

"That's right, Mom. Let's go now."

Back at El's apartment we all enjoy a departing cup of coffee before loading into our truck. Mother insists she wants to ride next to the window, so I climb into the middle seat. Before Don can get around to the passenger's side to help her into the truck, Grandma calls out, "El, come help me. Your mom and dad need to lower their truck so it's more like yours. Now give your old grandma a boost up or they'll have to put me in the truck bed back there, and I'll have to fart my way home." Peels of giggles come from

Grandma and El, as El pushes and Mother pulls and finally shifts herself up into the truck seat. "Now, El, I don't know when I'll ever see you again. It's been so many years since I last saw you." Tears well up in Mother's eyes.

"Oh, Grandma, it's really only been a few weeks--and now that you're closer, I'll try to visit you more often." El kisses Mother's cheek and helps her with her seatbelt.

"That coffee sure smells good, El. I could use a cup of coffee."

Despite having served us all coffee just a few minutes before, El splashes out about half a cup of her coffee into the gutter and hands the remainder to Mother. "Here, Grandma, you take this cup for the road."

We pull slowly away from the curb calling out additional farewells.

A few blocks down Mother leans over and looks toward Don, "My God, Don, did you pay for a full cup of coffee when you got this? You have to watch these gyps every place you go." Don laughs and Mother loudly slurps from El's half-filled cup.

Regardless of whose cup is half-full, we continue out of town and toward Whidbey. We're not very long on the road before Mother notes, "We're going north. I want to go south."

Don assures, "We *are* going south, Francine."

"Are we on Whidbey Island?"

"Almost."

Mother leans forward and casts a long look at Don. "Janice doesn't live on Whidbey Island, you know."

Don does not look away from the road as he assures, "Yes, she does."

Mother raises her volume a notch. "She does not. She lives outside of Chehalis."

I interrupt and look directly at Mother. "That's not correct, Mother."

Several miles tick by in angry quietness. Mother finally turns toward me, "Betty, you know this is not right. Dad won't want me going there."

I am non-responsive and look straight ahead.

Mother stares at the passing scenery. "I don't see anything familiar on this road."

"It's familiar, Mom. We're right now going over the Deception Pass Bridge where you and I had our picnic for my fifty-third birthday celebration."

"I don't want you dumping me out somewhere I don't know anything about."

"I'm not going to do that."

"Well, how will Janice know I'm coming? I didn't call her. I can't just move in on her. I don't know what she charges, but I know I can't afford to be there."

"Yes, you can."

"I came to her house last Saturday, and I stayed with her a whole week. I'm going to owe her my whole check at this rate. Why are you taking me to her house?"

"Because you can't live by yourself."

"Dad is not going to like this one bit."

"That's another reason--you can't remember Dad is dead."

Mother raises the volume. "Dad is *not* dead, and I don't need a bath, and I don't need these Depends."

I heave an exhausted sigh. My own memory hasn't been great lately, and today I'm not sure if she's sparring for a fight or if she's really that forgetful. I snap back at her, "You can't remember to wear Depends, and you can't take baths by yourself. Those are two more reasons to get you back to Janice's."

"Betty, you just came in and took over all the decision-making! You didn't do any work for me at all at the house in Ridgeview."

"I think I worked hard there for over four years. All those years after Dad had his stroke I came to Ridgeview every other weekend. And whether you think so or not, I worked very hard."

"You never gave Rolf credit for doing anything good."

"I haven't tried to discredit him, but he surely hasn't been much help."

"You're just trying to mettle and dominate over everyone."

"I don't think so."

"You're boarding me out like a dog. Dad is not going to like this one bit, and I'm going to call Rolf."

"That's fine."

"I should be at 516. Rolf could be with me at nights, and I could stay with my neighbor Ruthie in the daytime."

"I don't think so."

"You and Dr. Jones have cooked up a bunch of shit about my memory. I never had any mini-strokes."

"I haven't cooked up anything."

"Well, I can tell you there's nothing wrong with my memory. I need to get home and check on things. I need to fix Rolf's lunches. I have done my own washing and cleaning my whole life, and I've done it for these last few years, too. You haven't done a damned thing for me! I'll never leave home again without Dad, and I shouldn't have come this time. I'm leaving tomorrow."

At the end of an hour's ranting, we pull into Janice's driveway. I for one am happy--not just relieved--*Happy!*

Don gets out, and I move my limp body out of the truck on the driver's side. I hurry around and place the little stool for Mother, who seems to be moving better than I am. Don climbs back in and leans over toward the open door to tell me he's going to run into town for gas and to check the oil. Janice is on the front steps and comes down to greet us. She gives Mother a big hug, "Oh Francine, how nice to see you again. I've missed your company."

Immediate transformation. "Well, I've missed you, too."

Little Fern has heard all the commotion and come to the door. "Oh, Francine, I'm so happy to see you again. I've missed you terribly. Guess what? You have a new roommate."

"Oh?" Mother takes hold of the iron railing on one side and loops her other arm through Janice's. She labors up each step, and once at the top exchanges warm hugs with Fern. "Now, what's this new roommate stuff about?"

"Me--*me*, I'm your new roommate. Sadie is gone. Isn't that wonderful?"

Mother laughs appreciatively and hugs Fern again. "Well, that is wonderful!"

Fern and Mother chuckle as they continue into the house and chatter like school girls. A bit later I feel somewhat refreshed after a cup of coffee, and I go into the living room to bid Mother farewell. Fern and Mother are sharing their apple and still jabbering. All seems pleasant.

127

"I have to say goodnight, Mom. I have to get on my way."

"You don't need to think you can run my life for me."

"Huh?"

"You've always tried to do that with everyone. You first move in, and then you take over. You can't care very much for me to treat me the way you're doing. You could at least let me try to live at your house."

"Mother, you have just been to my house for a very nice week's visit."

"Dad built that house in Ridgeview for me to live in until I die. No one has said I'm unable to live alone. I've been alone a lot and done just fine."

"I know that, Mom."

"Dad isn't going to like this."

I sit down on the couch beside her. "Mother, I know you miss Dad. Is that why you're so angry? Do you wish he was here with you? Would that make it better?"

"Yes. I miss him a lot. I would like him here with me at Janice's. He'd like this place."

I pat her hand gently. "Mother, I know he'd like it here. I'm sorry he can't be with you, but he would like *you* to be here."

"Dad never agreed with a lot of things you did. He thought you were wrong a lot of the time. He isn't going to let you get by with this. He'll stop you."

"Mother, Dad isn't going to stop anything. Dad isn't here. Dad is dead."

Mother pulls her hand away and glares at me. "I know Don doesn't want me in his house and underfoot. He never wanted his own mother in his home. He would never have anything to do with the care of his own mother."

A huge pulsating glob engulfs my guts, my head--my whole body! I lean over close to Mother's face, lock her visual intensity with my own, and in a voice of quiet steel I rasp through clenched teeth, "Mother, you can degrade me as much as you like, but when you attack my husband, I draw the line. I've told you before, you will not hurt me ever again with vicious lies about me or my husband. Right now, you don't know what you're saying. You're being crazy!"

I feel my teeth and my facial muscles paining against the tightness. I force myself to breathe as I pull away slightly from her frozen face.

"Don's mother was one of the softest, most tender, most loving people I have *ever* known. And I love and adore her son who has many of her wonderful qualities. None of your lies and half-baked ideas can change that or ever hurt me again. You simply don't know what you are saying. Don loved his mother immensely right up until the day she died. He participated much in her care. You have absolutely no experience with his mom and *no* knowledge of her care in her life nor in her death. You are being a foolish, wicked old woman right now. I am trying to tell you that I care for you. *I love you! I want you to be in a place that is safe, clean, healthy, and with other people.* This place fits that bill.

Mother pulls away from my face and sits back on the sofa, maintaining her volume on high. "Well, I can't stay here!"

I straighten up, lean back from her and match her volume. "Yes, you can!"

"It isn't home."

"You're right. It isn't home, and I can't make it *be* that."

"Dad would want me to be home."

"Dad would want you to be well taken care of. For right now that means here!"

Frail little Fern who left us and went to her room a long time before reappears in the hallway above the living room and with all the possible power of her eighty-five pounds bellows, "Please stop all this and be quiet!"

Janice, who has been standing in the doorway nearby, comes into the room and walks up in front of Mother extending a hand, "Francine, let's get you to the bathroom. All this talk has been too much. Look here, the whole couch is wet, and so are you."

I lean back into the couch, wetness or not. Every part of my body is trembling. I am not so sure when I get up that there won't be a *brown* stain on my part of the couch, and Janice will have to come back and take me to the bathroom. Mother has beaten me up once again. I rise clumsily and round the couch on the other end, where I meet Mother and Janice on their way back. I mutter weakly, "I need to leave--*now*."

Mother pauses and leans her cheek toward me, "Goodnight. You be careful driving on the way home."

I give her a peck on the cheek. "Goodnight, Mother."
I let myself out and stand in the cool dampness of the woodsy night air.

God, what do you want me to do? God, I don't see any other way. I can't take her back to that filthy house in Ridgeview. I can't let her wander the streets. I can't let her sleep for two weeks between my cleaning trips on sheets and covers saturated in cat piss, as well as her own urine. That house is intolerable, and yet I know it is her home--the house that Daddy built for her to live in until the day she dies. Dear God, I know taking her to be with you is truly being "home," and I can't lie to you, I am ready for my mother to go to your home. After a day like today, you can have her! On the other hand, I'm really not asking you to do that. I'm not asking that at all. I'm just asking you to give me strength and wisdom. Bless Janice in her daily tasks. She says she doesn't listen to this every day, but, God, is she just being kind? Please allow us all to cope and to do the things that need to be done, and to just keep going one day at a time. I wish it could be different; but, God, I will do what you want me to do. I feel Mother hates me at this moment, but I know she really doesn't. God, please forgive my anger and personal retorts. I know I have shortcomings, but Mother is so wrong about Don's mom. Over the years I learned a lot from her in a quiet, un-pressured manner, and in addition I've had the privilege of enjoying intimately one of her greatest loving projects--a precious son. And for that I thank you.

Dear God, thank you for the good times. They do make up for so much that is irrational. Thank you for your servant, Janice. You truly have given her a gift to care for the elderly, a gift I don't have and I'm not asking for. I do think Mother can adjust to living here. Please help me to adjust and to complete the steps to secure the financing for this care. And, God, please work with Rolf in this regard to help him see Mother's needs and to take care of his own responsibilities. If possible help him get a job like normal people, and get him out of her house, so that I can take the next step there, too. I pray you will handle Rolf totally, so that I won't have to evict him. Emotionally I can't even do these visits with Mother very well. How would I ever do an eviction? Oh, God, please spare me that action.

Please shower me with purple tulips!

The headlights of the truck slowly jolt down Janice's drive-way and pull up near the steps where I am waiting. Don leans over and opens the door for me.

"Oh, God, Don, hurry up and get me out of here."

CHAPTER 17

Sometimes I'm Afraid To Say It

A FEW DAYS later Aunt Mavis calls. I update her on the recent trips. "What do you think, Mavis? It was so hard to drop Mother off at Janice's this last time, knowing she didn't want to be there. I have never had such a guilt trip."

"Betty, you're doing a good job. You have to do what you have to do. If that Whidbey property can't be sold because of the access problem, then the Ridgeview house has to be either rented or sold. As far as I can tell that's your only source of funds for her care."

"Mavis, I know you're right. I wish I wasn't so alone and that Rolf could see my point of view. I wish he could feel Mother's need. He continues to be unresponsive, and he always says, *I just don't know.* I told him he's going to have to start knowing pretty soon. In fact, Aunt Mavis, I've taken the first legal step in the eviction process this last weekend by notifying him in a personal letter that if he doesn't get out he will be evicted so that I can sell the house. I don't know exactly how the steps in the process go, but he knows I have to get money from somewhere in order to pay for Mother's care, and selling her house is the only feasible option at this time."

"Betty, Rolf will just have to take care of Rolf. Don't be worrying about him. They've always spoiled him and dished out for whatever he wanted. He'll have to figure it out for himself now."

"But, Mavis, I always get hung up on the fact that Rolf is my brother--and he's older. He should be the one doing this. At least he should help me in making decisions that are best for Mother."

"Betty, Rolf isn't going to do anything until he's forced. I think you're on the right path, and you just have to keep pressing on.

"I've been meaning to tell you, Betty, that Malcom, Mo and I are planning to come and visit Francine--maybe next month. They were both excited to take a trip with me. And we have all agreed to try and talk some sense into Rolf then."

The month passes quickly, and their trip actually happens. Uncle Malcom didn't do his usual last minute disappearing act as I thought he would. Despite a recent surgery, he makes the trip with his two sisters.

Upon arriving at Janice's, they all are pleased by Mother's living conditions and by Janice's care for her. Mavis recalls her last visit with Francine and Roger, and she is especially pleased by the improvements, despite the further mental deterioration and confusion now evident in Mother. All three of them note the ease with which Janice deals with Mother, and they agree whether Mother will admit it or not, they think she likes being at Janice's.

I feel an enormous sense of relief at the approval of Mother's brother and sisters, and that they also approve of evicting Rolf if that has to happen. They think the sale of the Ridgeview house must occur, and that can't happen with Rolf and all those guns in there. They say they will stop by Ridgeview and directly confront Rolf on behalf of their sister and try to help him fully understand the need for available resources and why he must get his stuff and himself out of her house.

Dear God, grant us all wisdom and courage in regard to this eviction business and clean-up and sale of that house. May all actions proceed according to your will. Help me to listen and be patient and to be aware of all the other persons and aspects of the whole problem, and to realize that you must orchestrate it all to your perfection, not mine.

Dear God, sometimes I am so tired I just want to run away and hide forever. About that time there will be one of your messages just for me--in scriptural readings Janice gives me, conversations with friends, or a call from Aunt Mavis or Aunt Maurine--or even cards or notes from some of Mother's friends whom I don't even know.

Oh, God, please forgive me for my shortcomings, especially my mouth and my impatience. Help me to continue to develop my faith and to rely fully on you for all my needs. I feel so much closer to you now than a year ago---or even in my whole life--and for that I am thankful.

Dear God, thank you for Alzheimer's and purple tulips!
Dear God, am I crazy too?

—⬬—

CHAPTER 18

The Dear Rolf Letter

FALL, 1991, IS a fuzzy collage of activities: Mother's adjustment at Janice's; trips to visit her; her deteriorating mental and physical health; land appraisals of her Whidbey tract; negotiations for an access to her land-locked property; appointments with lawyers in Coupeville, Everett, and Ridgeview; potential sale of the 516 property; a growing stack of back taxes and unpaid bills; and continued lack of cooperation from Rolf. Sometimes it's worse than a fuzzy collage. I feel as if I am walking a tightrope through a giant whirling blender! On more than one occasion I have been thoroughly pureed.

My attorney in Ridgeview confirms what Mr. Manilow in Adult Protective Services told me a long time back. "That's right, Betty, your mother cannot be forced to go to, nor to stay in, a nursing home--and that includes a foster home such as Janice's. It's one of those weird twists to the law, giving the senile party enormous power to aggravate. She doesn't have to live where she doesn't want to live."

"Mr. Oats, Mother has made it perfectly clear to me innumerable times she doesn't want to stay at Janice's. So, do I have to move her someplace else just because she says that? Can she really return to 516 and live by herself if she wants to? What if she walks away from Janice's by herself or calls a cab and catches a bus? Can someone like Rolf pick her up and take her back to Ridgeview?"

"Well, the answer is *yes* to most of those questions and *probably* to the others; but let's not worry about what has not happened. If she returns to 516 and has to have extensive nursing help that could easily cost as much as a nursing home. By law she *does* have a legal right to demand to live there.

If she has to go to the hospital for any reason, she must be there at least three nights and then she could go to a nursing home at Medicare expense. At that time you could put her property up for sale and if it doesn't sell in 20 days, then she could qualify for State aid. There is also another little point in the law that allows your mother to *reserve the right from the State to die in her home.* After she is deceased, the State may then put a lien against the estate and collect for any aid she has received."

"Oh, my God, nobody tells a person these legal points when they apply for a guardianship. And what does that mean in regard to the Whidbey property?"

"Betty, the best thing would be to sell the Whidbey property now to a cash buyer, and use those funds to keep your mother at Janice's."

"But I can't sell it--it has no legal access. Reputable realtors won't even list it."

"The next best move would be to sell her house in Ridgeview."

"I can't sell that either because of its deplorable condition and because Rolf and all his guns and things are in it."

"Betty, you're down to the third best thing, and that is to evict Rolf! Efforts to seek Rolf's cooperation have been well-attempted and document-ed. In fact, extraordinary effort has been made. Rolf seems to be in the house all the time now, and he is unlawfully occupying the premises and obstructing the preparation of the property for sale. You are required by law to provide care for your mother. I don't see any other possibility for you. A stronger course of legal action is needed toward Rolf-- and that is eviction!"

"How can there be laws like this? The laws and those who make them are crazier than the persons for whom guardianships are set up."

I make a special trip to Ridgeview to take pictures of the house and its contents as advised by Mr. Oats. This is a necessity so the court will understand why it cannot be sold as it is, if such a question arises in the future. In addition, I need to try to discern what belongs to Mother and what belongs to Rolf.

Though I had left things in some degree of order and cleanliness the day I drove Mother to Whidbey Island, what I find when I get to 516 isn't nice. Calculating that a cat poops twice per day, and there are two of them, it appears to have been over two weeks since the kitty litter was emptied. There are piles of cat manure on the rug in the living room and on the kitchen floor, and God knows where else. Rolf must be continuing the newspaper, as papers and books are flung haphazardly everywhere. There is a spot at the end of the kitchen table which looks as if he sits there to eat and work. God, how can he sit there? Or breathe? Or even think of eating? An open spiraled notebook shows his pick of lotto numbers day by day. His record goes back for weeks. It appears he is trying to develop some kind of system for picking numbers. There's a paperback book and a worn computer print-out on how to pick winners. I don't read it. I can't stay here and breathe long enough to read it, much less figure out his system. I move room by room and snap my pictures as quickly as I can.

In Dad's bedroom I snap a picture of fourteen guns laid out across the bed and clothing strewn across piles of boxes. When I proceed upstairs I find another hundred and thirty-seven guns. That's at least forty-nine fewer than when I was upstairs with Aunt Mavis. The guns that were scattered all over the floor are now gone. The glass doors on the gun cabinet are ajar. There are guns missing there, too.

I go back downstairs and take a few pictures in the front bedroom and the living room. Standing in the middle of the living room, I can now see the corner cabinets in the dining room, as several boxes have been moved from the dining table, otherwise known as Taco's dog house. I wonder where Taco is. I don't see the cats either, but they often hide out. Rolf did say he might give that one cat away. I don't need pictures of them--their deposits are sufficient record of their presence.

Mother's Old Salem Spode and matching blue crystal are still in one corner cabinet and the Fostoria is in the other. She always said she collected these dishes for me for *someday*. Is today someday? Oh well, the Spode and Fostoria are like the heirloom watch. Someday may never come, and I shouldn't be thinking about removing anything from this house. There are a couple of paintings and woodcarvings I would like to have, since I made them and gave them to Mom and Dad--but it would be wrong to take them. In fact, I think it's wrong to even *want* them right now.

If Rolf goes over the edge and becomes violent and destructive, these objects won't be very meaningful anyway. I hope I have determined correctly that a son who steals from his parents, bilks them out of their monthly income, abuses them physically and emotionally, and shows little or no compassion in the care-taking process is more of a puffed up, arrogant, blow-hard weenie and not likely to be destructive. If I have misjudged, there may eventually be destruction of property--maybe of people. I don't know. I have known very little for sure for four years, but I do know standing here thinking about taking anything from this house today makes me feel as if I am slipping into the same slimy ranks with Rolf.

In the midst of the clutter, the filth, and the treasures of fifty years of Malfait family history, I bow my head.

Dear God, forgive my thoughts of this moment. Please don't let me become like Rolf. I hate where I stand right now, and I hate what I am going to do. Please, God, take care of Rolf, because I can't. He shakes his head in the right direction every time and then ignores me, just as he ignored the pleadings of Mother and Dad for years. I love Rolf, but I can't reason with him. I can't help him. I don't even know him anymore. I do know I have to get him out of this house. What I am about to do is needed in order to care for Mother adequately. That's what I'm supposed to do, right? Dear God, I know the property is hers. It's not Rolf's! It's not mine! I want so much to do what's right and according to your will. Please help me now.

Despite my roiling guts and a throbbing headache, I feel I need to give Rolf yet another warning of the impending action, but I don't know how to make contact with him. I return to the kitchen and tear a couple of pages from the open spiraled notebook and write him a letter.

Dear Rolf,

    I haven't been able to see you or reach you by phone. I am in Ridgeview today, and I can tell from things in the house you've been in and out. I tried to call several times, and Mother has also tried to call. She gets very frustrated and worried when no one answers. I did ask Ruthie to leave a message on the front door for you, and she said she did that. You still did not call me, and I'm as frustrated as Mother.

Mother is otherwise doing fine. She is well cared for, sleeps well, is clean, and eats well. She likes Janice very much and says that Janice treats everyone like the president is there for every dinner and she's a wonderful cook. I think all these things are true, and Mother has adjusted well. There are only two ladies at Janice's now, Fern and Mother. Fern is a skinny little sweetheart, age 84, and she pretty well minds her own business. She and Mother have become friends.

Mother does say she wants to come back to her house in Ridgeview. As you know, it's $1200 per month to keep her at Janice's, and it's going to be more due to her increasing incontinence, as that's added work and expense for Janice. It's still cheaper than a nursing home, and Mother is very definite she doesn't want to be in a nursing home, regardless of where it is. As you also know, she has no other income, and as yet I haven't been able to sell the Whidbey property, because it doesn't have a legal access. If Mother comes back to Ridgeview, she will have to have live-in care, and that will be about the same expense as a nursing home. Rolf, you and I both know the financial situation here. Mother does not have enough cash flow to keep herself living in the manner she should be able to enjoy. If she comes back to Ridgeview, the house will have to be cleaned up, and a live-in care person provided. Either way means you must find accommodations for you and your stuff elsewhere and SOON!

If she stays with Janice, she needs her <u>FULL</u> income. That means if you continue to occupy the house, you need to pay $600.00 per month, which would provide $468.90 for *your* Fibex mortgage and for taxes and insurance on the house. If you are not here in the house, I still have to rent it out or sell it in order to cover her expenses.

Rolf, our mother deserves to live in a place that is clean and wholesome, the same as she provided and expected of us when we were growing up. This cannot be done unless the Whidbey land is sold or the Ridgeview house is rented or sold. I'm sure you have the ability and the ingenuity to help solve this problem. I am doing all I know possible to provide for her best interests. Your cooperation is vital to insure the best choices continue to be available for her.

I hope things will work out for you--for all of us, for that matter. I pray for you daily and ask God to help you find work and for you to be able to feel good about yourself again. Rolf, I <u>KNOW</u> you have the ingenuity, the ability, and the energy to find a job and get on with your own life. May God guide you and bless you in your search.

    Love,

    Betty

I place the letter on the open spiraled notebook obscuring Rolf's lotto scheme. They're both probably equally useless.

Dear God, please give me the courage I need for each step. Give me the wisdom to perceive your will. Give me a sense of your presence, of your loving, divine guidance. I don't want to do this legal course of action. I don't want to evict Rolf. I am afraid!

CHAPTER 19

―⊷―

The Eviction Notice

A FEW DAYS later when I am back in my home, it's late in the evening when the phone rings. Rolf's voice is crisp and upbeat, "Yeah, what's up? I was talkin' with Janice, and she said you wanted to talk to me."

"I left messages about every place I could think of, but you didn't answer."

"Well, I'm answering one you left with Janice. You musta' been talkin' with her. She said she told you I'd been in the hospital, but I was gonna get up her way for a visit."

"Yes, she said you had been in the hospital as a result of a dog bite, but you were fine now. She said you might be up to Whidbey to see Mother in a few days. That's great, but did you get my letter I left at the house?"

"Yeah, yeah, I did. That, and talking to Janice made me decide I better get up that way and visit Mom in a few days."

"Well, I don't know what a few days means. Mom has been sick this last week--more incontinence than usual and pain with urination. I have to go to Whidbey on Monday to get her in for blood work and a urinalysis. Janice can't leave the other ladies to take her in, so I hope your visit won't be on Monday or when she's having her medical appointments."

"Yeah, well, I'm not real sure I'll get up there that soon anyway. I'm at my place at Newcastle now. I been visitin' Eddie Eader, a friend of mine. I give the last piece of my Alaskan jewelry I had to his little 13-year-old girl. It's that jade and ivory cross. I paid three hundred and fifty bucks for it when I was up there fishin'. It's got little gold nuggets around the edge. You remember it, right?"

"Un-huh."

"Yeah, I'm gonna head up to Burien this afternoon. I want to see them guys who are still workin' on the Green River Task Force."

I ignore the issue of the Alaskan jewelry gift to a 13-year-old girl and his escapades with the Green River Task Force. Instead I ask, "But are you going to go to Whidbey to visit Mom?"

"Well, I don't know."

"Rolf, Janice told her you were planning to come and visit. I hope you won't disappoint them both. *Whenever* you make the trip, you need to know Mother thinks you're coming to pick her up, and she'll want to go home with you."

"I know. I know. I thought about that, and I thought I'd just park my car down the road and tell her I came up on the bus."

"No, tell her the truth. Tell her you came to visit, and you're not planning to take her to Ridgeview. Tell her she's in a beautiful place and has excellent care. You could also assure her the house is okay in Ridgeview-- and the dog and cats are okay, too. She worries about those things all the time. She also worries a lot about what Dad is doing or what he is having for dinner."

"I guess that's an easy one, since he ain't havin' any dinner."

"Say, Rolf, Taco wasn't in the house when I was there. What did you do with him? Was it Taco that bit you?"

"Well, yeah, that's what put me in the hospital. It was dark and Taco was gettin' in my way so's I couldn't get the door unlocked. I rapped him a good one on top of the head and he nipped me. When I went to the hospital--well, I didn't go right away--I went a couple of days later--anyway, they put me in the bed and kept me eight days. It was a couple of days or so before I could even think clearly about things. I asked 'em to let me out long enough so's I could put Taco in the vet's. They didn't want to let me go, but there wasn't nothin' else I could do. I thought about just shootin' him, but I didn't. I took him on to the vet. He gave me a lot of grief there, too, 'cause he didn't want to go in that place. I guess he don't like the smell. Anyway, he was at the vet's the last eight days I was in the hospital. He's still there."

"What did you do with the cats during that time?"

"I left 'em right there in the house. I just put out plenty of extra food and water that day they let me out of the hospital for a bit."

"You left the cats in the house for eight days?"

"Well, yeah. What else was I gonna do?"

"Oh, God, Rolf, I don't want to hear this. I could tell the last time I was there something was wrong. You keep hanging around in all that shit and you'll keel over in it too, and guess who will get to clean it all up?"

Rolf laughs gleefully. "Yeah, I guess you'd really have your hands full then."

"No way. I'm not that much of a cleaner-upper. Are you okay now?"

"Oh yeah. I been okay for a couple weeks now. I'm back to work."

"So you're well enough to make a trip to Whidbey? I'm not sure if I heard you say if you were going to visit Mother or not."

"I don't know what's gonna take place until I see these guys on the Green River Task Force and all."

"Well, I don't see what that has to do with visiting Mother. The doctor has already said she may have to be in the hospital for a day or two with that kidney problem. Whether she's in the hospital or at Janice's, she'll think you're coming to take her home, and I don't want that to happen."

"Well, it'll probably be better if I don't go."

"No, I'm not saying that. She really needs the visit. She'd enjoy a visit from you more if she could be with you--to go somewhere or do something with you--or just visit with you there at Janice's. We had her over here a couple of weeks ago for a visit."

"Yeah, how did that go?"

"Overall pretty well. We all had to concentrate to keep ahead of the incontinence problem, but we managed. She had one kind of bad time of not being able to hold her bowels, but I'm not so sure that wasn't my not watching what she ate."

"Nah, nah--I don't think I could take care of that."

"You wouldn't have to. It's not like that usually. You wouldn't have to worry about any kind of incontinence on a day visit. Mother wears Depends regularly now, and Janice would prepare her for an outing. She would be fine for a short ride or out to lunch at a restaurant. She loves doing stuff like that."

"Well, I don't know."

"Rolf, Janice will help set it all up; whatever personal attention Mother needs she would take care of before you guys go anywhere. When I visit, a much harder part for me than the Depend issue happens when I take her back to Janice's."

"Yeah, how's that?"

"She doesn't want to go back. She wants to go to Ridgeview. Janice and I have discussed whether a trip to Ridgeview would be helpful for her--maybe help her to let go of Dad somehow. You might be able to do that if you want to--you know, for a couple of nights--but the house would have to be a hell of a lot cleaner than it was the last time I saw it."

"Yeah, yeah, I know, but remember I've been in the hospital. I ain't been able to do no cleanin'."

"I thought you'd been out for two weeks and back to work. Were you in again?"

"Well, no, but you know what I'm sayin'. The house ain't up to par, because I ain't been able to do much. When I get completely over this hand thing, I'll be able to get a little more done. I'll be gettin' more drivin' time, and things'll be pickin' up. I'll get a lot of stuff done then."

Our conversation ends as it often does, and I don't know how many times he's promised "things'll be pickin' up." Oh well, it doesn't really matter. Rolf's going to do whatever he wants to do, no matter what it costs Mother or me or anyone else. I personally don't care what he does with his dog, his jewelry, himself, or anything else! That's a horrible thought, but I really don't care!

I try to refocus on Mother's needs, as fragments of my conversation with Pastor Ted come back to my mind. *If your mother is ever going to snap back, it has to be away from Rolf and in clean, healthy, positive surroundings--be prepared for her to hate you--it won't matter--it will be the right thing--if necessary use a law enforcement agency as protector--don't hesitate about evicting Rolf and his gun collection--it's not his house--Rolf will have to worry about himself.*

Rolf does not make the trip to Whidbey, at least not in the days before or during Mother's hospital stay with kidney problems. He does call and assure her all is well in Ridgeview. He talks at length to Janice, filling her in on his report to the sergeant of the Green River Task Force. In fact, he gives Janice so much detail she calls me to ask if Rolf is all right. Is there something wrong with him that she ought to know about, especially if he does come to visit?

Dear God, how should I know if Rolf is all right? I don't know if anyone in my family is all right. I don't know if I'm all right. God, please, I've said all along I don't want to get dead over trying to do what's right, legal and honorable! Please help us all.

Summer vacation time at Decatur Island again rolls around. We are all in need of a break. I can't take Mother to visit Aunt Mavis until she feels better, but I had hoped we would be able to take her with us to Decatur. I even got her a little light-weight fishing pole. That trip for her is not to be. It's too remote with no ferry service. Considering her recent kidney problems and hospital stay, it just won't work.

For my family, being on Decatur Island is a massage to mind and body. The tide goes in; the tide goes out; the fog presses the water, the beach, and the land in the early hours; the fog lifts mid-morning. Afternoon skies are usually a faded blue tinged in orange and magenta by early evening. Summer temperatures hover between 70 and 80 degrees with a slight marine breeze. Seagulls cry out a scavenger rap-beat at frequent intervals; the dog across the bay challenges them. Other gulls sit in amicable clusters on the beach or cruise quietly above the constantly moving salt water. A blue heron sits proudly stone-cold still. It may be the same one from summers past on the same post on the boat dock. A bald eagle perches high atop a fir crag and misses no small detail of the entire bay. The eagle most likely views me as a small detail of the entire bay. I view myself as a small detail of a larger world.

When we leave Decatur, we stop by Janice's place on our way home. She invites us to stay for dinner. She's expecting Rolf to show up. I have my doubts about that, but she says he called that morning. We decide to stay.

Don and I brought fresh crab from pulling the crab pot the last thing before leaving the island. If anything tastes better to Mother than fresh salmon, it's fresh crab. Janice, Mother, and Fern join in the cooking preparation, Mother and Fern each squealing as Janice expertly drops the fearsome Dungeness, pinchers fully extended, into the boiling water. Minutes pass and the dull brownish red shells turn to bright orange, indicating progress toward doneness. When it's ready Mother, and Fern "ooh" and "aah" around the kitchen sink as Janice expertly cleans the crab and lays out the resulting cracked claws, legs and body parts with nutcrackers, picks, and hot seasoned butter.

A little later we all sit down to a dinner of baked chicken-rice casserole, deviled eggs, corn on the cob, and a tray of fresh garden vegetables with home-made dill dip. Dessert is pineapple upside down cake. Such a repast well disguises personal shortcomings of any of Janice's regular guests--or her visitors.

As coffee is served, Rolf arrives. He has never met Janice personally, but within minutes he is seated at the dining room table, has heaped his plate with gargantuan servings, propped both elbows on the table, and begun a frenzied feeding motion. He shovels food continually from plate to mouth, talking incessantly, his mouth full or not. Topics cover a whole gamut from "yarding logs" to an update on his personal Green River killer theory and details of his latest interview with the sergeant on the Task Force.

"Yeah, you know these Task Force guys are real interested in my theory as to who the killer is. I've collected a lot of info on this one particular guy, and I've been able to talk to people the Task Force may have missed out on. A lot of my information makes sense to them guys, and they'll be doing the necessary follow-up investigations. You know, my friend Hansel--you know, Ingrid's husband down there in Newcastle--well, he seen a check to this guy for $600,000 supposedly paid as an insurance adjustment to him because he'd been in a building in Florida when it collapsed--"

As Rolf continues spouting off, I recall his talking previously about the large settlement his *suspect* had collected. In today's version the amount of insurance money is ten times greater. And Ingrid's husband Hansel saw it? Oh well, what do I know? Don and I, as well as Janice and Fern and Mother, sit in a mummified stupor as Rolf blathers on.

"You know, that's a hell of a lot of money. So, I call Florida--guess what? There's no record of any building collapsing in the whole state.

"Now, another thing about this guy--he owns a flat-bottomed river boat. It's quiet and fast with surface jet power. So I ask the sergeant if the Task Force had ever considered this Green River Killer kills his victims elsewhere and dumps them from a boat in the river. I shared with him, too, I had made a little trip to Portland to this guy's old neighborhood. I talked to several of his former neighbors, and little bits of information I collected there implicate him time-wise to the murders. You know, one thing was real peculiar about his property in Portland--he had a huge fence built around his yard--actually taller than the law allows. He told his neighbors the nature of his work subjected him to danger from intruders.

"Another thing I learned from the people who bought his house, he had a mass of pornographic literature stowed throughout the place. The people were still grumblin' 'cause they had to clean all that stuff out of there. Neighbors will tell you all kinds of little details like that."

Rolf shakes his head, "Nah, you know, there's just somethin' all too peculiar about his place there. You know all his victims disappeared quietly--I'm thinkin' some of them right from that house. A guy ain't gonna pick up that many women, mostly hookers, right off the street and not one out of forty-nine of 'em make a peep. These hookers know how to make plenty of noise if they think they need help. They wouldn't of been shy."

Little Fern scrapes her chair back, "I need a cup of tea." Janice offers the rest of us coffee refills. Mother leans toward Rolf, "You better be watching out with this Green River Task Force thing. You'll get yourself into something you can't get out of."

Rolf laughs smugly, "Yeah, Mom, you ain't the first to tell me that."

On and on and on...

Janice goes to the kitchen where Fern is putting the final touches on her cup of tea. Mother takes herself to the bathroom. Don and I have no escape and remain trapped at the table, a less than captivated audience while Rolf continues to stuff his face and talk.

Finally a dog's bark overpowers Rolf's volume. Don jumps up, "Maybe that's Mandy. I left her tied to the front bumper of our truck."

Rolf rises also, "Oh, I'll go with ya. It might be Taco. I left him in my car."

Out on the front steps, Rolf pauses and separates a long white paper from among the pens, notebooks, lotto tickets and other papers in his front shirt pocket. "Say, Don, I don't suppose you know anything about this?"

I step out onto the front porch as Don is scrutinizing the paper. The bold print at the top of the page announces, "NOTICE OF EVICTION." Rolf expounds as to how he hadn't planned on getting sick, and eight days in the hospital had really thrown him for a loop. He nods toward me. "I suppose *you do* know somethin' about this?"

"Yes, Rolf, of course, I do. It has my name on it. I would say to you again the eviction is not directed to you personally--it's an attempt to free up money that can be used for Mother's care. I want her to stay right here. This place is $1200 per month. *I* am now buying the Depends, bed pads, rubber gloves, and medications in addition to that amount. She doesn't have that kind of money coming in--at least she can't pay to be here and pay your mortgage, too. You and I have talked about this many times. I stated it clearly to you in my letter. She can't get any kind of help or subsidy because of her assets, and the law says her assets must be used for her care. Other people transfer assets early on--Malfaits didn't do that. There's nothing else I can do to finance assisted care for her. You're using her house, at least for storage of your stuff, and you're preventing it from being made ready for a sale. I have to sell either the house or the land. Since I can't sell the land without legal access, it has to be the house."

"Yeah, well, I wasn't prepared to get some notice that says I have to be out in three days. We never talked about that!"

"Rolf, that's not what it says. It says you have three days to *respond* as to *why* you shouldn't have your things out of there. Anyway, we *have* talked about Mother's needs repeatedly. She cannot be paying your bills and have anything to live on."

"Yeah, well, I don't expect to be able to be out of there in no three days, and I ain't gonna live under no log. *You* better call that lawyer of yours *and* that judge of yours and tell 'em that."

"No, Rolf, it's not *that judge of mine.* He is a superior court judge, and I don't even know which one signed the eviction notice. If you want to send a message to my lawyer, *you* call him and tell him yourself. It's not my responsibility to speak for you. You have to speak to the lawyer yourself and the same goes for the judge."

"Well, if I go to your lawyer's office or over to that courthouse speakin' to some judge, I'll be settin' 'em both straight; and I may just end up in jail as a result!"

"Rolf, that will be your problem, too. Don't threaten *me* with what your behavior might be with my lawyer or a judge."

"I'm not threatening you. I'm just tellin' you, they both better be white men about this whole thing. After all, they each got theirs all figured out, so's they know just how much they can collect for this kind of stuff."

"Rolf, *I* need money for *Mother's* care. You can add numbers as well as I can. You know what she needs each month. How hard is that?"

Rolf yanks the Eviction Notice from my hands and shakes it in my face. "I'm tellin' you, just like I said before, truckin' is pickin' up. I can't pay you by this deadline, but I can pay you my next paycheck. And, *you* better call that lawyer and tell him that!"

"No, Rolf, *you* call him and tell him yourself."

"Okay, then, I'll just go in and see him Monday morning and set him straight."

Mother opens the front door and comes out on the porch. We both fall silent. "What kind of no-good scheme are you planning now, Rolf?"

"Nothin'. I ain't plannin' nothin'."

Mother continues to direct her comments to Rolf. "I've been packing my things. When are we going to get going?" No one answers. She turns to Don, "What have those two been arguing about?"

"Oh, mostly they've been disagreeing--some of it about what to do with Taco."

I don't know how Don came up with that, but I am relieved. Mother looks in disbelief at Rolf and me. Rolf crams the Eviction Notice back in his shirt pocket.

Mother continues speaking in Rolf's direction, "Well, you two hurry up and finish your talk. Rolf, I'm going home with you."

Rolf folds his arms over his chest and looks at no one in particular. "No, Mom, you're not."

"I'm going home to Ridgeview with you tonight."

"No, Mom, you're not going home to Ridgeview with me. You better just keep breathing the nice fresh air up here. Things are fine in Ridgeview, and I didn't come up here to pick you up and take you home. I only come to visit."

The two of them begin a repetitive tune, one I easily recognize and have already danced to too many times in the last few weeks. Rolf deserves a turn. Don and I need to catch the late ferry. We excuse ourselves and move toward our truck, leaving Mother and Rolf on Janice's front door step. Our departure is hardly noticed as the intensity between Rolf and Mother increases.

On the way to the ferry I ponder aloud, "Don, do you think right about now Rolf if doing his usual *Rolf routine*?"

"What do you mean?"

"You know--like he did when he and I talked frankly that time before, and then he shared *every* bit of our conversation with Mother and Dad. Do you think he's telling her about the eviction? Do you think he'll show her the notice?"

"I don't know--maybe. He certainly doesn't hesitate to share his personal woes and bad luck with Janice, Fern, or anyone else."

"Yeah, as much as I would like to think otherwise, I bet he'll show Mother the official notice and tell her this is what Betty is up to and this is how it really is in Ridgeview, and 'poor me I've been in the hospital because of a dog bite.' I don't trust Rolf at all. I don't understand what has happened to him these last few years. We used to be great friends. When did he become a stranger? I really do care about him."

"He's a genius of his own unique brand, but he has no consideration for other people, whether in sharing dinner table conversation or in sharing their bank account, as he has for all these recent years with Malfaits. I can't believe he has much concern for Mother's welfare now. He lies repeatedly, and sometimes I don't even think he knows he's lying. What is all that stuff about the Green River Task Force? Is that a lie, too? Does he imagine that? My feelings are further complicated because I don't feel completely right about the eviction process--he's still my brother, for God's sake! But, in my head, and by law, I know I have to do it!"

"Betty, I know what you're saying. I wish things could be different for the two of you--for all of us for that matter. We used to have such good times with your folks. It was almost like that for a little bit tonight when everyone was there at the kitchen sink whooping and hollering and eating crab. Your mom was so relaxed and jovial. It was like old times. Then Rolf arrived and her whole demeanor changed. All of her attention went right to him, and she immediately became suspicious of everything and everyone. She's drawn to him. He's pretty overpowering."

We pull into the ferry waiting dock. My eyes are heavy. In fact, my whole body feels heavy. The lights of the boat are bobbing in the distance.

Dear God, please strengthen me. Will You please deal with Rolf? I really can't. I can't think and feel like he does. I don't live my life like that. Please protect me and my loved ones from his abuse and any possible harm that he might want to direct toward us. Please bless and protect the lawyer and the judge who must deal with this complicated process and employ the laws which will force Rolf to respond to the notice.

Oh, God, please forgive my short-comings, and help me to keep trying. I feel as if I'm so far out to sea now, I couldn't return if I wanted to. There's no end in sight. I'll go on tossing forever. Still I know that isn't true. I know there will eventually be calm water.

After the visit with Mother and Rolf on Whidbey, I receive a call from Aunt Mavis. "Rolf called me about the eviction notice. He, of course, is very upset. I knew he would be. It did seem a bit of a short notice. He says he had only three days."

"Mavis, that was three days to *respond*--not to get out of the house. He's told Janice, and God knows how many others, he's being kicked out in three days."

"Rolf also told me with his hospital stay and all, he probably couldn't pay the kind of money you were asking for."

"What I asked Rolf for was $600 per month rent. I guess if he's not been working and was in the hospital, he won't be able to meet that demand, but I didn't know about the hospital stay when I told the lawyer to proceed with the eviction, and it's so long from one step to the next I am never quite sure where the process is. I was instructed to ask for sufficient funding from him that would be a comparable rental amount for a house in Ridgeview of that size. That's the figure that was recommended by the attorney. I feel as if I have to press on. I can't make decisions with regard to Rolf's financial status or health status. Are you beginning to think I'm moving in the wrong direction?"

"Well, Rolf is kind of hard-pressed right now, but he'll just have to figure it out."

"Mavis, I'm really sorry for all the stress and hurt and upset I'm causing by these legal moves. I'm sorry to you personally, because I know you worry and are unhappy with the whole situation. I know you love both Rolf and me, but I don't have very many options. I don't see any way to get anything done with Rolf not really living there but sort of holed up in the house and storing all his belongings there. You don't have to agree with me, but you do understand, don't you?"

"Yes, I know. I told Rolf you had to have the money for Francine. That's all there is to it. If he would pay his own mortgage, you would about be able to make it, wouldn't you?"

"Not quite, but close. Mother only has $1019 from Social Security and her pension each month, and Janice charges $1200. She's already told me she's going to have to charge a little more because of the increased incontinence--and lately some spells of bowel incontinence. I guess that's Janice's call when the work load increases to such a degree that she needs to increase her price."

"Yes, I suppose so. How much longer does that mortgage continue for the Ridgeview house?"

"You asked me that the other day, and I looked it up. There's $7,502 remaining spread out over sixteen more payments. Malfaits have paid about $60,000 so far."

"What about a second mortgage or some other type of loan?"

"Aunt Mavis, I've tried for a second mortgage and been refused twice--by the bank and by the credit union. I'm not willing to risk my personal finances for such a mortgage, especially with Rolf ensconced in the house and unwilling to help or to move his stuff out. You aren't suggesting something like that, are you?"

"No, no--you shouldn't have to jeopardize any of your personal assets to do that, especially since it's really Rolf's mortgage. What about this new thing called a Reverse Mortgage?"

"I've investigated that, too. It's an attractive idea, but they are expensive and probably not a good deal for Mother. The person has to go back to live in the house until their death to get the improvements made. Then when the person dies, the Feds get their money back--or if the person lives there long enough, the Feds get the house. I don't think Mother should go back to that house, regardless of what improvements are made to it. Then, of course, there is the Rolf problem--bilking, abuse, thievery or whatever. I couldn't be guaranteed of any changes in those behaviors?"

"Yes, I see what you mean. Maybe Rolf could sell enough of his guns to pay the rest of the mortgage off. He told me the collection is worth forty thousand or more. Then would you be able to make it?"

"Yes, of course, and I have suggested that to Rolf myself. I haven't been able to get any response. When I was down there last time there were 49 fewer guns upstairs than the time you and I climbed up there. All those ones that were all over the floor are gone, as well as some from the gun cabinet. Maybe he does trade guns. I don't know. I don't have time to deal with whether he bought guns or traded for them. He's such a liar. I can't trust him or depend on him for anything."

"Well, Rolf has talked to me about going to Alaska. We've all told him the house is Francine's asset, and he needs to deal with his own property that's stored there. When he called about this eviction notice, I told him there would be an even bigger mess if Francine needed nursing home care. That would be twice as expensive. And when she dies, with no will and all, that will be another mess. I asked him again if he had seen a will when he took the insurance policies. He said no. I asked him if he thought maybe Francine tore the will up when she was so mad at you and Don about the missing money and grape juice or whatever. He said, no, he didn't think so. He thought it was around, and he was going to look some more."

"Mavis, the will was kept for thirty years or more right there with the insurance policies. It had been kept in Mother's dresser on the right-hand side in a little black metal safety box. That box was gymied open--remember? You were there when we found it. Who did that? Mom? Dad? Rolf? Or Don or me?"

"Well now, I know you and Don didn't take anything from there--grape juice, wills or anything else. I'm certainly not suggesting that."

"Aunt Mavis, I don't want to fuss with you. I'm just angry all over again about the insurance policies and the wills. I can't help but think Rolf has the will just like he had the insurance policies. He'll probably show up with it when *he* thinks it's needed."

"You may be right, but Rolf said he'd look around. Maybe it will show up yet."

"Even so, Mavis, what difference will it make? She's not dead, and the problem is not about dispersing her property. The problem is about how to pay for her care. I have repeatedly told Rolf her assets are hers. He is as stubborn about that Ridgeview house as Mother is. Neither one of them is rational about it. I just don't get it. We simply can't agree."

"No, I don't think you can either. Well, I've lived in West Virginia and griped about our laws, but I don't think it's as bad as in Washington."

"Mavis, it's not totally a matter of poor Washington law. It all could have been so much easier if Mom and Dad had arranged their business better--if they had just *arranged* it! A Durable Power of Attorney, even if it was to Rolf, could have saved everyone a lot of grief. It would have given someone the authority to make decisions instead of all this court business and trips to lawyers."

"Well, they named you the executor, didn't they?"

"Yes, but that's meaningless. That *honor* just means I'll take care of all their business when they are dead. I'll pay their outstanding bills, see that they get buried, and disperse their assets. Right now I can't even find the wills that indicate either one of them felt I could, or should, take care of that much of their business. They trusted me enough to ask me to be that after they were dead, but they never trusted me enough to give me a copy of the document. Anyway, a will isn't needed right now. What is needed is a Durable Power of Attorney. A guardianship doesn't allow the necessary power to make the decisions that need to be made. Then there's the fact that Mother cannot be forced to live in a nursing home, a foster home, or anywhere else she doesn't want to live. She has the right to go back to her home--that means the house in Ridgeview. God, Mavis, it just doesn't make sense!"

"Well, for myself, I don't think I'll be giving any such power to anyone either."

"Yeah, but, Mavis, even if they had given it to Rolf, it would have been clearly a choice and one person making decisions. They would have excluded me, and I would have been hurt and felt they were unfair. Their checkbook shows that anyway, as well as all the little lists of debts to be paid back that Mother wrote out in her famous angry red ball point pen ink. None of those unofficial little notes will ever be collectible debts, whoever is executor of their wills. I think I could have gotten along better without all this hassle and fighting. I could have accepted the hurt of unequal treatment better than the current grief of trying to work with Rolf. And who knows, Rolf may have made better decisions if I were not in the picture."

"Well, I know I need to update my own will, and I'm not going to be designating any Durable Power of Attorney. I understand how Roger and Francine didn't want to do that. I don't want to give that power to anyone either."

"Mavis, I understand that, too. You've been around these situations more, and you've certainly had experience dealing with greedy family members. Maybe all families have familial vultures hanging about somewhere in the wings of the household, waiting for death to creep in and benefit them. However, there aren't any assets in this family that are worth what's happening here. I should have my head examined for even trying to sort through this shit and pursue a guardianship. I'm angry at Dad, and he's dead. I'm angry at Mother, and she's irrational and demented. And, I'm angry at Rolf, because he's as bad or worse than the two of them put together!"

"Well, Betty, you certainly have your hands full."

"That's for sure. I'll do the best I can, and I don't even know what that means."

Our conversation ends on an less than encouraging note. Aunt Mavis *knows* I have to proceed with the eviction, but somehow I think she's changed her mind.

I again feel very alone!

CHAPTER 20

Damn!

IN ADDITION TO loneliness, there is a greater depth to my personal abyss. In the first week of November, Nick, our now twenty-three year old son, is diagnosed with a brain tumor. It is an invading mass the size of a golf ball between his cerebrum and his cerebellum. His surgery takes place three days later.

Damn!

The doctors believe they got it all and that it was benign.

Thank you, God. I'm sorry.

CHAPTER 21

─◦◊◦─

Eviction Day

MONDAY MORNING, NOVEMBER 18, 1991, my classroom lesson is sharply interrupted by the principal's voice on the inner-com, "Mrs. Alder, please come to the main office for an important phone call. Your party is on hold."

I scurry to the office, arriving somewhat breathless, as it's a good long city block away. My breathing becomes more labored when the deep commanding phone voice of a County Sheriff apprises me that the eviction will be Wednesday, November 20th.

"This coming Wednesday--day after tomorrow?"

"Yes, Ma'am. You should meet me promptly at 9:00 AM in front of 516, and you may want to have some additional labor with you in case you have to move Rolf's personal things out yourself."

"I might have to move his things out?"

"Yes, Ma'am. The person bringing the eviction procedure sometimes has to literally put the stuff out on the sidewalk or the street."

My breathing continues its accelerated rate as I return to the classroom.

The evening before I am to meet the Sheriff, Nosy-bill, the neighbor to the 516 property, calls. "Kid, what's going on at your mom's house? Do you know?"

"Yes and no. Rolf was served with eviction papers, but I don't know exactly what's happening now. What does it look like?"

"Oh, Betty, this looks like nothing I've ever seen before. Rolf has been working and moving stuff out all day. He has three people helping him, and I mean they've really been working since early this morning."

"Well, all I know is he is supposed to be moving. He was served with eviction papers November 1st, and he didn't show up in court November 8th to explain why he should be allowed to occupy Mother's house. I've been ordered by the court to sell the house, and it can't be sold with him and his stuff there."

"Oh, Betty, I knew something was going on. That server guy come to your mom's house several times. Finally he come over here. I told him Rolf's hours were real irregular. I guess he finally got him real late one night. He told me serving Rolf was the hardest case he'd ever served, and he'd been doing this job for about twelve years. He said Rolf acted real chatty and friendly when he finally made the contact though. I told him that was all just a bullshit act--and I used just that word, too. He said he could tell I was glad. I told him glad was not the word for it.

"My husband didn't want me to call you, kid, but dog-gone-it, Rolf shouldn't be able to keep Francine from having what's hers for her care. That's not his house. He hasn't lived there for a long time, and I'm not so sure you'd call it living there now. He's in and out of there at all hours of the day or night. And he never does anything around the place. Oh, kid, it's just horrible. The grass and weeds are clear up over the fence. I can't even see the side of their house any more. The kid from across the street keeps the front mowed down though--Oh my, there goes another load-- Oh, gosh, kid, I hope he isn't moving out her stuff, too."

"I hope not, because I guess I'd have to charge him with theft then. I took pictures of the house contents several weeks ago. Her things had better still be there."

"Well, there goes a truck load of somebody's stuff. I don't know where he's taking all that. It looks like he's already taken more than that house could possibly hold. I mean a whole houseful has been moved already! Kid, he's gotta be moving her things, too. All that just can't be his!"

"I don't know, and I can't really do anything about it. My appointment is with the Sheriff at the house tomorrow morning at 9:00 AM. Whatever he's doing today is really none of my business."

"Is Don coming with you?"

"We'll both be there."

"You guys come over and have some coffee when you get here. You'll need it."

"No, thank you. I don't think it's going to be a coffee kind of day. Rolf has had ten days since the court hearing date to vacate--not including weekends. Tomorrow is the tenth day. I guess he waited until the very last minute. If he doesn't finish, I have to put his stuff out on the sidewalk myself. It's just not going to be a coffee day."

"Oh, kid, but I'm tellin' ya, he's moved more than a whole house already."

"Good, it's that much less for Don and me to do."

"If he doesn't finish, do you and Don really have to do that? Do you have help?"

"The Sheriff informed me that I should be prepared to put his things out on the sidewalk in front of the house if necessary, and I should show up with the manpower to do that at the time. I have one hired worker--the fellow who dug the ditches for Mother for the new sewer line last year--plus Don and me. I've lined up a U-Haul truck and a storage place nearby. Frankly, I hope whoever is in the house today keeps moving--and moving--and moving!"

November 20, 1991, Don and I pull up in front of 516 in the rental truck at five minutes to nine. Piles of Rolf's belongings are spread out on the sidewalk on sheets of black plastic about four feet wide, forming staggering, lumpy mountains the length of the sidewalk in front of the two fifty foot lots which comprise the 516 property. The piles abruptly end at the fence by Nosy-bill's house. Eight sheets of plywood form crude A-frames over most of the mountainous lumps. I thought Nosy-bill said Rolf and his helpers had moved more truckloads than a house could hold already. It looks like another houseful piled on the sidewalk.

Rolf and a longtime family friend, Lars, emerge from the front entry of the house carrying boxes. They pause and look at the overflowing sidewalk and drop the boxes on the grassy parking strip near the curb. Down the street parked on a neighbor's driveway is a black pickup piled high, looking like a modern version of a *Grapes of Wrath* vehicle. Another old beat-up red pickup of similar appearance sits in front of the house laden to more than full capacity.

Don and I see no Sheriff's car in sight, and neither Rolf nor Lars acknowledge us. I don't know if they see us or not, and I don't know what to say or do if they do notice us. We stay in the U-Haul and watch this grim sight. We decide they are working hard, but they're not finished. Maybe we should drive up the street and choose a viewing spot further away. As we are preparing to pull away from the curb, a Sheriff's car swerves over from the on-coming lane and pulls up close to the driver's window of the truck and motions us to stop. I get out and go around the front of the truck to the car window and introduce myself.

The uniformed officer responds officially. "Yes, Ma'am, I know who you are. We've been watching you from both directions on the street. There's another officer down the block behind you folks, and we also have a car in the back alley."

"We didn't see any official cars, so we were going to move a little further up the street away from the front of the house."

"That's probably a good idea. I'll go on down to the corner and turn around and come back and pull in behind your truck. Then we'll all go up to the house together."

I run back to the passenger's side of the U-Haul and climb in. Don moves the truck slowly up the street, easing over close to the curb four houses away. The officer continues in the opposite direction, pausing momentarily in front of 516, then going on to make a U-turn at the corner. He cruises slowly back up the street pulling in at the rear of our truck. Don and I are both leaned over in the seat trying to share the outside rear-view mirror on the driver's side for a view of the house.

Rolf must have noticed the truck and the Sheriff's car and walked up the street. His booming voice through the open window on the passenger's side shatters our concentration. "Yeah, what's happenin'?"

I lurch away from Don, conking my head on the rear-view mirror mounted high up on the front windshield. I mutter some inane comment about the uselessness of a mirror placed in that position and turn to confront Rolf's head and both elbows leaning on the window frame on the passenger's side. "Oh, God, Rolf, I'm really sorry it has to be like this. I'd rather be just about anyplace else in the world right now."

Rolf leans further in, crosses his arms over each other with his elbows hanging inside the cab, causing me to scoot back to the center of the seat close to Don. He locks eye contact with me. "Yeah, yeah, I'm sure."

"I do hope you understand why all this is necessary. There just isn't any other way to pay for Mother's care, and I've been ordered to sell the house to gain the funds. I can't do that with you in it."

Rolf shrugs his shoulders and mutters, "Them's the breaks." He continues to maintain his silent window vigil with his elbows and head inside the cab of the truck.

The Sheriff steps up behind him and stands on the sidewalk. Another Sheriff's car arrives from the opposite direction, darts across the north-bound traffic lane and quickly pulls in almost against the front bumper of the U-Haul truck. The officer steps out, pauses momentarily behind the vehicle door, looking as if he's adjusting his gun belt. He then approaches Rolf. Rolf pushes himself away from the truck window, stands on the curb, stretches to his full nearly six foot height and re-crosses his arms high over his chest not looking at either officer. Both men move closer to him, one on either side. Rolf does not acknowledge either one of them. He continues an icy glare back into the open truck window.

"Well, I've about got all the stuff out, but the weather's been bad. It's been rainin' on and off all night. From the looks of that sky, the real storm is gonna let go here any minute. I need some plastic, but I ain't got any. I got all my guns and gun loading manuals and books out there on the sidewalk. All I got to protect them with is them plywood sheets. I don't know what I'm gonna do."

From the open window I mutter, "I'm sorry, Rolf."

Rolf doesn't acknowledge my apology, and I don't expect him to.

"Rolf, do you have a place to take the things that are still on the sidewalk?"

"I don't know what I'm gonna do with it!"

I persist, "Do you have a place to live?"

"Not really. I guess I'll be sleeping in my truck tonight. I don't know what I'm gonna do." Rolf turns and looks toward 516 and then in the other direction to the loaded truck parked on the neighbor's driveway. He takes a step toward the neighbor's house, and the officer on his right moves back to allow him to pass. We all watch as he walks up the street to where the loaded black pickup is parked. Both the Sheriff and the Deputy keep an eye on him.

Don asks me, "Shall I go get him some plastic and help him cover all his belongings?"

My heart is in my throat and my stomach is churning. "I suppose it wouldn't hurt to help him that much. Maybe we could--"

Before I can suggest anything further, the huge uniformed frame of the Sheriff blocks out the already limited light in the truck cab as he leans into the open window on the passenger side. I turn back to Don, "No. No, we should not do one single thing to help Rolf at this point. He has had weeks and months--*years* to make this move! If he had been responsive to anyone but himself, this gentleman wouldn't be leaning in our window now!"

The Sheriff speaks to both of us, "Okay, folks, perhaps we should all go down to 516 to talk. We'll do a walk-through and see how much more they have to do."

Before anyone can respond, the drab olive green uniform is highlighted in the window frame by jagged bolts of lightning followed almost instantly by frightening thunderous rumbles. This part of the state is known for its rainfall, usually rather a constant drizzle. This is not a drizzle! A blackened sky suddenly rips open and sends torrents of rain thrashing the aging maple trees, the truck windshield, the Sheriff, Rolf, and all his belongings. The uniformed shape jerks away from the truck window, and both the Sheriff and the deputy run to their cars. Another sequence of jagged torches burns across the sky followed by a prolonged deafening cadence of thunder. I crank up the resistant truck window, and Don and I huddle close in the cold darkness behind the steering wheel. The rain pelts viciously for several minutes, turns to a quiet patter, and suddenly ceases. After a moment or two of eerie stillness, a surging wind sweeps down through the huge maple branches which arch over the street, throwing small broken branches against the truck window and stirring up fallen leaves and street debris. The whole truck, a sizable twenty-two foot U-Haul, is jolted several times by the force of these gusts. As quickly as it began, the wind ceases. We are engulfed in black, chilly stillness. Before either of us can utter a word, an instant torrential downpour pummels the truck windshield, drenches the earth and all its contents steadily for at least five full minutes. Abruptly the climatic wrath ceases. The sky above the trees turns a dull gray. No more rain.

Don and I sit in stunned silence.

A distorted shape of uniformed law enforcement appears through the water droplets on the truck window on the passenger side, and a hand raps on the wet window. I again tug at the stubborn window crank and lower the squeaky glass.

"Well, Ma'am, perhaps we could do that walk-through now." The officer turns toward the house, and I get out and walk with him. Don moves to the back of the truck and busies himself assembling storage boxes in the haul space. As the officer and I reach the front steps, Rolf comes out of the house. He must have returned via the alley. I didn't see him go down the sidewalk during the storm.

Rolf yanks a red bandana from his pocket, wipes his brow and faces the Sheriff, looking only at him as he explains, "Yeah, we been workin' steady all night. We've about got it, but we ain't quite through."

As if I am unable to hear, the Sheriff turns to me, "Ma'am, they haven't quite finished with their part, and they are not able to meet the deadline as required. What do you want me to do?"

I ignore the interpretive step for non-speaking opponents, which the officer is probably obligated to do, and face Rolf. "How much more time do you need?"

Lars, a family friend who is helping Rolf, walks up and joins our circle. He's a tall, gangly farm boy, who was a hunting partner for Rolf. I don't think I've ever seen him wearing anything but checkered flannel shirts and blue jeans. His blond curly locks still fall across his forehead and sometimes partly over his glasses. Despite wearing glasses so thick they make his eyes seem too big for his face, he could often beat Rolf at hitting a bulls-eye on the paper target secured to a bale of hay down in their orchard, a good 600 feet below their barn.

Ignoring the awkwardness of our situation, Lars steps across the circle and gives me a silent bear-hug. Over Lars' shoulder I see the Sheriff's deputy, and note his right hand move to his gun belt. I step back from Lars and tell him, "We have a way of seeing one another only at unhappy times, Lars. The last time was the sad occasion of your Dad's funeral. I'm sorry about today."

The Sheriff keeps his eyes on Lars as he returns to stand beside Rolf. "You're working with Mr. Malfait, here, right?"

"Yes, sir."

The Sheriff continues, "Well, how much more work do you fellas have to do?"

Lars and Rolf agree they need about an hour more.

Nodding toward me, the Sheriff directs, "Ma'am, will you step over here with me for a moment, please?"

I follow the officer a few paces away. He looks at me and shrugs, "What do you think? You can demand they leave immediately as ordered or you can give them their hour to work. It's your call. What do you want me to do?"

"I don't know what to tell you, because I haven't been in the house for several weeks. We didn't go in when we first arrived."

"I know you didn't go in, because we've been here since 8:00 AM. We've been watching both the front and back of the house. It's been the same two rigs and the same two guys working steadily."

The Sheriff is distracted by movement in the back alley. A small gray inconspicuous Chevy Citation emerges from behind Malfait's garage. The Sheriff glances toward it, gives a thumbs up sign and a casual goodbye salute. A hand waves back through the top of a partially opened dark tinted window. The drab little automobile continues down the alley, disappearing behind Nosy-bill's garage.

Turning back to me, the Sheriff explains, "That's one of our guys. There's been no suspicious activity at the back of the house. And, like you say, I haven't been in the house either. How about if I walk you through like I suggested earlier? That way, we both can determine if we think everything is okay."

The officer moves back to where Rolf and Lars are standing and explains his intent. I glance about the outside of the house and notice the family in the home next door. The mom, dad, and three kids are perched on the back of their couch watching the activity in the yard at 516. They have rarely had their shades open in the past five years. I guess they're as fascinated as Nosy-bill on the other side of the house.

Across the street Mrs. Saunders is in the front yard with her garden hose watering her lawn. That's hysterical after the thunderous ground-soaking downpour we had a few minutes ago. Other neighbors down the street appear to be doing yard work as if it's April instead of November. Even the kid whom I hired to mow the lawn is more than curious. As he leaves his house for a walk with his girlfriend, they stumble all over themselves and almost fall off the curb trying to coordinate holding hands and at the same time observe our family activity. Nosy-bill has a seat on the 50-yard line, as she rushes from her house to her garage carrying a small "this or that" and then strolls back slowly toward her kitchen door partly obscured by Malfaits' fence, shriveled raspberry canes, and overgrown shrubbery.

The Sheriff and I enter the house. The interior is now an uncluttered but filthy disaster. The only indication of any kind of order is a row of guns lining the entire wall from the front door to the bathroom. Rolf follows us into the living room and pauses offering an excuse to no one in particular, "Yeah, it's pretty much of a mess in here. We tried to be as careful as we could though. We put down lots of papers, you know, to protect the carpet as best we could. It's pretty hard though to keep the floors clean and move out of a house in a hurry."

I bite my tongue, knowing the papers on the floor are the same ones that were on the floor when I was in the house weeks ago taking pictures. I can see the telephone notes I wrote on one of them. As far as *move in a hurry*, I silently remind myself if he had done what he should have done, he wouldn't be having to move in a hurry, or maybe not at all. I walk behind Rolf and open the door to Dad's bedroom. All the boxes and guns which had been piled on his bed are gone. Dad's remaining clothes and personal items are still in his closet and dressers. At least now I can *get* to the closet and have room to open the dresser drawers. In Mother's bedroom some of her clothes have been removed from the closet and are laid out on the bed. That's strange. Maybe Rolf's been looking through her things. I can't tell if anything is missing, as I haven't seen this room so empty for years.

A trip upstairs reveals that *all* the guns *and* the cabinets are gone. All the storage boxes are out of the big bedroom, which was Rolf's room. The built-in shelving and loading table have been ripped out of the hallway and dismantled. A few boards are still scattered on the floor. The little guest bedroom is no longer piled floor-to-ceiling with bows and arrows, crossbows, pistols and holsters and such. Only a few crumpled empty paper bags, a ratty looking military blanket, and a couple of empty boxes for handguns are strewn haphazardly on the floor.

I go back downstairs, where the Sheriff is waiting for me. The deputy is across the room standing by the front door. I can see Rolf and Lars out on the sidewalk loading things into Rolf's old car. The Sheriff asks, "So what do you think?"

"Several men must have worked very hard in the past few hours, or perhaps days--and not very neatly. It's a mess--but mostly cleared out."

The Sheriff follows me to the kitchen. The sink has the usual stack of dirty dishes and moldy food. I'm sure the Sheriff couldn't care less, but with a sweep of my arm toward the sink and a discouraged scowl, I tell him anyway, "In years past I cleaned up stuff like this after Mom and Dad. I guess this time I'll have to clean up after Rolf. A Malfait Mess is a Malfait Mess! What difference does it make?"

The Sheriff is unresponsive. I move back into the dining room. The table is un-stacked, and the lace tablecloth that once was the background for beautiful china place settings and luscious food presentations at family holiday dinners is stuck to the table in an oily greasy film. I pick at the grimy lace and ask the unresponsive Sheriff, "Rescue?" I answer myself, "Maybe. It was pretty once." I drop the tablecloth and point to the built-in corner cabinets. "Those dishes are treasures. I'm surprised he didn't take them." The china and crystal pieces sit in their proper places, held captive in layers of oily grime. Dining room pictures and carvings are still on the wall, even the cross-stitch calendar of the old Mayberry Mill, year 1983. "Oh, God, I remember that year. It seems like things have been screwed up ever since!"

The unresponsive Sheriff moves ahead of me into the living room, where he notes a discolored area about four feet by six feet on the knotty pine paneling. "What hung there, Ma'am?"

"It was an oil painting of two fishermen in a stormy sea--a painting once used in a saloon in Alaska. It had a small hole in the canvas right where one of the fishermen's eyes had been painted, so the saloon owners could spy on their patrons or cheat at poker or something like that. It was a very powerful piece. It belonged to Rolf."

Near the front door the deputy snaps a double barreled shotgun closed and places it in the row of other guns extending along the living room wall. He gives a thumbs up signal in our direction. The Sheriff steps over by him and they exchange a few words in whispers while motioning toward the row of guns.

I move outside. A light, misty rain refreshes my face. Don meets me at the bottom of the front steps. "While you and the Sheriff were walking through, the deputy picked up every single one of those guns leaned up in the living room, checked it, clicked the trigger, and put it down. There are seventy-three of them. He didn't talk to me at all. I've been standing here by the front steps most o the time. Lars kept working out there on the sidewalk, but Rolf was in and out. Every time he went in the house, that deputy stuck to him like glue, always to the side or right behind him. If Rolf went to the back bedroom, the deputy went. If Rolf went to the front bedroom, the deputy went. Man, I'm glad they were here and it's not just us by ourselves with Rolf."

Rolf and Lars come up the walk, and the Sheriff and the deputy come out of the house. The Sheriff asks, "Well, Ma'am, is everything as it should be? What would you like me to do?"

"I have some errands to do, and I can see there's still some unfinished work. I can give them until 11:00 AM. I'll come back then."

"Is that agreeable with you, Mr. Malfait?"

"Yeah, yeah. I think we'll be done by then."

"Rolf, I'll *have* to have you gone by 11:00, because I have work I have to do *today*, and I don't want people in and out while I'm trying to work."

Rolf squints his eyes and speaks through clinched teeth, "Like I said, we'll be *completely* out in time."

The Sheriff speaks up, "Well, I don't want any problem here."

Rolf turns to the Sheriff, "There won't be no problem."

The Sheriff nods, "Good. I'll be going on then. I'll be back at 11:00 AM sharp."

Don and I depart with the Sheriff and walk in silence in front of him up the street to the U-Haul truck. The Sheriff and the deputy chat for a moment on the sidewalk. Then the deputy moves his car from in front of our truck, and the Sheriff gets in his vehicle behind us and pulls out. We move the U-Haul into the traffic lane behind the Sheriff's vehicle and slowly follow him down the street. About two blocks away at a corner stoplight the Sheriff turns right and we wait to continue through the intersection.

A purplish-black sky opens up, and we are the recipient of yet another torrential thrashing. The rain is so intense the truck's window wipers switched on hi-power cannot keep it clear enough to drive. We pull over and wait. Whatever is worse than torrential exerts itself for several minutes.

When the rain slacks off, Don and I find a nearby cafe and pass the time trying to eat a bite and relax over coffee and a newspaper. Near the appointed hour we return to 516 in the truck and pull up in front of the next-door neighbor's house. We open the back truck doors and begin assembling more moving cartons. Rolf and Lars are still making trips in and out of the house. He's never kept his word about anything--why should I expect him to be out, even by the extended time limit? Lars notices the truck and comes around to the back.

"Hi, Betty. We really have about got it this time."

"Thanks, Lars. Thanks for helping Rolf. This day--this whole thing is awkward--embarrassing. I'm sorry. It's just that Rolf and I disagree about a lot of things."

"Yeah, my brother and my sister and me have our disagreements over what's best for our folks, too."

"Well, it's that for us, also, but the worst part is over his humongous mortgage."

"What humongous mortgage is that?"

"You do know why this eviction occurred?"

"No, not really--Rolf feels like you're trying to take something from him--kind of take over, that's all."

"That's not exactly right. Rolf got into financial difficulties after Mt. St. Helens blew up. He persuaded Mom and Dad to sign a second mortgage on their house, which so far has amounted to their paying some $60,000 over the last ten years. He promised to take over the payments when he got back to work. That never happened."

"Yeah, I can imagine that not happening. Getting money out of Rolf is not an easy task, regardless of who you are. A fair number of people around Newcastle can attest to that, even my own brother can't get him to pay him back some money he owes him. I've read the letters Bud wrote to Rolf related to debt collection and avoidance of responsibility. That kind of cooled their friendship as a result of Rolf not paying up. Nah, Rolf just doesn't pay up very well to anyone."

"Well, he never paid his folks. They paid his way, and now Mother needs the money for her own care. Over the years of the guardianship, I have not been able to get him to pay either. This house has to be sold, and Rolf has had a lot of his stuff stored here. He has not been cooperative at all about moving anything out, so the house could be made saleable. Eviction is the only thing he would respond to."

Lars turns away and spits a stream of tobacco juice under the laurel hedge behind him. Turning back toward me, he runs his fingers through his curly hair and pushes the errant strands back up atop his head. "Well, I understand the situation better--but Rolf is my friend, you know?"

"I know, Lars, and I don't want that to change. I'm glad you're here today."

"Well, I'm just trying to help him. I don't want to be on anyone's side, you know?"

"That's fine. I'm glad. You might also help him by reminding him the taxes on his Newcastle house and property are overdue. He's going to lose it at the county auction if he doesn't pay them."

"Oh, God, that's serious." Lars takes a notebook from his shirt pocket and asks, "What's the deadline? I'll really work with him on that. It would be a shame to lose that. It's a real nice piece of riverfront land."

Rolf appears at the back of the truck. I scribble a quick date in Lars' notebook and hand it back to him. Looking at no one in particular I ask, "Did you guys get those loads delivered somewhere before that last storm let loose?"

Lars speaks up, "Oh, yeah, we didn't have far to go. We just had to run it over here a few blocks and unload it into a couple of storage units."

Rolf crosses his arms and glares at Lars. Without any prior notice, the Sheriff appears, stepping between the two of them at the back of the truck.

I try for one more point with Rolf while he's in front of the Sheriff. "Rolf, despite this action today, I want to be able to get in touch with you regarding our common interests, and I need a way to contact you."

"I don't know where I'll be. I'll be sleeping in my truck tonight, I suppose."

"I mean if I need to contact you regarding Mother or maybe about something you may have left in the house. Your truck doesn't have a phone, does it?"

"Nah, I don't have no phone in the truck. Are you gonna be around a few days?"

"Not really, I'm only down for a limited time, and I have some very specific work to do, and then I'm going home."

"Well, I still have a few things in my room--my bed, desk and some gun catalogues. Can I come back and get them?"

"Yes, but at this point I want to work in the house, and I don't want you in and out while I'm working. I would like to have your keys today; and I will be changing the locks immediately, but I need a way to contact you in the future."

Reluctantly Rolf writes out his boss' name and phone number of the company for whom he drives log truck and also Lars' phone number in Newcastle.

The Sheriff speaks up, "Mr. Malfait, I'd like you to give her the house key now in my presence." Turning to me, he asks, "Is there anything else you want from him?"

"Yes, I'd like the keys to Dad's old Buick."

Rolf shrugs, "Well, I don't know where those are at the moment."

The Sheriff points at him, "Do you *have* them, Mr. Malfait?"

"Yes, I have them."

"Rolf, I have to have the keys, as I have been ordered to account for the old cars to the Department of Health and Social Services, and I have to respond to the city's abatement notices and get rid of the one that is still sitting there on the driveway."

Rolf digs deep into his pocket and struggles with the content. "Well, maybe I have it right here on me." He pulls out a huge chain of keys and fumbles trying to get a key off. Both his hands quiver furiously.

The Sheriff offers, "Can I help you with that?"

"Nah, nah."

Lars reaches for the keys. "For God's sake, Malfait, what's the matter with you? Give me them damned keys." Lars takes the house key and the Buick key from the ring and hands them to me and returns the remainder to Rolf.

In the same monotonous repetition, the Sheriff asks, "Is there anything else?"

"There were two saws upstairs earlier when I inventoried the inside of the house for a court record. The saws were paid for by Malfaits, and they are not there now."

Rolf sticks his chin out and leans back. "No, there were not *two* saws upstairs. There was *one* upstairs."

"Okay then there was one *upstairs,* but there *were two* saws."

"Well now, Mom told me I could have those saws for doing some of the work around the place."

"Rolf, those two saws were the crux of a terrible fight between you and Mother and between you and me. They are not yours. They belong in the house, and I would like them returned."

The Sheriff's authoritative drone takes over, "Mr. Malfait, do you have the saws?"

"Yes, I have the saws."

"You need to return them. Can you do that?"

"The saws will be back this afternoon."

The voice is directed to me, "Is that all right, Ma'am?"

"Yes, that would be fine."

The Sheriff continues, "If the saws are not returned, you may call me and I'll attend to it. Is there anything else?"

"Well, I want to work in the house, and I want to be on the property undisturbed."

"And is that agreeable to you, Mr. Malfait?"

"Oh yes, we'll not be in the house. You'll be undisturbed." Rolf glances at his watch. "In fact, I have to get to work here in a little bit. Do you care if Lars continues for a couple of more trips? He can return the saws."

The Sheriff speaks to me, "Is that all right with you, Ma'am?"

"Oh sure, Lars wouldn't be a bother at all."

"Then I don't see any further problem here, and I'm going to leave. I don't feel there is any danger of altercation from either of you." The Sheriff looks directly at Rolf. "Is that correct?"

Rolf's response is immediate, "Oh no, there ain't gonna be no altercation. There'll be no trouble at all."

Lars chimes in, "I won't be in nobody's way, and I won't cause no trouble."

The Sheriff concludes, "Then I think at this time all is peaceful for both parties. If there should be anything further, Ma'am, you just call 911."

Rolf reaffirms, "There ain't gonna be no disturbance."

The Sheriff turns and walks to his car. There is an awkward silence as Rolf and Lars stand on one side of the sidewalk facing Don and me on the other side.

Lars breaks the silence, "Where's your dog, Malfait?"

"I took him to the vet's for a couple of things. He's still there."

I try to be conversant. "Rolf, the kid across the street really likes Taco. He asked me about him, and he expressed an interest in having him. He said his mom didn't mind. You might consider that."

"Yeah, yeah. I might do that."

Lars continues, "Well, Malfait, have you got them cats still in the house? It sure smells like it."

"Well, now that you mention it, you know that little scrawny one named Lizzy? That's a story all in itself. She was gone for a long time, but

I found her. Course there wasn't much left of her when I moved the furniture out and discovered her."

"Oh, God, Malfait, you mean she died in there?" Lars turns and spits under the hedge behind him, rearranges his chew, and shakes his head.

Rolf smiles, "Yeah, you might say that--and there was even less left of the maggot infestation when I found her. Both the cat and the maggots was pretty well dried up."

"Oh, Jesus, Malfait, how could you be in there with that?" Lars chokes and gags, and spits some more, shifting from leg to leg.

Don and I stare at one another slack-jawed, speechless. At least now I know on my last trip down what the dirty mop and pails of water were for in the living room. That's one cleaning job I'm glad I don't have to do.

Lars turns to me, "How's your mom doing?"

"Pretty good. She likes the foster care place and the woman who runs it, but she still would like to be here in Ridgeview. Rolf and I would both like that for her, but she can't take care of herself independently, especially with her forgetfulness and wandering along the streets looking for Dad. . then there's the incontinence."

"Yeah, my family is having some of the same problems with Dad. I don't know, maybe it's harder when a man is incontinent. He's gone down hill real fast since Mom died. He's just not doing very well. We can't let him be by himself anymore either. I guess we all go down hill when we get old and bad things happen and we gotta have someone else help us."

"Well, Lars, I've been thinking lately it's not just when we're old. Sometimes bad things happen to a person when they're young. By the way, Rolf, did you know about Nick's brain tumor?"

"No, no. I didn't know anything about that."

I recall Aunt Mavis telling me she had shared that news with him, but why bother arguing? I describe the surgery briefly to Lars, as he seems interested. Rolf asks nothing, not whether his nephew is okay, dead or alive.

I think today is a greater family separation than I had thought it would be.

I turn toward Don, "We have a lot to do. Shall we get at it?"

"I'm with you."

"We'll see you guys." Don and I turn and walk up the walkway and into the house, locking the front door after ourselves. Rolf and Lars stand and talk for a bit on the sidewalk. Then Rolf leaves, and Lars loads the few remaining boxes in his truck.

Eviction day is over.

CHAPTER 22

---⊶⊷---

The Day After The Eviction

EVEN THOUGH ROLF cleared out his property and vacated the house, the work Don and I see before us is formidable. That which we do not see is even scarier, but we make a list and launch into the tasks before us. We schedule a locksmith for this afternoon to change all the locks in the house, garage, and shop. We do a preliminary clean-up of the *protective newspapers*, scattered boards, and any other flotsam and jetsam from the eviction. We box up the china and crystal collections and the remaining art work. We select as many pieces of furniture as we deem deserving of storage space, pack these items in the U-Haul truck and take them to a nearby facility, hopefully not the one Rolf is using.

The wee hours of the morning and several degrees past physical exhaustion force us to quit and go to our motel, a low-budget competitor of The Sterling located a ways out of town. If Rolf comes looking and just happens to see our truck, at least he'll have to search several miles further than The Sterling.

A hot shower partially revives me. As Don is showering, I struggle with a stubborn warped nightstand drawer, finally unclogging a couple of phone books. I push aside an array of tourist and entertainment brochures, cheap notepads advertising our cheap motel, and several two-for-one restaurant coupons, and retrieve a Gideon Bible.

Dear God, I need some kind of affirmation that what I've done today is right---that it's in your will. Please, God, guide me now through the words of this Holy Bible. Let me know by your written word that I'm within your will.

I let the book fall open arbitrarily and squint to read, *Hebrews 13:1 - Let brotherly love continue.*

Oh, God, this is not fair! This is too much!

I slam the book shut and throw it back in the drawer with the pandering community literature and phone books and force the drawer back to its jammed condition. I turn out the light. The tears spill over. I'm glad Don's shower water is still on. What kind of affirmation was that?

The next morning I call my aunt. "Oh, Aunt Mavis, yesterday was an ugly scene, but we all made it through the day." I give her details of the eviction, and conclude, "But, good god, Aunt Mavis, it's still an ugly scene. House-cleaning at 516 may take years, and *clean* may never happen! I know you said you'd come if I needed you--and I do need you--but all I can promise you is a bed, bathroom and kitchen as clean as Don and I can make them, but it still stinks. I don't know if we can ever get the odor out."

"Betty, you and Don have worked awfully hard. I know you have. Of course, I'll come. That is, I'm willing to come and help if that bathroom sink is fixed. It is, isn't it?"

"Oh, yes, the plumbing is in good working order. We did that a while back. Don did a preliminary cleaning of the bathroom today, and tomorrow he's going to scrub the whole room floor-to-ceiling. I'm pretty sure the bedroom, bathroom and kitchen will be clean by the time you get here."

"Okay, just tell me when you want me to come."

Mavis and I agree on a date, and Don and I return to 516 for a second day's work. The immediate tasks before us are a bit more bearable, anticipating Aunt Mavis as a third worker, an especially comforting thought considering my relationship with Rolf.

Don gathers a collection of sponges, brushes, buckets, cloths and cleaning solutions and attacks the bathroom. My goal is to clean out Dad's bedroom, which is next to the bathroom and the room intended to be Aunt Mavis' bedroom.

Dad was a mill worker for most of his working years. He worked hard in his job and at home. He enjoyed gardening with flowers, fruits and vegetables. His favorite hobbies were making jelly, fishing and hunting. His clothing for these tasks was mostly sturdy, durable labels and in ample supply filling the drawers in two bureaus, a mirrored vanity, and a few boxes stacked on top. I go through each drawer and box, sorting and refolding, placing useable items in heavy fifty-five gallon plastic bags and the rest in a pile for the garbage.

Several hours later I finally face Dad's closet, which is also filled beyond capacity but is the antithesis of blue-collar content. The man loved to dress up. On the left-hand side of the eight-foot closet protected by plastic wraps and dust covers hang twenty-four beautiful brand-name suits, and placed in orderly fashion below are twelve pairs of shoes of matching quality, Florsheim being by far his favorite brand--especially wing-tip styles. Thirty-six dress shirts--some starched cotton and some monogrammed soft silk, some still bearing a vague odor of Old Spice--hang in a group on the right side of the closet, mostly stiff and yellowed by age. In the center between the suits and shirts hangs a necktie collection of more than sixty on rotating and vertical organizers, gift gadgets of Christmases past. Searching suit pockets I consistently find an unused handkerchief in the outside front left pocket and often a partially used wrinkled one in the inside breast pocket crammed behind one or more ball point pens. Several of the suits contain partial packages of Dentyne gum. It was his favorite, as it never stuck to his dentures. A few pockets contain one or two individually wrapped red and white peppermint candies. These would have been for Mother, when she got a coughing spell in church or for some little kid who needed a diversion from a long-winded preacher. Other pockets held an occasional comb, a torn concert ticket stub, or a dated church bulletin. I fold each garment and add them to the plastic give-away bags.

It's after 10 PM when Don and I drag six burgeoning bags of clothing to the pickup and throw them in the back. Dad's bedroom is empty and clean, and the bed is made up for Aunt Mavis. The bathroom floor-to-ceiling scrub-down is complete and dry. The living room is clean--clean being relative since permeating odors of animals and years past may never be eradicated. The big sectional couch Goodwill refused in their afternoon pickup to the house has been cleaned with the power and efficiency of the mighty Rainbow Vacuum brought from home, and it looks reasonable for a garage sale.

I make my way to the dark alley at the back of the property dragging the last bag of trash. Four huge city dumpsters, cylindrical units measuring six feet across and five deep, are now full to the point of refusing their lids. I struggle for several minutes in the darkness hoisting my trash into the fifth dumpster and trying to force the dumpster lid to obey. I finally surrender to the strength of the dumpster and return to the house.

Don is at the kitchen table making a list for a future work day. We are both bone-tired, and formulating a simple list is a blurry challenge.

The ringing of the front door bell shatters our fragile concentration, startling us both. I make my way through the house, turn on the porch light, and peek through the metal wicket. Rolf is standing there in dirty, cut off logger blue jeans, oil stained hickory striped shirt, arms crossed over his chest. I open the front door a crack keeping my foot wedged behind it. "Yes?"

"Yeah, I was just drivin' down the alley and I saw you back there by the shop. I wanted to get my antique bucking saws, but the shop's all locked up. Don told me yesterday it'd be okay if I got them. You got the keys?"

"Yes, Rolf, I've got the keys. You probably noticed I had all the locks changed. Don and I have worked like dogs yesterday and all day today since early this morning. We're just about ready to leave. I really don't want to open that back shop at this hour. It's after ten o'clock."

"Oh, oh--all right. I'll try another time."

There are no other words from either of us. In the awkward silence Rolf backs off the steps. I close the door and lock it and return to the kitchen and the list.

The doorbell chimes again. I plod back through the living room and open the wicket. There stands the same unwelcome, hickory-striped form.

"Yeah--I wondered if you had seen my Absorbine and my medication."

"We found a bag with that stuff in it yesterday. I gave it to Lars. He said he would make sure you got it."

"Well, I just thought I'd step in and look around and see if I could see it."

"No, Rolf, I don't think that's a good idea. There was a paper bag on the television that had Absorbine and some kind of medication in it. I gave it to Lars."

"Well--okay." The bulky figure again backs off the step and I close the wicket and recheck the lock on the door.

Don is now standing directly behind me, and he turns off the house lights and the porch light. The two of us edge through the darkness to the front bedroom and peek out the cracks of the blinds. By dim street light filtering through the leafless maples lining the parking strip, we can make out Rolf's hunched, motionless form in his car. Both of his hands are gripping the steering wheel, and for several seconds he seems to be staring straight ahead. Finally one of his hands moves away from the steering wheel down by his side.

If we can see him, can he see us peeking out?

A thundering belch splits the late night neighborhood quiet, evidence that Rolf has not yet bought a new muffler. He pumps the gas pedal several times. The engine settles into a rhythmic roar, and the vehicle moves slowly away from the curb.

Don and I drop the blind slats over our peeking spot, hurry through the dark living room and out the front door. As we cut across the lawn to our truck, we can still see the lights of Rolf's old car at the end of the block and we hear a faint rumble as he shifts down and makes a right turn. Don hurriedly starts our truck and we make a quick exit from the drive-way before Rolf has time to drive around the block or down the alley and come back to the house with some other feeble excuse to gain admittance.

I can't help recalling an episode from years back when he bragged about sitting in his car in a parking lot pointing a rifle at the store window of the establishment where the man who stole his logging truck piece by piece from him worked. He said, "It was a real pleasure to know he could bring him into sharp focus and he could choose to shoot him in either the right or the left eye."

I don't want him to place either one of us square in the sights of one of his hundred-plus weapons which he just removed from 516 in yesterday's eviction process and relish the idea that he could choose to shoot one of us either in the right or left eye.

I am probably being paranoid now, but I wonder if earlier he watched me in the alley and out by the shop through a rifle scope or from the shadows. He said he had seen me, but I didn't see him.

Paranoia or wisdom, it doesn't matter. The cab of our truck feels safe and comforting as we make our escape. We're not staying in Ridgeview tonight but going home to our home. Despite our tiredness and a long trip ahead of us, it's better to be dead-tired than dead.

CHAPTER 23

Family Thanksgiving At Janice's

DESPITE NEGATIVE FEELINGS of what's to be thankful for, when Thanksgiving Day, 1991, rolls around, my family and I spend the time with Mother, Janice, and Fern. Janice outdoes herself preparing turkey and all the trimmings, real mashed potatoes with real gravy, broccoli-cheese confetti, orange-cranberry molded salad, pickle and olive trays, and two kinds of home-made bread. My contribution is pies: two pumpkin, a custard and a coconut macaroon.

Thanksgiving at Janice's: The author's husband, the author, their son Nick, and Francine's brother, Malcom

Dear God, I do have much to be thankful for--for BEING—for surviving up to now--for sharing--for Janice--for Mother being here--for my family. And, if I really do all my thanking adequately, I will have to spend all this day talking to You, and we'll have no time to eat!

Mother is jovial during dinner, as we all are. Fern readily adopts my family as her own, and I don't ask why she is not spending this day with her people who live nearby. Though Nick and El are quite grown up, at least semi-sophisticated in their collegiate roles, they seem to enjoy being *the children* at this celebration. I myself enjoy that illusion as their childish giggles make Mother and Fern giggle, too.

Francine's brother Malcom, sister Mavis, Francis and her grandson Nick at Janice's Place

At Janice's Place everyone helps: the author and her husband on kitchen duty

Grandma eventually asks, "Now, Nick and El, will you kids be coming down to visit your grandma at Christmas time?"

They're both quick and simultaneous, "Of course!"

"Well, you'll have to come to Ridgeview for that, you know, because Dad will want to be there, too."

There's a stifled, not at all childlike, giggle.

Grandma continues, "I just don't think Dad and I can drive up to your place any more. We'd get lost for sure.

"What would you two like for Christmas?"

From across the table silent, pleading glances are cast my way.

Grandma pursues her Christmas plan, "I think I'll give each of you ten dollars. Would you like money?" Turning to me, "Would that be enough for them, Betty?"

"Yes, that would be fine, Mom. May I have the broccoli-cheese confetti?"

Grandma passes the dish and turns to Don. "You know, I've been having a lot of dreams lately, Don. I dreamed the place in Ridgeview was grown over with weeds so high I had to wade through and swing my arms like I was swimming. I couldn't even see the fence. Betty, you call Dad and ask about that!"

I wish I could do that for her. I can't tell her the current status of the house in Ridgeview. Maybe in her own way she knows. For sure I can't discuss the eviction of Rolf nor the court order to sell her house. I can't tell her Aunt Mavis is coming out to help this event happen. She would probably have more than a mini-stroke.

Oh, God, there isn't any other way...Is there?

CHAPTER 24

—∞∞∞—

Dismantling The House That Daddy Built

AUNT MAVIS ARRIVES in Portland the evening of December 4th. We waste no time heading back to Ridgeview where we survey the tasks and plan our subsequent days. We decide to attack the dismantling of the house one room at a time, the first priority being the front bedroom. In recent years it was Mother's bedroom, and before that both of them slept there when Dad was recuperating from his stroke. Despite Rolf's plundering prior to eviction, the closets and chests are still packed tight. Mother was a master at packing beyond full capacity!

Friday and Saturday pass in a flurry as the three of us work fifteen-hour shifts, mostly in that bedroom. The carry-out trash fills three of the alley dumpsters, plus two trips to Goodwill. All of this in that one room *after* Rolf moved out!

By Sunday we all reach our limits of well-aged cat fumes. We decide to work outside for a breather, attacking the leaky roof problem, which we noted from stains in the dining room ceiling and the little upstairs bedroom after the recent torrential rains on the day of the eviction. It takes all three of us to stretch heavy black plastic over the places where shingles blew off. Don tacks two-by-fours down to hold the plastic in place.

The leaks ought to be repaired, but there's no money. I can't get a loan. Mother has no cash. Debts for her care have accumulated. The only immediate potential source of cash is the garage sales we are planning. I don't think there's $10,000 in garage sale items on the premises, but that's the minimal amount I need at this moment just to catch up with Mother's debts. Aunt Mavis thinks I may be surprised at our potential garage sale income, and I want to believe her.

189

Aunt Mavis, Don and I are exhausted after our first work weekend of cleaning up 516. Monday morning Don and I find our classroom responsibilities to be refreshing and restful compared to our past weekend. Mavis uses the days until our next trip to Ridgeview to prepare and advertise our upcoming garage sale.

Such advertising in local papers draws a special breed of human being. Don and I have not met them before, but on the next weekend our naiveté is erased--bartered, stolen, smashed, devastated! Hordes of humanity clamor through 516. Mavis and I struggle to keep up with customers. How much? Will you take less? Oooh, this is nasty. Why would anyone have this in their house? Where's your bathroom?

Don is a crew of one to evaluate items in another room--sort it, sell it, trash it. He also has to be ever vigilant to keep people out of restricted areas of the house, garage, and shop. Some people even ask to dig up clumps of starter plants from the yard. By the end of the first day, five city dumpsters in the alley again have more than their normal weekly contributions, and some of our sale customers do additional follow-up freebie-shopping in the alley dumpsters.

At the end of the weekend the house doesn't look as if we've made much of a dent in the total content, but the coffee can on the kitchen table holds $1,303.53.

In coming days and weeks we stay the course working our way through the house one room at a time. We hold a sale each weekend for three and a half months. We become so familiar with the alley dumpsters we name them: Old Green, Splotch, Nosy-bill's, and Cat-pisser. We have several satisfied repeat sale customers who anticipate the content of the next room in the house far more than any of us do. When will you get to the upstairs part of the house? Both Rolf and your dad hunted and fished. There must be some good stuff up there. Have you got any guns for sale? Where are all of your mother's ceramic molds? Hey, I looked through the garage window, and you got a bunch of tools in there and enough wood to build a house. When will you open that up?

The approaching Christmas season comes upon us with almost no notice. We bring Aunt Mavis to our house for a Christmas break, but the celebration and real meaning of the season is obscured with a trip to Whidbey to deliver a huge economy container of Depends for Mother and fruit jars for Janice. Actually our truck load is thirteen *cases* of empty quart jars and eight *cases* of half-gallon jars *full* of grape juice. I guess whenever Don *stole* those items he must have stowed them upstairs in Malfait's house for this special Christmas celebration! Sarcasm? Yes. Hurt? Yes. Tears? Yes. And there's at least another full pickup truckload of fruit jars in the attic of 516. And only God knows how many more tears.

Frustration and tears aside, I am thankful the garage sale money is keeping things afloat. Janice is happy with my efforts to pay her, even though I can't pay in full. We all see progress, but our room-to-room strategy has turned up additional personal items belonging to Rolf. Legally, they can be sold, but should we do that? My attorney's advice is to give Rolf another written letter and have Aunt Mavis hand deliver it.

December 29, 1991
Dear Rolf,
You may not think so, but I have thought about you daily during these recent days and hope all is going well for you. I'm so sorry
Nov. 20th had to occur. I wish we could have worked out our differences, but I have agreed to disagree with you.

I am sorry for the stress and unpleasantness which the eviction action has caused both of us. However, the day of eviction did not seem to allow you enough time to remove the entirety of your personal property, and we are still finding things in the house which we recognize as yours. In regard to the remaining items, I have two requests: 1) Please refrain from stating publicly or to old family friends that I am selling your stuff. That statement is untrue, and any items which have been inadvertently sold were impossible to distinguish as yours. In fact, Aunt Mavis did sell your old doll, but only after asking you, and she made sure you received your $45 from that sale. 2) The eviction date itself was a definite time by which you were to have <u>all</u> your effects off the premises.

However, since that did not happen, and since you have expressed a desire to take other items, would you please do so as soon as possible? I will consider <u>any items belonging to you and left on the property after Sunday, January 12, 1992, to be abandoned, and these items will be sold for the benefit of Mother's estate account.</u>

If you have some notion the proceeds from the garage sale or from the sale of the house itself is for my benefit, please rest assured every penny can be accounted for and is being spent in Mother's behalf. I do confess to getting angry with you for making this total process more expensive than necessary. The thing that comes out short due to your lack of cooperation is Mother's pocketbook. It cost her over $150.00 to serve legal papers to you, and she's just now catching up on the lumber bill and the bill at the hardware store. I will never be able to understand your position regarding this, just as I will never understand your allowing your mother and father to pay out $67,500 from their retirement and Social Security incomes to satisfy a debt which you have made absolutely no attempt to be responsible for--at least not during the past four and a half years that I am aware of. I do hope in your own private reflections you understand my anger over this.

As I have told you previously, however, my anger does not prevent me from loving you. I hate what you've *done*--but I do love *you!* I care about you, and I care what happens to you. Even though you are the older one, I wish you would finally just plain grow up and take responsibility for yourself. And most of all, be honest with yourself. You are enormously creative and ingenious and very capable of being a constructive and contributing citizen and caring about other people, at least as much as you care for Rolf. Contrary to what you seem to believe, the whole world is not out to do you in. I know you've been screwed more than once by people and by the system itself, but you were never screwed by Malfaits! We both know Mom and Dad slaved long hard hours for years to make things better for you and me! Enough of my sermonizing. If you feel no direction from your own

soul, then you need a bigger voice than mine. I remain your loving but angry sister. God bless.
Love,
Betty

CHAPTER 25

Garage Sale Vultures

CHRISTMAS BREAK DOES not slow the garage sale vultures. At the first weekend opportunity they reappear, hovering and pecking on the front door each Saturday morning beginning at 7:00 AM, despite the ad and signs on the door clearly stating we open for business at 9:00 AM. However, as I gain experience in this frenzied phenomenon of merchandising, I learn garage sale junkies come in second in *unethics* compared to unscrupulous timber companies and independent gypo loggers. I hope to sell the timber on Mother's land as another source of income, and several logging companies and gypo loggers have been asked for estimates. The first timber cruise estimate comes from Gladstone Gypo Timber Works, offering four to five thousand dollars for the timber on twenty acres. "That's the best we can do right now due to a downturn in the foreign market."

Ha! I just read a local newspaper article yesterday about the glut on Northwest timber by the Japanese and how timber prices are skyrocketing. I can eyeball Mother's timber better than that myself.

The second offer is to buy the 20-acre parcel for $10,000. I do need the money, but that's ridiculous.

A few days later I receive an estimate from Soloman's Sno-Island Timber Company for twice as much as the Gladstone people had proposed--and that's only for the timber--not the land. Now I know how Gladstone got to be called *gypos!*

I don't have time to think about these offers right now. I need to stay focused on the preparation of 516 for sale.

As the weeks progress, Don and I get our fill of marketing to the vultures, especially those who want to buy the house for little or nothing. *Yes, we know there's an odor in the house, and it will probably never come out.*

It will probably never come out of our nostrils! Yes, there's a hole in the roof. What did you think we were hiding under a hundred square yards of heavy plastic tacked to the roof? Yes, it's a buyer's market right now. Yes, we know the economic reality lesson relevant to this declining neighborhood. Yes, the stairs are broken. Yes, electric heat is passé. Yes, you will have to pull out all that old carpeting; and you might even have to remove the flooring. Yes, you might have to haul away $1,000 or more in lawn debris. You might even have to bull-doze the whole yard to gain control of an agricultural bonanza that grew beyond the wildest expectations of someone named Ortho--or Scotts--or just plain Guano!

Yes! Yes! Yes!

Days and weeks blend into a haze of flea-defoggers, rubber gloves, and eleven more dumpsters. Our intense work schedule forces us to have fashionably late suppers at various places with flashing neon lights--sometimes red and green with a cactus around it, sometimes red and white splashing from around some happy old man's image, sometimes massive and golden directionals beckoning from miles down obscure stretches of freeway--food for comfort, food for survival, food for more stress pounds on a frame that's already sagging under forty or more overweight pounds.

Food for health has not been an option for months! Maybe years!

Finally we're down to cleaning out the shop behind the garage. More ads--more vultures. I hate this! I never truly know what fair price is, and most of these career shoppers are looking for something for nothing. They thrive on the haggling, and a final agreement of about one-third the value of the item is usually the going price.

One family stopped after church and insisted their three kids stay in the car while they came in, definitely three tired kids who should not have been left anywhere by themselves, much less crammed in a hot car. Signs posted in the house ask people not to go into certain rooms, but these folks go anyway. Plywood boards placed across the stairwell ask people not to go upstairs, but these church-going saints go anyway. Geez! Either one of these rude, disobedient, neglectful, haggling Sunday pew occupants would scam their own mother if the price was right and then hide behind their righteous Sunday best persona!

Dear God, please forgive my crudeness. I am so tired--not just from these weekends, but of the past four and a half years! Help me to be calm. Help me to be nonjudgmental. Help me to rest. Help me to be patient. Help me to continue to trust that you have this all worked out in your own divine perfection.

I am not immune to difficulties, whether this Ridgeview situation or otherwise, and I ask you for peace and your continued guidance. Please forgive my shortcomings, and allow me to progress one step at a time according to your will.

Despite special challenges with varieties of bargain hunters, I am pleased overall with the results of the garage sales and with the cumulative work in the house so far. I appreciate the support of my family and the incredible job my aunt is doing. I can't help getting angry every time I see Don dripping in sweat and crawling around through all the mess and hauling unbelievable tons of garbage. This is shitty work, figuratively and literally. He actually swept up one whole box of poop from behind the plywood stacks in the garage and from the loft--I mean a whole full-sized wooden apple box--FULL! Rat shit, dog shit, cat shit--you name it. I'm no scatologist, but the volume and variety was incredible.

Then when the garage was finally swept out, and all those treasures of wood sold, it brought in $432.00. It probably cost that much in dust masks, gloves, washing powders, showering soaps and disinfectant. Why was such treasure saved all those years? I don't know, but I have definite feelings about *who* should be doing these clean-up jobs, and it's not Don. He is such a gracious, kind person.

One of my blessings from all of this is that I have been able to see repeatedly what my loved one is *really* made of--what strength--what positive support--what courage!

I love and appreciate him all the more.

Rolf continues to show up sporadically and visit with Mavis but usually not when Don and I are present. Mavis says he took a clock mounted on a huge tree burl off the wall and down to Sally's cafe as a gift to remember Malfaits by. She hopes that was okay. Sally had asked me for a photograph or a plate from Mother's everyday dishes to add to the collection displayed above the booths in her cafe, but Rolf thought the clock was better. It doesn't exactly fit into the decor in the cafe, but it definitely is a Malfait memento. Actually it's a piece he gave Mom and Dad and despite the court deadline, it's okay with me for him to give it to whomever he wishes. That's one more piece I don't have to barter about.

Aunt Mavis doesn't want to violate any legal requirements, or add to the conflict between Rolf and me, over clocks, dolls or otherwise. I don't blame her. She does say though that Rolf has told her someday he is going to raise holy hell about all this. I am troubled by this remark, because it isn't I who owed Mom and Dad $67,500. And it isn't I who stole their money and pushed and shoved them around, and swore like a raving idiot. I can't imagine what he'd have to raise holy hell about!

At this moment my only regret is that I did not perceive the total situation earlier, especially with my father. How many times I've wished I had believed Dad when he told Don and me in his halting fragmented speech, "Rolf...is...mean to me. He does...fah...goochi... ka...ra...tee...chops...to me." "No, Dad. Rolf wouldn't do that to you. You must be wrong. He would never hurt you." Dad was always a wonderful story teller and tended to embellish his stories, so Don and I laughed on those occasions when we should have been listening.

Dear God, I'm so sorry!

On a more positive note, Mother's health and overall attitude are improving in her new environment. Janice appreciates how hard Aunt Mavis, Don and I are working to make payments to her. Each time I pay she expresses her appreciation, but she has begun lately to tell me she herself is running kind of short each month as she only has Fern as a steady paying client. She also suggests to me Mother's degree of care is increasing and she may have to raise her rates. She reminds me nursing homes cost twice as much as foster care.

Dear God, does every soul have a dollar value? Is Janice now becoming a garage sale barterer? Please, God, don't let me think this. Please send me purple tulips by the gross to continue this venture. Help!

CHAPTER 26

—∞∞—

Legal Vultures Too?

IT's DIFFICULT TO recognize blessings in my life--which I have come to refer to as *purple tulips*--from all that is transpiring about me. This thought becomes particularly evident one evening about 8:30 PM in a phone call from Mr. Casner, a lawyer on Whidbey Island from whom I had sought advice regarding Mother's property and the lack of access. Other than one consultation I have had no contact with him. He sent me a bill and a brief cover letter in which he mentioned one of the owners bordering Mother's property may be interested in purchasing it. The words of his letter were almost like a postscript to our conversation, *"I don't know if he's shopping for a deal or exactly why I got a call from him, but you may want to speak with him about selling your mother's property."*

At the time of my office visit, Mr. Casner told me there wasn't much he could do for me in regard to gaining access to her property. I needed to understand no one was required by law to give me an access. None of the surrounding property owners needed me nor my access. I needed *them*, and I may have to give them a fourth, or even a half, of Mother's property in order to gain access.

With this unsettling thought in my memory bank and my current lack of trust in people magnified from recent garage sale warfare--and Janice's subtle pressure for a raise in rates--Mr. Casner's letter is of little interest to me, and his late evening phone call is more than dubious.

He is loud and persistent. "Several weeks ago you got a letter from me indicating you had a potential buyer for your Mother's land. Why haven't you responded?"

"Your letter didn't say I should respond to a potential buyer or to you. It said I *may* want to speak with the man."

"Well, he called me and wanted to know why you hadn't called him."

"I've been more than busy in Ridgeview every weekend working on garage sales and cleaning up a house containing more than fifty years of living--*mostly dirt*. I haven't had time to give any consideration to the party you named, and he didn't seem seriously interested. He's the same person to whom I spoke previously about gaining access. He told me at the time I would have to jump through every legal hoop there was before he would ever give me any kind of access over the south end of his land where I just *thought* Malfaits had a legal access. I didn't think he would have changed his mind since that conversation in which he was so uncooperative."

"Well, you had better give consideration when people show an interest and have the money. You're supposed to be raising money to pay for your mother's care and this is probably an excellent source of cash. We can't afford to overlook or ignore such inquiries when perspective buyers come to us."

The sudden *we* and *us* stabs into my numbness--or dumbness--or both. I haven't contracted with Mr. Casner for *any* legal services. *We* do *not* have an attorney-client relationship. I sought his advice on one issue. He recommended I see another lawyer. He sent me a bill for the time I spent with him. I marked it *Paid in Full* and took care of it long ago.

"Well, Mr. Casner, I don't have a clear access according to you. I tried to sell the property for $89,500 privately to an adjoining land owner, probably the same one you are referring to now, and he was not interested. Realty agents refuse to list the property because of no clear access."

"That's right, you don't have an access. I myself went to the title office and your access doesn't go anywhere. You don't have one!"

"It's not just Mother's access, you know. Don and I own the forty acres to the north. If I sell Mother's land, that would leave our property land-locked. What good would that do?"

"I don't know where you get your information, but you don't have any access, and if you don't move to name a price to a willing buyer like this one, you may carry your land-locked property into eternity and give *your* children a problem to work on."

"That may be true," I concur quietly.

Mr. Casner booms on at top volume, "You may be able to condemn an access, but you will pay for it, and that will probably cost $10,000 or more and take a long time."

"But I don't think it's fair to sell the Malfait property at some cheap price to avoid a legal battle over access, and turn around and pass the tab for seeking access to Don and me--or our heirs. These properties were purchased at different times but as a dual family venture, and I know that justice will not allow for them to remain land-locked."

"You seem to be confusing two problems. Your job is to raise money for your mother's care *now*, and you have a buyer interested *NOW*!"

"And at what price?"

"He's not in a position to name a price. *You* need to do that and tell *him*."

"And how do I set a value on a land-locked property? Maybe that's advice you need to give me."

"Betty, you can't just do nothing. When we have a buyer come to *us*, we need to respond."

"Well, he wasn't interested before, so I figure he probably isn't serious now."

"Maybe he didn't have the money before and he has it now. Does it have un-harvested timber?"

"Yes, a couple of timber companies have been interested, but they don't offer much. Another owner of bordering property on the other side had an offer from a local logger for $20,000 for their timber. Recently I had a professional timber cruise of Mother's land, and it's described as having more marketable timber than the adjoining properties, so what does that make her land worth?"

"Well, we should probably ask them for $5,000 per acre and see what their response is. If you feel the deal would land-lock your own land, you should sell the whole acreage--your forty and your mom's twenty--in one deal."

"Yes, you may be right."

"Then do you want me to offer it that way?"

"As my mother's guardian I speak solely for her land. I don't make decisions for *our* land without consultation with Don. I can't tell you that tonight on the telephone."

"Well, you had better hurry up and make a decision, or as I said, you may be sitting with that property into eternity. This is a special opportunity of a lifetime."

"Thank you, I'll talk to Don and let you know."

"All right. Goodnight." SLAM!

What brought all that on? Who's been chewing on Mr. Casner's ear? Why is he yelling at me? I didn't hire him for further service. Why are we now *we* and *us*? I wonder if Mr. Casner shops garage sales? How many kinds of vultures are there? Am I being paranoid? Maybe our easement really doesn't go anyplace.

God, nothing goes anyplace anymore!

Dear God, I need purple tulips again! I NEED them in abundance! God, I will keep trying. I'll go back to Mr. Casner's potential buyer, even though he was rude and threatening when I talked to him previously. I'll try again. Somehow I know there is a way through this. God, I just pray that I will recognize it. Please help me to do it right according to your will!

CHAPTER 27

A Brotherly Vulture

BY EARLY FEBRUARY garage sales dwindle. Clean-up is becoming manageable. Mavis has not seen nor heard from Rolf since she personally handed my letter to him. He made no response in regard to his things left in the upstairs bedroom and in the shop at the back of the property. We include those items in our final sale.

In conversation with a neighbor across the street, I learn Rolf stored some things with him.

"Oh, yeah, Rolf's got seventy or more guns in my garage plus another seventy bows and cross-bows and some pistols. He was by a couple days ago and picked up six pistols which he said he needed to sell, as he needed cash. I told him then my garage space was temporary. I was real firm. I told him I had to have my garage back by summer, because my wife wants me to build a play area for her day-care kids and I'd have to do that in the summer. Rolf said he's been interviewing for jobs in Alaska, and he's going to go if he lands a job."

"Well, sir, all I can tell you is you better be a bit more than firm if you want your garage back. Firm never seemed to get Mother and Dad anyplace--nor me either."

"Oh, I was plenty firm. I says, 'Rolf, if you go off to Alaska or don't keep in contact with me, I'll have to give your guns to your sister'."

"Now, wait a minute, you can just tell Rolf something else. In no way do I even want to touch his guns, or any of his other stuff. Personally I don't want to, and legally I can't. You are not returning anything to me that belongs to Rolf Malfait."

"Oh, well, Rolf probably thought I was kidding about giving you the guns. I did tell him outright if he didn't keep to our agreement, I wouldn't hesitate to proceed legally. I says, 'Don't be forcing me to have to do any more legal action in this neighborhood'."

"And if I were you, I'd stick to my word on that."

As I go back across the street I think to myself, Another person reached out to help Rolf. Should I have tried harder? Was the neighbor criticizing me for the eviction? I'll see how he feels *when* he gets his garage back.

I relate the conversation to Aunt Mavis, and she tells me, "Oh, yes, Rolf was by a couple days ago. He said he was only working two days a week now, and it's a bad job situation. He even has to wash and service his own truck. He's living on a shoestring and barely makes enough to feed himself. His dog is costing him, too, since it's still at the vet's. He says he's going to have to go on unemployment again. I've gone to dinner with him a couple of times, but I make sure to pick up the tab. I told him again I thought Alaska would have better opportunities for him."

I am disturbed by Mavis' sympathy for Rolf. She's labored long hours in this 516 mess, much of it Rolf's mess. It seems like the same old ploy I succumbed to of feeling sorry for poor Rolf and his streak of bad luck has worked on her, *and* the neighbor man. Rolf's bad luck has now lasted ten years--maybe longer! I can't argue with Aunt Mavis, because she's caught between us and she loves us both. I wouldn't want her to feel differently, but I hate the fact that Rolf works on her emotions this way. I think he's sick--and maybe sicker than I think with over two hundred rifles and all those pistols, bows, scopes, and accessory equipment. He habitually puts on his poor-me persona and wheedles his way into using other people's assets. I don't think he has any perception that what he does and says is wrong in any manner.

Rolf's unreal perceptions are affirmed when he stops by unexpectedly the next day and speaks with Don in the back alley. I'm raking leaves under the grape arbor, but he doesn't speak to me, only to Don. Well, maybe it *is* to me.

"Yeah, you know Betty just doesn't realize how much I did for Mom and Dad and how hard I worked. I spent a lot of time cleaning up and sorting out things here in the shop. They had shit all over the place and themselves, too. I found out they hadn't been paying their bills, and especially that Neilson Insurance. I helped get all that straightened out, you know."

I stop raking and look up. I know which one of us drove to Portland to rescue the Neilson Insurance. I grit my teeth as I hear Don say, "I'm sure you tried to help."

"Well, Betty gives me *no* credit for doing anything around here that benefited Mom and Dad. You know, there was stuff all over the place--tires, old flower pots, sinks, garden wire--I just couldn't get it all in order."

"Yeah, I know what you mean. There's still a lot of stuff around here."

"Yeah, Dad was a real pack rat. I don't know why he kept all them tires--and all those freezers, too. They had four freezers. Oh man, that one in the garage was a mess. I cleaned that freezer up, too, after Dad cut the cord on the thing."

My inner voice is screaming: *Don, how can you stand there and let him say that? You know it took you all day to remove the rotten meat and bloody ice out of that freezer! Rolf just wired the cord back together and plugged the freezer up again--rotten thawed food, meat, blood and all. He left that frozen mess for you. Okay, if you can bite your tongue, I can bite another hole in mine.*

Rolf drones on, "Say, Don, have you seen my boat anchor and my metal truck plating?"

In the battle to keep my inner voice silenced, my teeth are clamped so hard my jaw throbs. *Damn it! The eviction was November 20th. The last extended date for picking up anything--actually a date of courtesy--was January 12, 1992. It's now March! We're trying to get this property ready to sell.*

"No, I didn't see any boat anchor or metal plating. You might ask Mavis."

"Yeah, okay, I will. Maybe I can get a pickup truck and get some of this stuff next Saturday when you're here again. All this movin' has just been too much for me. Storage fees is eatin' me alive. That damned eviction notice was so sudden I didn't have time to do nothin'. Hell, Taco is costin' me six bucks a day. It costs more for him than me!"

I want to pound Rolf with my lawn rake! Don, how can you listen to him? You know he's full of baloney! Don't you dare offer to loan him our pickup or to haul anything for him. I clinch my teeth and walk across the lawn away from the two of them where I see Nosy-bill. She and I begin to chat idly. Rolf raises his voice, I'm sure to accommodate the two of us.

"That damned bitch! She reported me for allowin' Taco to howl. How the hell was I supposed to stop that? That's the nature of a Siberian Husky. She also reported me about the old cars. I don't know why *I* should have gotten all that shit. They weren't *my* cars. They belonged to the folks!"

Don remains agreeable as he continues to work. "I don't know whose cars were whose, Rolf, but I saw the notice on the one in the front yard."

"Yeah, and I wrote a note back to them guys and really told 'em what I thought. Them inspectors are just a bunch of power hungry little tyrants."

"You may be right, Rolf. We got a notice ourselves this past week for having too many garage sales. It said neighbors were complaining and it was against the law."

Rolf's volume victoriously shoots up even higher, and he waves an arm toward Nosy-bill and me. "Yeah, well there you go--you can bet that's the work of that damned bitch. Now if I lived here, I'd get my friend and we'd bring girls that look like hookers and we'd really raise hell and give her something to complain about."

Don pauses from his work and leans up against the fence near Rolf. "Aside from all that, Rolf, your mom really needs to be taken care of--and we both know it requires professional help, more than what any of us can provide."

"I fully understand that, but things could have been handled differently. She could have been put in a foster home here in Ridgeview. I don't see why she had to be dragged off up to Whidbey Island. All her friends are here in Ridgeview."

"I don't think Betty exactly dragged her to Whidbey. She and your dad always liked Whidbey. They talked about wanting to live there, and your mom said she was willing to try Janice's place. It's a good place, and she's being well cared for."

"Yeah, Janice's a great person, but it's so far away. Anyway, I've been shit on before, and I'm just gonna let the Man Upstairs take care of it one day at a time."

"You're right, Rolf, we *all* should be doing that all the time anyway."

"Yeah, I realized that when I got that blood poisoning here a while back and ended up in the hospital. Life can be snapped away pretty quick, and I thought for a while there it might just be my lucky day. Anyway, I just wish Mom was closer so I could visit her, too."

"Betty did check with Western Heritage House here in town. It costs about twice what foster care does, but your mom doesn't want to go to a nursing home. She is very vocal about not wanting to go there."

"Yeah, I know, but I think she'd be better where her friends could visit."

"I don't know if Betty can arrange that or not. I certainly hope whatever happens the two of you can someday get together on things. This situation is a real shame for a brother and a sister.

"I don't know if gettin' together's ever gonna be possible again. I've tried hard to forgive and forget, but I ain't been too successful. I got a long ways to go."

"Rolf, if that could happen, it would be better for all concerned--maybe sometime in the future?"

"Yeah, maybe so."

I walk back over to where the two of them are standing near the fence. "Hi, Rolf. How's it going?"

"Oh, so-so."

"I know we don't have a whole lot to say to one another, but there are a couple of things I'd like to ask."

"Yeah, what's that?"

"Number one, I hope you will plan to go see Mother. Especially if you're going to Alaska, you should make an effort to visit her before you go."

"Yeah, yeah--I'll probably do that."

"Secondly, I know you don't want *me* to know where you are, and that's fine. But would you please give Mavis your address and an emergency phone number if you go? I assume you'd want to know about Mother's health, improvement or decline, or possible death. I really hope you'll do that."

"Yeah, yeah. I'll see to that. I'll tell you what, if I do make it good in Alaska, or if I win the lottery, the first thing I'm gonna do is buy this house back."

"At the rate things are moving, it will still be on the market."

"Yeah. And then I'd buy the house on the other side of Nosy-bill, and I'd spend day and night makin' that bitch miserable."

"Rolf, you can spend your life making her miserable—or making anyone else miserable--if you like, but that's sick."

"Yeah, well her husband ain't doin' so good--you know he had heart problems and prostate cancer. If he died, I'd be sure and be at the funeral dressed just like I am right now in my work clothes, and I'd write in the guest book in red ink two spaces high and really tell her what I think."

"Rolf, that would be mean and miserable, a really sick thing to do."

"Yeah, well, I'd enjoy doin' it!" Rolf laughs deviously. "It would give me a real sense of pleasure." He wipes his dirty sleeve across his smirk and chuckles again.

"Rolf, you *are* sick!"

"Well--I'd enjoy that! I would!" Rolf crosses his arms defiantly over his chest, glares toward the fence and chews on his lower lip. "Yep, I really would enjoy that."

I turn and walk back to the grape arbor and resume my raking. Don goes into the shop. Rolf stands alone, arms still crossed, an evil smirk playing at his lips. He squints towards Nosy-bill's house, jerks his head in a bizarre gesture of private triumph, then turns around and ambles toward his car which is parked in the alley. He climbs in, fires up the noisy engine, and drives off down the alley.

Dear God, I've said before--I can't deal with Rolf. He's crazy—call it sociopathic, psychopathic, whatever! He has no sense of right or wrong and no feelings of compassion. He reinvents scenes to suit himself. Rolf is out for Rolf! I don't think any kind of change is possible short of a miracle. I do indeed pray for that for him. I believe you can do such miracles. But until that happens, please keep us apart. Help me to continue to do what is best for Mother. What a holy mess! Oh, God, I'm so sorry.

A short time later Aunt Mavis returns to West Virginia. Rolf goes to Alaska.

Mother has been at Janice's almost two years, and I feel moving her from the house in Ridgeview was a right move. Janice is a wonderful caretaker. In many ways much has happened in this time, and yet nothing has happened. I am torn by my inability to progress fast enough. The house has been on the market almost a year and still hasn't sold. Mother's Whidbey property can't sell. The timber deal was on, then off, and now it may be on again.

We've all worked so hard, and yet I feel as if nothing has been achieved--nothing, at least, unless dismantling fifty years of living in the house that Daddy built is an achievement!

CHAPTER 28

———— ⚭ ————

Decline And Distance Take A Toll

WHILE I AM consoled by knowing Mother's move to Janice's was right for her physically and emotionally, nothing I have been able to accomplish has been enough to keep ahead of her deterioration. She now uses a walker. Her speech is slurred. She's dragging her left foot when she walks. She either won't or can't be up and about as much as she used to be. The recent hospital stay for surgery for a urinary problem was a turning point for the worse.

Janice's work with Mother has become more difficult. It is harder to get her up and down from the couch. Mother won't walk anymore for pleasure and exercise, and sometimes she is ornery and uncooperative about bedtime and baths. Her incontinence is more serious and with occasional bowel failure. Janice still enjoys Mother, and Mother and Fern continue an evident friendship, but Janice and I have talked about whether Mother's situation is getting beyond the level of foster home care.

It's heart-breaking to watch this slow-motion decline. Mother doesn't complain of any specific pain, but her body is shutting down one bit at a time. It's so gradual, so insidious. In some ways I think she knows what's happening. Sometimes I feel as if *I'm* becoming stronger, more focused as Mother becomes weaker. Other times I feel like an unmanaged, erratic glob, oblivious to people and things, a complete failure.

Dear God, I see Mother more tottery and weaker on each of my visits. Is this the beginning of death? She's too far away from me. I know she'll be gone before Don and I can retire and be on the Island near her. Is it too much for Janice now? Do I need to move Mother to a nursing home? Oh, God, if I have to move her, please help me know when and how--not too early--not too late.

Dear God, I feel incapable of doing the care-taking of my own mother. I don't know if it's that I can't or I don't want to. I don't think I could do it physically or mentally. I know I couldn't do it in our home--a daylight basement with spare bedrooms in the basement--doors to the bathroom too narrow for a wheelchair--kitchen facilities on the upper floor. God, I feel as if I have to keep my teaching position and work because we still have two kids in college. I love my job, and sometimes that's the only place I feel as if I'm having any success. It's one of the few places I feel I operate at a level of personal sanity.

God, are these excuses, or are they reasons?

Oh, God, I can't be Mother's care-taker, but I need her to be closer to us. Please help me figure this out.

My prayers may not be traditional by any religious or denominational standards, but I am comforted by shutting myself off in private moments and muttering my concerns. I believe God hears me. Whenever the next bit of adversity occurs, I can choose to let go and fall apart or I can hold on tight and cry out to Him in my helplessness. It doesn't matter who I am, where I am, or even how I ask. He hears. He responds. Many times I literally feel His strength seep into my being. I constantly tell myself He won't give me more than I can bear, despite how often I've been to the helpless, broken, crying out point. Each time I am incredulous at the depth of the abyss, but I come back up ready to try again. I feel like a little kid taking swimming lessons and jumping in for the first time, popping up buggy-eyed, terrified, gasping, flailing, then going down again--then miraculously surfacing. Part of my strength comes from feeling God may consider me strong enough, faithful enough, smart enough, or whatever-enough to deal with the challenges of continuing to become the parent of my parent.

About the time I sense some progress, security, confidence--maybe even some smugness--down I go again!

I have always been a healthy, strong, energetic person, but tiredness is now a chronic condition. I spend a lot of time sleeping. I sleep through rented movies. I sleep at theaters. I sleep through automobile trips, boat trips or any other trips. Ferry boat workers often have to rap on my window to get my car out of the way so others can disembark. I even sleep in church. I haven't fallen asleep in my classroom yet, but I occasionally put my head down on my desk during planning period for a little rest. It's a good thing a bell rings before the next class. I know my physical health is not good. I've gained forty-plus pounds. I'm not exercising. I catch more than my share of colds. I have excessive stomach gas, and my bowel function is irregular. I either don't want to know or don't care about going to the doctor. All these signs are unhealthy. I need to get a better hold on my own life. I can't manage Mother's affairs nor help provide a healthy life for her if I can't manage myself adequately.

Dear God, please--enough! I'm expending myself, and I'm just spinning my wheels. God, I'll be dead before Mother at this rate. Please help me to hang on and guide me to complete the necessary tasks which you set before me. Help me to let go of the things you don't expect of me. Forgive me of my shortcomings and guide my every thought, word and deed! May your will be done. In Jesus' name, Amen.

CHAPTER 29

―∽∞∽―

A Road Trip With Mother

WINTER PASSES. I survive a number of late-night passages on the little ferry from Keystone on Whidbey Island to Port Townsend on the Olympic Peninsula. On more than one occasion I've wondered if *sinking into my agonizing abyss* might not really happen as the boat is tossed harshly in the sometimes stormy waters of Puget Sound.

By summer 1992, I decide I *have* to move Mother to the mainland closer to my home. I don't want to make this move any more than I wanted to make the move from her home at 516, the house that Daddy built, to Janice's. I hope I'm not being selfish because of the severity of the past winter's traveling.

In researching possible new homes in my area I use recommendations from my family doctor, local senior citizen agencies, and friends who have needed care for their loved ones. I find several local facilities. I visit and interview each one and narrow my choice to a foster home close to my home. The caretaker, Patty, has had nurses' training, and she will not be overwhelmed by the incontinence problem. She wants to provide a home atmosphere as much as possible in her care-taking. She is licensed for five but enjoys a usual work load of three and only takes ladies. I like her personally, and I like the general set-up of her facility. Mother will have her own sitting room, bedroom and bath at the back of the house. The walls of the rooms are knotty-pine, reminiscent of the Ridgeview house. Mother will like that, and I think she'll like Patty. I'll be able to see her more often, as she'll be less than fifteen minutes from my home.

Dear God, you know what is best here. I sense your approval for moving Mother, but I don't see any way to do it financially. Patty's service

217

costs about the same as Janice's in dollar amount, but she can't afford to keep any of the billing on a tab. Right now Mother's income is insufficient for the monthly expense of Patty's place. Dear God, I still have time on summer break that I could move Mother, but I don't have the financial means. I'll do whatever you want me to do, but if this is a right move and the right time, I need purple tulips for sure. I give the financial details to you and ask you to make them happen if it's the right thing.

My purple tulips never have really come up in the cracks of the sidewalk in the snows of December, as I indicated years ago in one of my desperate cries to God for help, but the sale of the Ridgeview house occurs so suddenly after meeting Patty I'm not sure I even recognize it at the moment as an answer to my prayers. I am caught up in a flurry of activities--maybe that's *my special snow flurry*--rushing from my home to Ridgeview, to the realtor, to the lawyer, to court.

When *all the snow settles,* Mother has the necessary financing for wherever she lives for several years. The available cash is also sufficient to pay the balance of Rolf's loan and to pay Janice in full, an amount that has reached $11,692.65. Payment of this debt will alleviate Janice's financial stresses, and moving Mother to Patty's foster care home will relieve some of my own stress over long distance travel and stormy late-night ferryboat rides.

The day I arrive at Janice's for Mother's departure it takes only half an hour to pack her meager belongings--clothing, family pictures, cards and letters, a quilt, her down comforter, and toiletries. Accumulation of things has been unimportant at Janice's. Everything Mother needed while she was here fits in two large boxes. I roll up her quilt and comforter and stow them in a large plastic bag and load everything in the bed of my pickup.

When I go back into the house, Little Fern comes into the living room teary-eyed. "Oh my, I've enjoyed you so, Francine. I've tried so hard to get you to share that apple with me every day." She turns and speaks in my direction, her tiny frail hand seeking mine," Oh, Betty, I've peeled the two of us an apple every day. Now I know Francine doesn't always change her pad, and she says 'I just did' and I know she didn't, but does she have to leave? She's really no trouble at all, and I don't want to be here eating apples by myself." Fern's lip quivers and she squeezes my hand repeatedly.

I fold my arms around her delicate frame, "Thank you for all the apples, Fern. I'll come back and visit you, and I'll bring Mother if she feels like making the trip."

Mother hugs Fern. "I liked those apples, too. Good-bye, Fern."

Mother hugs Janice too, but she sheds no tears in either case. I doubt she understands exactly what is taking place, and I don't press to fill in details. She may think this is just a little daily outing. Or, she may think I'm moving her to my home--Or, God forbid, she may think I'm moving her back to Ridgeview.

It's hard to say goodbye to Mother's friend, Little Fern

Dear God, please deal with this. Please don't let her think that's what's happening here. I'm afraid to clarify any of today's activity. I need your help.

By the time we're down the front steps and I get the truck door open, Mother has leaned the walker up against the hand railing at the bottom step and shuffled over near the open door without any help. She steadies herself on the door and steps up onto the little stool before I can adjust it to the right place.

The author and her mother leave Janice's place with all of Francine's belongings.

219

"Mom, wait a minute for me to help you."

"I don't need any help. You just stay back a bit. I can do this fine."

When we're both settled in the truck cab, we exchange further good-byes with Janice and Fern through the open windows. Then we slowly drive out the drive-way waving as we depart.

It's an incredibly beautiful day as we travel north over Deception Pass Bridge and off Whidbey Island, across the rich productive farmlands of the Skagit Valley and on toward the North Cascades. I have planned a short trip for the two of us, hoping it will soften the transition from Janice's to Patty's for Mother. Really for both of us.

The author and her mother take a road-trip across the North Cascades

Mother is very vocal and excited to be traveling. What is this highway? Has Don ever been here? I don't want to cross this windy bridge ever again, but it sure is beautiful. What town is next? Did you tell Janice I'm going? Are we coming back down this same highway tonight? Janice will be worried about us."

I give minimal answers to her questions. We're well up into the mountains when Mother finally asks specifically, "Are we going back to Janice's tonight?"

"No, Mother, you're going to another place to live. We're not going back to Janice's at all."

"We're not? Why not?"

"I need to have you closer to my house and nearer to doctors and medical help. Besides, Janice raised her rates."

"How much?"

"Two hundred per month."

"Oh, that's a lot. I can't afford that. I've been there over two weeks already."

What town is next? Have I been here before? Has Don ever been here? Did you tell Janice I'm going? Are we coming back this way tonight? It's really beautiful here. Did you tell Janice I was going? Janice will be worried about us. Are we going back to Janice's tonight?

I answer the questions hundreds, seemingly thousands of times. Mother's speech becomes more slurred as she gets tired, and I can't always understand her words, but she seems satisfied whether the answer fits the question or not. After a considerable time, we pull into a roadside rest stop.

"Boy, Mother, I need a bathroom break. You must be about ready to burst."

"I don't need to go."

Without responding to her comment, I park the truck and hurry around to her door, put the single-step stool in place, and open the door. She slides down to the stool, pauses a moment to balance, and then takes my arm and steps down. Her walking is shaky, and I can feel her grasp my arm tighter than usual. I wish I hadn't forgotten the walker. In the restroom I am especially thankful for an empty handicapped stall. I enter with her and help with her clothing. She makes no objection, and she goes big time!

A few miles further up the road in the next town, there is a motel. I haven't seen any others in the last hundred miles, so I decide we better stop. I leave Mother in the truck admiring the motel landscaping while I check us in. It's well past the dinner hour, and the clerk tells me the only open food establishment in town is the tavern a couple of blocks back, but they have the best fish and chips in the whole county. Mother will probably raise hell on this issue, as she has never been in a tavern in her life and she is definitely opposed to drinking, but I can't feed her potato chips, candy bars, and cookies from the machines at the motel. When I return to the truck, her first comment lets me know she is hungry.

"Did you get us a hamburger while you were in there?"

"No, Mother, this is a motel, but we're going right now to get something to eat. We'll come back here later. The lady at the desk said the best fish and chips in the whole county is just two blocks back up the road from here. Would you like to try that?"

"Oh, that would be better than a hamburger any time."

I don't know if it's because she's hungry or she's excited about fish and chips, but we park and shuffle into the tavern at a pretty good pace. Mother is oblivious to the various neon beer signs. She doesn't say anything about the loud music, the smoky blue haze hanging against the ceiling, the handful of cowboys lined up at the bar, nor that we're the only two women in the establishment. A multi-purpose cook-waiter-bartender notices our presence and ambles over to our table. He wipes his hand on an already well-wiped apron, pushes back his Stetson which looks as if it has been worn a lot of other places besides here, and poises himself with one sharp-toed cowboy boot hoisted up on the seat of an empty chair at our table. His leans toward us a bit, puts his order pad on the leg resting on the chair, licks a stub of a yellow pencil which he has retrieved from over his left ear, and curls his left hand up over the pad.

"Good evenin', ladies. What can I do for you all?"

Mother squints up more at his hat than at him, maybe at the cigarette over his other ear. "We're starved!"

I speak up quickly, "The lady at the motel desk said your fish and chips are reputed to be the best in the county, right?"

"Yep, that's right!" He glances at Mother who is still staring at him and winks. "You all like beer batter, right?"

I hurriedly respond before any connotation of beer is perceived by Mother. "Yes, we do. Make that two orders, two green salads with thousand island dressing on the side, and two coffees--black!"

"Yes, ma'ams!"

Our cowboy waiter scribbles on the pad, uncurls his leg from the chair and moves toward the bar. He draws a couple of mugs of beer for bar patrons, plunks them down on the bar, piles two coffee cups on top of each other in one hand, grabs a glass coffee pot of very black liquid and returns to our table. He lets each cup slip down onto the wooden table with a slight clunk and fills it with the black steaming brew. "There you go, ladies."

With a definite lack of speed our multi-tasking waiter saunters back to the kitchen, gives his Stetson a firm yank, and assumes the role of cook. Mother sits quietly, head tilted as if straining to discern from the nasal twang of the female vocalist *why she is leaving her man*. She continues to appear equally attentive to the musical beat and rich male voice in the next song lauding *having friends in low places*, followed by another tune by a different deep rich voice assuring that *the circle won't be broken by and by*.

When our food arrives, Mother's eyes light up. She is delighted with the colorful, appetizing plates. We are both indeed starved, and the reputation of the fish and chips is well deserved.

Once we're back in our motel, Mother refuses to shower but willingly lets me help her sponge bathe. While I enjoy a long hot steamy shower, she settles in contentedly to watch the Republican Convention, despite her lifelong allegiance to the Democratic Party.

She's still staring at the TV screen when I am ready for bed. "Mom, I'm exhausted. Shall we turn that off now and turn in?"

"No, I want to watch the rest of the Convention."

"That will go on all night."

"That's okay. I'm not tired."

"Mom, it's almost midnight. We both need to go to bed. Tomorrow is a big travel day, and there will be lots to see. I'll never be able to drive, much less enjoy the scenery, if we don't get some sleep." I click off the television.

"Oh shit!" Mother shuffles over to her bed and climbs in.

Dear God, thank you for the purple tulips of this day!

I awaken at 6:30 AM, somewhat refreshed but desperate to go to the bathroom. Loud gurgling snores are coming from Mother's bed. At Janice's she often slept until 9:00 AM, so I should be able to sneak out of bed and make the few steps to the bathroom without waking her. My toes touch the cold floor, and I stand.

"Bettyeee! Bettyeee!" A slurred, high decibel alert blasts from the darkness.

"Oh, my God, Mother, hush! I'm just trying to sneak into the bathroom."

I take a step toward the lighted slit at the bottom of the bathroom door as the same slurred volume blasts again, "Wherrrrre are you goin'?"

"Mother, Mother," I call back in my loudest whisper, "lower your voice. Remember we're in a motel. I don't want our neighbors to know I need to pee."

The slurred voice growls, "*I* don't need to pee."

"Good. That's good, Mother." I shut the bathroom door for a moment of peace and quiet. When I'm finished I unplug the nightlight, stand on the cold floor, and listen. I hear the regular deep nasal snores. I ease the door open and tiptoe back to my bed.

As I pull the covers up, my assumed success is shattered, "Bettyeee! Bettyeee! Are you back in bed?"

"Yeah, Mom, yeah. I'm right here. It's still dark and I'm sleeping. Okay?"

The slurred speech seems satisfied and the volume goes down, "That's good. *I'm* sleeping, too."

An hour later I give up on sleep as Mother gets up for her bathroom trip. I help her dress and get her situated watching the Convention results while I make a run to the lobby for a continental breakfast tray to take back to our room. Mother thinks the food is a little skimpy, but it's awfully nice of these people to provide it.

Our morning drive takes us through a beautiful craggy gap in the North Cascade Mountains. On the eastern side of the range the highway winds along a river and gradually to lower elevations. It's a gorgeous day and a collage of early autumn yellows, oranges, and reds emblazons the hillsides and gives emphasis to the jagged greens and blues of the rugged mountains behind us. We are both soothed as each little town passes by our windshield viewing screen--places like Twisp, Carlton, Methow. Each has its own charm and quaintness, each a unique paradise. Each also has a restaurant, and although it's 10:00 AM, none of them are open. I guess no one eats breakfast in these paradises. Our continental breakfast is seeming even more skimpy as the miles rack up.

Further into eastern Washington, the landscape changes to rich agricultural scenes. An array of varied green squares crisscrosses the rolling hillsides, each orchard or field laden with the bounty of the fall season, particularly a bumper apple crop.

"Oh, Betty, this is so beautiful! Dad would die to see this! We should have brought him with us."

I don't want to even try to unravel that comment. I am saved from the challenge by a roadside advertisement hand-painted on a sheet of plywood propped up against a rocky ledge at the side of the road. The large colorful letters extol the appeal of fresh-pressed, chilled apple juice and home-baked apple fritters. Five hundred feet down the highway I pull off onto the graveled strip and run up to the cut-out window of the little fruit stand. I order two large cups of fresh-pressed, chilled apple juice and two of the home-baked apple fritters. I hurry back to the truck and get the cardboard food tray situated on Mother's lap, hoping she won't get the lids off or the bag open before I get around to the driver's side. We move a short ways down the road and pull over into a wider graveled spot to enjoy our treats while we watch workers harvest luscious big red delicious apples. There's an energy and excitement in the morning air as pickers trail back and forth from trees to a big fruit bin pulled through the orchard by a tractor. Above the chatter of the mostly Spanish-speaking workers there's a thumping, hollow rumble each time a worker's bucket is dumped into the large bin. An aroma of the thousands of bright red jewels being picked and hauled wafts gently through the open truck windows. Actually, it's more likely we smell the fresh squeezed apple juice in the truck cab. It doesn't matter, we both sense the joy of a successful harvested crop.

"Oh, Betty, Dad would love this so. We should have brought him with us."

"I know, Mother. He would have loved it."

By noon we reach Pateros, where we have a good selection of restaurants. We settle on one overlooking the river, and though it's well past noon, I indulge in a taco omelet which is piled as high as the mountain range we have crossed. Mother chooses an equally delectable western omelet. Neither of us can say lunch is skimpy.

Leaving the restaurant the temperature is 85 degrees. As we continue to Chelan the thermometer rises with the miles. All the truck windows and vents are open, and hot air blowing through dishevels our hair but does little to cool us. Mother doesn't complain but concentrates on the changing scenery. She seems to be enjoying herself.

There are a number of nice motels and restaurants in the Wenatchee area. I consider stopping early, having a nice dinner, and staying overnight to be well rested before we arrive at Patty's. But by the time we get to the junction just north of the city limits, I have vividly recalled the events of our motel experience last evening a number of times, and the exterior temperature is well over one hundred degrees.

A nice dinner in Wenatchee? Maybe. A restful motel overnight? I don't think so.

The big green highway sign indicating Hwy.2 – Leavenworth looms into view. I move to the right-hand lane, exit, and head westward.

Late in the afternoon higher elevations on Stevens Pass provide lush green beauty and lower temperatures. A road-side rest stop is appealing to both of us. After we use the facilities and take a short walk along the sidewalks, Mother says she's tired and we return to the truck. She shuffles around the truck a couple of times and then tells me, "Betty, I'd like to just sit on the tail-gate for a while."

"That's a bit high for you, Mom. I don't know if you can get up there. Besides the bed liner is cold and hard. Wait a minute--there's a sleeping bag in the truck cab behind the seat. I'll get that and spread it out for you. That would be a little bit softer."

I grab the little single-step stool and the sleeping bag and place them both so she can get seated on the tail-gate. She watches chipmunks running up and down nearby trees for a minute or two.

"Oh, Betty, look at them. They look like they're playing tag. I wish I had some peanuts. Help me get back further in the bed of this truck. I'd like to lay back for a minute."

"Mother, I don't know if that's a good idea. You can't stand up in the truck bed, and I don't know how else you can get back there—but wait just a minute--maybe I could slide you on the sleeping bag."

I scramble up behind her in the truck bed. "Hang on." I pull the bag a foot or so toward the cab, and Mother breaks into peals of giggles.

"Are you okay?"

"Yes, just get my old frame a little further back."

"Okay, here we go again." Amid another round of giggles, I pull the bag several feet back into the truck bed near the packing boxes and the big plastic bag which holds her quilt and comforter. When I let go of the sleeping bag, she doesn't bother to look behind her, she just flops backwards into the makeshift pillow formed by the soft puffy plastic bag.

Francine takes a nap in the bed of the pickup

"Good heavens, Mom, you could crack your head flopping back like that!"

"Oh, Betty, the pine trees are so beautiful, and the sky is so blue."

Dear God, thank you for things great and small--great like the sky but small like properly placed puffy comforters.

I jump down from the truck bed, and Mother is already snoring. I can't leave her, so I occupy myself cleaning the glove compartment. About twenty minutes later she awakens as suddenly as she had fallen asleep.

"Betty, Betty--what happened to those chipmunks?"

"You scared them away with your snoring."

Mother smiles. "I guess they never heard anything like that."

"No, I guess not. Even the family in the Volkswagen camper next to us left. I guess they never heard anything like that either."

Mother giggles aloud.

"Mother there's a sign over there advertising 'free coffee'. Would you like some?"

"Oh, that sounds good. I haven't had a good cup of coffee for months."

"Well, Mother, I don't know how *good* this coffee might be from a roadside rest stop. It may have been in the pot all day. Want to wait until the next town?"

"No, I'd really like a cup of coffee right now."

With some gentle tugs on the sleeping bag and a few more giggles, I get Mother into an upright seated position back on the tailgate. "Okay, you stay right here and rest."

Keeping an eye on the truck, I cross the parking lot to the shelter and get a cup of coffee for her. Lemonade sounds more appealing to me.

When I return with the drinks, Mother takes her coffee and immediately sucks in a giant slurp, oblivious to the heat of the drink. Then she leans over and squints into my cup. "What's that?"

"Lemonade," I answer, as I take a sip.

"I'll have that."

She reaches out and relieves me of the lemonade and leaves me holding her cup of coffee. "Oh well, Mom, I like coffee, too."

Once we're back on the road, Stevens Pass provides its usual grandeur, and we both ooh and aah on several occasions. I get out a few times to take pictures, but Mother says her legs just aren't what they used to be, and she doesn't want her picture taken anyway. Just before the town of Monroe we pull over in front of a tiny little chapel called Rest-by-the-Wayside Chapel. Mother chuckles in childlike glee.

"Isn't this beautiful! Why, this is the smallest church-house I've ever seen. Do they let people go in there?"

"Yes, it's open to the public. Would you like to go in?"

"I wonder if I can even fit through that door." Mother opens the truck door and slides down to the ground before I can get around to her side with the step stool. Her feet hit the ground a bit roughly, but she maintains her balance. "Betty, this church is wonderful. It's not much bigger than a doll-house, but it's got a little steeple and a bell and everything." She hobbles over to the door and shoves it open. "Betty, quick, get over here. It's open, and there's four little pews in there." Without waiting for me, she shuffles into the building and plops down in the back pew. "Oh, God, I'm so tired, and my old legs kill."

"Is that your prayer, Mother? I'm sure God can hear you."

Mother giggles. "Oh, I'm sure He can, too. I tell Him about these old legs all the time, but He hasn't done much about them."

"Do you mind if I take your picture, Mom?"

"No, that would be nice."

I snap the picture and ask, "Would you like to pray?"

"No, you pray for me."

I slide into the pew next to her and take her hand.

Dear God, thank you for this day and for this trip. Thank you for this special place for travelers such as Mother and me. Please guide us on the rest of our trip and strengthen both of us, and especially her legs. In Jesus' name, Amen.

The author and her mother visit The Wayside Chapel on Hwy. 2 near Monroe, WA

"Thank you, Betty. That was nice."

Back in the truck and on the road, Mother recalls past trips with Dad when they traveled through Monroe. "This has always been such a pretty part of the state. I don't know why they had to ruin it by building a prison here. I couldn't live anyplace near something like that. What if one of those hoodlums got out of there? I don't think I've ever been any place Dad or I either one liked better than right where we are. Ridgeview suits us just fine and always will. Where am I staying tonight?"

"Well, I've found a new place for you which is close to my home. You'll be staying with my friend, Patty, because I have to go back to work next week."

"Who's Patty? What if she doesn't like me? Are we coming back on this same road tomorrow? Well, I'll stay one night. Will you come and get me tomorrow night? Will Dad come and visit me there? Will Dad be there too? What if Patty doesn't like either one of us?"

CHAPTER 30

Patty's Place

PLACES LIKE WOODINVILLE, Bellevue, Renton, and Tacoma pass in a fuzzy vocal blur. When we arrive at Patty's it's late afternoon. Patty immediately comes out to the truck and greets us. Introductions are warm and friendly. Patty helps Mother from the truck, and offers her an arm as we walk around to stretch our legs and view her yard. I can tell Mother doesn't think much of the house as she tells Patty, "You got a lot of work to do here, Patty. It looks like you need to get started by painting your house."

Francine is welcomed to Patty's place, a new adult foster care home nearer to the author's home

"That's definitely on my list of chores, Francine. What color do you think would look nice?"

"I like white houses. A white house shows off all your flowers so nice. You have a lot of pretty flowers, too, but you need to get some weeding done. You better put that on your list, too."

The grounds and gardens do have a plentiful array of flowers, shrubbery, and trees. Mother enjoys identifying many of the plants with Patty as we stroll along a

Francine likes Patty's place

231

walkway around the house. Occasionally Mother stops, hangs on to Patty's arm, and leans over and pulls out a weed.

When I least expect it, along comes another *purple tulip*.

George is a huge orange furry feline. He rounds the corner of the house on scraggly legs, stops, and points what's left of his ears straight up and surveys us all. Then he walks directly to Mother and begins repeatedly brushing each of her legs in irregular bumping motions. He's the ugliest cat I've ever seen. His head is the size of a cantaloupe, far out of proportion to his scrawny body. His coloring is more like the insides of an overly ripe, deteriorating cantaloupe. His emaciated body is scarred, and his back and tail show evidence of recent injurious struggle. He moves in a slow figure eight pattern, continuing to bump Mother's legs each time he passes. I don't know if he's purring or growling. It's sort of a guttural rumble, much like Mother's snoring. Bracing against a tree trunk, Mother leans over and scratches him. He grumbles appreciatively, turns and leads the way to the front door. The three of us obediently follow.

When we are seated in the living room, George paces back and forth at Mother's feet, pausing and stretching his cantaloupe-head upward, but he makes no attempt to jump onto her lap. Finally she bestows her full attention on him, "My God, George, you look about like I feel. Come on up."

It doesn't take a second invitation. George springs up with surprising agility and nestles into her lap. George has found a new home. And so has Mother.

My decision to move Mother to Patty's place is good. I see her more and we do more things together. We frequently go to restaurants, as she loves to eat out. We go on picnics to local parks, and she comes to our home for occasional weekends. She is enthusiastic for these outings, and we usually have a good time, but whenever I get ready to leave, she always makes me promise to call Dad and be sure he had as nice a lunch as we did. This routine request has become part of our good-bye ritual. Maybe it's because I've given up trying to teach her that Dad has been dead for years.

If she is very tired or not feeling good, or if something I say or something we see is not agreeable to her, things are not so wonderful. She may abruptly become angry with me and ask, Are you going to come and get me tomorrow? I need to go home. If you're not going to take me, I'm going to call Dad and have him come and get me.

Patty says she is quite alert compared to other clients she has had, and she never shows any kind of anger with her. Patty is especially good about having Mother help with activities around her home--simple tasks like folding wash, drying a pot or a pan while Patty does the dishes, pushing a vacuum cleaner, even if it's in circles while Patty sweeps the kitchen, or just holding things while Patty works. Patty takes her on errands and sometimes to do the grocery shopping, although Mother usually needs a wheelchair for lengthy ventures now. When I have gone with them, I marvel at how Patty manages Mother, the wheelchair, and the grocery cart in the store.

There are serious moments: "Why can't I go home with you?"

Being close affords me more time to help with Mother's care. I secure suplementary insurance for her and establish her with a new doctor. One who is willing to take Medicare patients and has a nice manner in treating them is somewhat of a rarity, but I find one. I for sure count that as one of my *purple tulips.*

Then there's George—that's a whole bouquet of purple tulips all by itself. His presence and devotion have been unceasing from day one in the front yard. All things considered, I think Mother is relatively happy at Patty's.

CHAPTER 31

The Timber Snag

ANOTHER PURPLE TULIP arrives almost at the same time that Mother is settling in well with Patty. I am able to sell the timber on Mother's property through another gypo outfit, Duke Logging Company. I net enough profit to pay for foster care for another three years, an amount that is almost six times what Gladstone Gypo Timber Works and Sno-Island Timber Company offered together previously.

Even so, the timber project with the company I selected is not without adversity. This logger, despite his good reputation, turns out to be a gypper! He sells several loads of logs from Mother's property as if they are his personal property, and he doesn't split with Mother on those loads. Inadvertently in phone conversation with one of the places where he hauls the logs, I discover his scam and confront him with the information, of which the value is a little over $18,000.

Yes, he feels like a rotten heel for doing that, but his loader broke down and some other machine blew a piston. He hadn't counted on that--blah, blah, blah!

During these last few years I have learned there are innumerable *Rolfs* in the world and my heart has hardened toward them, so I sue the culprit on Mother's behalf.

Mother isn't totally aware of the details, but she knows it was *her* timber on *her* property, and she wants *her* money back. She says, "Betty, I hope I live long enough for you to catch that bastard and make him pay!"

It's quite a while later, but the day I share with her that I have collected $13,500 from the logger for her, she is happy in her own unique way. She doesn't ask about the $4,500 which went for legal fees. She doesn't ask to see the money or a bank statement. Even without the details, she cherishes the outcome. Her response is, "Serves the bastard right. We need to go out to lunch to celebrate."

Having Mother at Patty's provides me greater time to be with her but also more separation time from her confusion and the poor family relationship with Rolf. I feel like I almost have some relaxed breathing space since that fateful day of false accusation some ten years ago. In many ways the whole decade has been a sequence of stress and mess, but I try to focus on the positive things which have happened during that time and how fortunate I am currently. I really have managed, to a considerable degree, to become the parent of my parents, and to do that lovingly and kindly, even though it meant excluding a brother who felt he could, and should, do a better job using sheer physical dominance and brute force.

I buried my father honorably almost five years ago. I moved my mother to safe, secure surroundings. I took her finances from chaos to order--except for the Whidbey property. It has not yet sold, but the likelihood of an access appears possible since the logging operation. In my own family relationships, I have a wonderful, loving husband. I have two beautiful children. And I have a very enjoyable teaching career.

Dear God, you are awesome! I know you're in command. You always have been, but I haven't always known that. I am just an observer in this process. It's hard for us all right now because Mother is confused and she doesn't talk as much. Over her lifetime she has been so conversant. It's one of the reasons Patty and her other ladies enjoy her so much. Though my recent conversations with Mother are often fractured, I have enjoyed these times with her, especially our recall of earlier pleasant family events and her own growing up years.

I am so thankful to have been able to reconnect with her after our family rift. I'm not sure if she ever understood she was wrong and that we all forgave her misjudgment, but I understand. I thank you for the opportunity I have to feel forgiveness. In this silent painful decline I feel helpless. My main weapons have become liquid nutritional supplements and Patty's expertise in providing clean sheets, baths and other daily nurturing. I do thank you that Mother is in this loving environment.

By summer, 1994, Mother's funds are running low. I still can't qualify her for Medicaid because of her ownership of the Whidbey land. I was able to negotiate with land owners on the west side for a legal access, and a reputable, real estate attorney did a thorough legal, registered workup of the paperwork for that. I have had the property listed for over a year but it hasn't sold. There have been several interested parties, but the court deems I must have a cash buyer and can only accept Fair Market Value or better. My potential buyers have not been able to do that. The money from the timber sale will last until December, as her foster care expense is generally five to six hundred dollars more per month than her income. I couldn't sell her property before because it didn't have a legal access. Now that part is settled, but it's a terrible real estate market for undeveloped land and cash buyers.

Don and I don't want or need any more land, but we have talked about buying it ourselves when her money runs out in December. El will graduate at the end of fall quarter, and we could afford to buy it then by using the money we've been spending for her schooling. We don't really want it because then we'd go into retirement with a huge debt.

An even more pressing reason is that Rolf for sure would never approve--not that he would have to. The law states that a guardian can make such purchases of assets by paying 90% of Fair Market Value with court approval. However, I'm sure Rolf would object to our buying it for any price, even though the money is needed income to keep Mother in foster care. He would think we were trying to pull a fast one and cheat him out of something. On the other hand, upon Mother's death, Don and I don't want to have Rolf and his 200-plus guns for a neighbor on property adjoining *our* property. Our ownership of property on the Island was way before Malfaits' purchased theirs, and somehow having Rolf as a potential inherited neighbor after Mother is gone is a formidable thought. Her Whidbey property just has to sell!

Betty Alder

Dear God, you know we really don't want this land nor the indebtedness in our retirement. Our own Whidbey property was supposed to be part of our plan to supplement our teacher retirement, and it well could be, but not if we buy Mother's land--and yet, the only quick market for this piece is probably us. I've had it listed for a long time, and privately I've asked every one of our friends and acquaintances whom I think could afford to buy it, and none of them can buy right now. Don's brother is the only one whom we haven't asked, and he probably could well afford it, but, God, I don't want to sell it to anyone with the same last name as ours--and that includes us! Please help us find some other way to solve this dilemma.

CHAPTER 32

—∞∞∞—

Going Home In Slow Motion

CHRISTMAS, 1994, DON and I make a special effort to celebrate with Mother. She didn't come to our house for Thanksgiving this year as she had a cold, and though she's over the cold, she doesn't seem up to coming for Christmas either. Celebrating at Patty's is the only option. We both have an ominous feeling this may be our last Christmas with her.

Such worries are wasted energy and detract from celebrating Christmas at Patty's, which has twice proven to be a very enjoyable experience. The whole holiday season there is sort of an open-house with a constantly brewing coffee pot, a well-supplied goodie table, beautiful decorations, fresh greenery strung from the kitchen to the bathrooms, and happy music ringing softly in the background. The living room is dominated by a huge flocked noble fir with little colored flashing lights and a fascinating array of angels, Santas, gingerbread men, delicate see-through glass balls and some sturdy shiny metal ones on the lower branches for George to occasionally attack. Parents and friends of Patty's clients stop by frequently sharing with their loved ones. Everyone brings treats to the table. There's a genuine holiday spirit in Patty's foster home.

When we arrive at her place Christmas Eve, I am discouraged to learn Mother doesn't want to even get up and come out to the living room. Don and I go to her room wearing our big red and white Santa Helper hats. I ring my handful of sleigh bells, and sing out, "Ho, Ho, Ho, Francine, and have you been a good girl this year?"

Mother is dressed but lying on her bed. Her eyelids flutter a few times as if just coming to wakefulness from a nap.

"Ho, Ho, Ho, Francine, did I catch you taking a little nap here on Christmas Eve?"

She opens her eyes wider and breaks into peals of giggles reminiscent of when we were on Stevens Pass and I was pulling her back in the bed of the pickup for her rest at the roadside park. I take off my hat, "Hi, Mom. It's Don and I. Wouldn't you like to get up for a little bit?"

I see a flicker of recognition, then her eyelids droop, "Oooooh, noooo."

I put my hat back on and repeat the Ho-Ho-Ho routine. Again she laughs, her whole body shaking pleasantly. She makes some rough, guttural sounds, but there are no distinguishable words. We don't really have a conversation, but she seems to enjoy our efforts at light-heartedness.

I point out her Christmas cards arranged on her television and dresser. I pick up each one and show her again, pausing to see if her tired eyes follow the various Santas, trees, bells, angels and snow scenes. Her eyes are open, but they don't follow. I read the words of each card and any personal messages that have been written, skipping a few parts. There's no use explaining Mavis' eye surgery or her recent fall resulting in a broken arm-- nor does Mother need to know about her brother Malcom's diagnosis of diabetes.

As for Rolf, there is no card from him, so I avoid mentioning his name.

As I describe each friend and acquaintance who has sent a greeting, Mother speaks no words, but I know by the way her eyes light up and by the way she squeezes my hand in signal to my yes-no questions she still understands and feels fondness for Annie, Hazel and Stella, Evelyn, Mavis, Maurine, Malcom and others.

Don and I sing Christmas carols along with Diana Ross and a backup symphony orchestra behind us on the TV screen. When I ask Mother if she would like us to sing more, she squeezes a definite yes. I'm sure she can't tell which one of us is Diana.

After we leave I feel renewed anger toward Rolf for his omission of such a simple thing as a Christmas greeting. I tell myself my anger only belies my failure to forgive him. For my own well-being, I need to be more charitable. I write a Christmas note to him and send it to Mavis to forward.

I sense an enormous void without a brother, and not just at holidays. I've needed him so many times in these last years, but I can't change anything that has happened. Furthermore, if I had it all to do over--perish the thought--a part of me says I would do the same things again. Another part says: If you knew all that you know now, you would never have pursued a guardianship. You would have made a 180 degree turn from Ridgeview and run away to a far away place, changed your name, built a new identity and never pursued any of these problems nor tried to bring justice and closure to anything!'

The Christmas season this year is especially stressful for me and I develop some sleep disturbances for the first time in my life. Often I wake up in the middle of the night tearful and wishing things could be different, both with Mother and with Rolf.

These are not the disturbances that bother me the most. On my usual teaching schedule I need to awaken at 6:30 AM and be up by 6:40 AM. I hate hearing the alarm go off. Most of the time for the past twenty years, I have awakened at 6:25 AM and punched the off button. Recently my eyes have begun to pop open at precisely 5:16 AM. It drives me crazy because I need sleep so badly. I don't know why it can't be 5:20 or 5:30--or 6:00 AM. I wouldn't consider it a sleep disturbance, except for the eeriness of the numbers, and it's happened over twenty times this month. My brain must make it happen. What's wrong with me? Did I do something wrong in regard to *the house that Dad built*? Do I have a mental problem? I try to talk myself into accepting coincidences. About the time I think I am convinced, I get caught off guard in some unrelated event such as topping off the gas in my car and the amount of the fill-up is $5.16. Okay, it's still coincidental. I check the oven to see how much longer my cake must bake--it's five minutes and sixteen seconds. I check a map destination--it's five hundred and sixteen miles. Coincidence? I don't know. I'm the one who says I have received so many purple tulips throughout recent years that I no longer believe in coincidences.

On a more rational level I tell myself I have been thoughtful each step of the way in this long family trauma. I have sought professional help for Mother and for myself. I have constantly sought God's guidance. I have learned incredible lessons in faith and grace. I have experienced humility and humiliation. I know I have been strengthened as a person, and I have been able to share with others and to be helpful and comforting by example. I have learned that the efforts of a single unlikely person can be the most important thing in the world to another person. And just as quickly it can be totally insignificant, useless, worthless.

I feel somewhat insignificant--useless--worthless--at the present time as I watch death stalk Mother. God will take her when it is time and not a moment sooner. The greatest paradox in all of this is knowing when to hang on tight and when to let go. Much of the time I feel as if I'm doing both actions at the same time as death hovers, weakens, bruises, and chokes her!

A couple of weeks after Christmas Patty calls to say, "You know, Betty, I'm just a little bit worried about Francine. She's getting up now to use the potty chair beside her bed, but she won't stay up for any length of time. Also, she's running a slight fever."

"What does her doctor say?"

"I talked to him yesterday, and he put her back on the same antibiotic he used during the bout of pneumonia last summer."

"Does she have pneumonia again?"

"I don't really think so, but the doctor doesn't want us to move her or bring her in considering her history and overall condition. What are your thoughts, Betty? I'll do whatever you want me to do."

"Patty, I have to trust you and the doctor on this one."

The next day Patty calls again. "Francine's fever has dropped back to normal, but she won't take any solid food."

"What about liquids?"

"Oh, yes, she continues to take liquids, but she's taking less. She totally refuses the nutritional drinks, and she pulls away when I try to offer them. She will take a little bit of apple juice and occasionally some water. She sleeps on and off throughout the day and the night."

"Is there anything you can think of to perk up her appetite, Patty?"

"I was thinking maybe a little change in flavor, maybe some of her favorite Ruby Red Grapefruit juice might perk up her interest in food."

"I'm coming up tomorrow. I'll pick some up."

The next day I leave right from school to go visit Mother. I stop at a grocery store and pick up the Ruby Red. The whole store smells of fresh-baked

French bread, and I can't resist buying a loaf of the warm bread and some rolls. Don has come with me, and I get him a small bottle of Ruby Red to drink in the car, as he isn't going in to visit because he feels he may be catching a cold. I wait patiently through the heavy Friday night customer lines, and by the time it's my turn to check out I am not very attentive.

The checker mumbles, "That will be five dollars and--"

"Again, please?" I request.

He looks up and in an irritated voice growls, "I said five-sixteen, please!"

I hurriedly lay out the exact change and flee from the store.

I am upset by the 516 incident in the store, and by my having awakened that very morning at 5:16 AM. My visit with Mother further adds to my agitation. I'm glad the fever is down, but she's so lethargic. Maybe it is pneumonia again. I hope she has the strength to battle it this time. Despite her weakness, she does take a few sips of the Ruby Red. That's good.

Later in the evening in a phone conversation with Don's sister, Annie, I tell her about my "5-1-6-Stress Syndrome." She offers her perspective, one which I hadn't thought of. "You know, Betty, I think it's an omen. Your mom's no longer speaking, but God is telling you she's going home. He's just using the grocery store man to tell you--or those other instances--you know, 5-1-6 was the number of her home. Friday the 20th was the day you were visiting her--that's part of the message. That was the street she lived on, right? You get it, don't you? She's going home--well, she's really going to her heavenly home--but she is going home. And God wants you to know that."

"That's weird, Annie. I don't know if it's good-weird or bad-weird."

"Betty, God's been telling you for a long time, if you'd just listen."

I visit Mother again Sunday evening. Her temperature is still normal, but there is an eeriness about her, about the whole room. Her eyes have a bluish, veiled, unfocused appearance, eyes that are usually deep pools of dark chocolate brown. Even in the times when her brain wasn't functioning rationally and her body wasn't up to par, her eyes were a vibrant brown--and in moments of anger, they were a piercing, intense brown. Now they seem drained, faded, and bluish around the edge of the iris. When I look into her eyes, it's as if there's no one home. I know she hears my voice, and the heavy bluish-tinged orbs strain laboriously to focus. She opens her mouth and I feel air being forced out as if she is trying to speak, but I can't distinguish the sounds. I pat and stroke her arms and legs. I talk to her about the weather and how cold it's been. I tell her she feels cozy warm. I feel stupid as if I'm talking to myself. I offer her a drink using a medicine dropper, and though there is no enthusiasm or urgency to the motion, I see faint attempts by her lips and throat, as she swallows a tiny bit of the liquid.

This is spooky. I'm not exactly afraid. It's more like a deep kind of respect or awe. I feel as if I'm alone here at her bedside, and she's not really in her body, at least not completely. There is some kind of "presence" here, and it's not just me. It's gentle, protective, waiting--I don't know. I feel too calm. Is it mystery? Is it evil? Is it God? Is it an angel? It doesn't feel natural. It's not tangible, but I'm not afraid. I lean over and kiss her cheek and whisper, "Mother, you don't have to fight anymore. You go on home any time you want to." There is no response. I feel shallow air movement near her nose. She is warm and looks peaceful. I straighten up and leave her room.

Dear God, I don't know exactly what I experienced tonight. I thank you for the peace and calmness, maybe even the quiet protection, that was in that room. I know you'll take Mother whenever you are ready, and that the glory of life after death as promised to believers will surely make up for the loneliness of life without Dad, for the hurt of estranged family, and for the fear and confusion resulting from incomplete brain functioning. Oh, God, I truly wish I had Rolf's companionship and support to make these last gaunt, flaccid visits somehow more tolerable. It may be that he has his own wrestling match over his health issues. I know he has been sick with his diabetes. I do pray for him in this regard, but I can't change past events. I pray that I heard your guidance correctly. May the understanding of purple tulips be Rolf's as well as mine. God, may you send us both a continuous, ample supply!

Patty calls Don's office on Monday, January 23, 1995, with news that Mother died at 11:08 AM. I am called from my classroom and go to Don's office. When I call Patty, she tells me, "Francine awakened with a little fever this morning. Her breathing was shallow and labored, and she had some "rails." I could hear the rattling clearly. I really thought the pneumonia had returned, and I called her doctor. After we discussed her condition this past week, he was concerned about her quality of life and that the antibiotics had not been effective. He opted not to reorder them, but instead ordered a medication to relax her. It was to be delivered this afternoon, but it hasn't arrived. Francine just slowed down throughout the night last night, Betty."

"Was she comfortable without the medication?"

"Betty, I think she was as comfortable as is possible. She was very peaceful. In fact, in my experience with other folks, I would say Francine was very comfortable, relaxed. I have spent quite a lot of time with her throughout the last couple of nights. She would sleep, stir, sleep again. Each time it seemed with less effort. Last night I had difficulty getting her to take any water, even with the little dropper."

"How did you arrive at an exact time of death, Patty?"

"You know, that's kind of strange, but I know the time is correct within a minute or two. I was with her at 9:00 AM this morning, and then we both fell asleep. I was sitting in a chair beside her bed and was pretty tired, as I had been with her on and off throughout the night. I awakened and checked her at exactly 10:00 AM, and she was asleep. I set my timer and checked her again at 11:00 AM. She stirred, but her responses were very weak and she wouldn't take any water. I went to the front porch to the mail box right after that, even though I know the mail-man doesn't come until 11:30. I was surprised when I opened the box. The mailman had come early, and there was a card from her sister, Mavis. I took the card in right away and read it to her. Her eyes flickered--like she was trying to open them and wake up. She just took a few more breaths and slipped away right then. I couldn't get a pulse or any further air movement at all. She just slipped away. I looked at my watch--it was exactly 11:08."

"I'm glad that's how it ended. Thank you, Patty."

By 11:45 AM a substitute is in my classroom and Don and I are headed home. I am on automatic pilot as I enter my house and pick up the file

I have prepared to use in the event of Mother's death. The first call is to the funeral home in Ridgeview. They are experienced and proficient, and they set the tone as they assure me of the arrangements to transfer the body within the next hour from Patty's home to a local funeral home for preparation and then further transport to Ridgeview. A coroner call is not necessary since the death was expected. I make more calls to Aunt Mavis who will notify Rolf. To the minister. To Mother's other sister and brother. To Nick and El. To the lawyer to stop the land purchase process. To cousins, close family friends, previous neighbors, fellow workers and Ridgeview friends. To Social Security. To retirement fund administration, bank and credit union. To motels in Ridgeview and back and forth to Patty.

Despite all of my preparations for the end of Mother's life, I missed an important detail. The funeral home director told me to bring a complete set of clothing for her: full dress, slip, panties, bra, and hosiery. I don't have suitable clothing for her. None of her dresses fit now, as she lost considerable weight. On the way to Ridgeview I stop at a department store and pick out the burial clothes. I want her to be pretty. She needs all new things--all of it.

Rolf and I meet at the funeral home to plan Mother's service with the guidance of the funeral director.

I haven't seen Rolf since his eviction from the Ridgeview house. I don't know where he has been, and I don't ask. I only know he is here now in response to Aunt Mavis' contact.

He is domineering, angry, rude, very directive--and I let him be so, unchallenged.

"Yeah, we don't want no short-changing here. We don't want to cheat no one. I want Mom to have the exact same casket as Dad had. I want that picture on the lid to be the same, too."

His words are to the funeral director, but I know the implications of cheating or short-changing are to me.

Despite his attitude, we are fairly agreeable in our choices, except for the pall-bearers. Rolf has chosen his long-haul trucking friend, Mike, to serve in this capacity. "Rolf, you and I both know neither Mother nor Dad cared much for your friend Mike, especially in recent years. I would like Nick to be a pall-bearer."

"Well, Nick is kind of young for the task, don't you think?"

"I think Nick will be fine doing that. Age is not significant, and besides, he is twenty-seven years old, for God's sake. I agree that you should be a pall-bearer, and so should the three who are long-time family friends. The others you have chosen are not friends of Mom nor Dad. They are your personal friends. Nick is her only grandson, and I want him to have that part in her funeral service."

"Yeah, yeah, okay by me then."

To myself I say, It had better be! I would have liked Don to be a pall-bearer also, but that's okay. I can understand how that might be offensive to you.

Actually, Rolf, you've spent so much time in between our choices today here at the funeral home telling the director about your work with the Green River Task Force that I'm surprised you didn't have Sgt. Dave Reichert or Mr. Malcomb Chang on your list to be pall-bearers.

You are so sick!

CHAPTER 33

---⟨∞⟩---

Another Funeral, Another Eulogy

SICK TAKES ON new meaning a few days later at Mother's funeral service. The chapel is beautiful. The coffin is draped in flowers, and there are twenty or more arrangements standing at the front. It's a far greater expression of sympathy than I had expected. Many of the colors and kinds of flowers were favorites in the yard at 516, especially roses, gladioli, and chrysanthemums in orange, yellow, purple and white. All of the flower arrangements, as well as the indoor potted plants, are beautiful tributes to both Malfaits.

My family and I share the viewing time, and we take some photos to send to Aunt Mavis, as she will not be attending this time. She said she would prefer to hang on to other memories, but she would appreciate the photos. We conclude that mission and leave the viewing prior to the funeral in plenty of time to allow Rolf and his friends a full hour of privacy.

We return a little before the designated time for the service. There is a rush and a blur of friends with condolences. Finally the director taps me on the shoulder and asks to seat me and my family. He ushers us up to the first row pew, leaving the second row vacant. The funeral director returns to the back of the chapel for Rolf, who follows him up to the front. Limping on his foot that was operated on due to a diabetic condition, he moves slowly, using a cane. The director stops at the family pew and motions for him to be seated next to me.

Rolf stares at the empty space on the pew, turns and squints back over the audience, and shakes his head. "No, no. I don't want to sit there."

The director leans toward him and whispers, "Rolf, remember I need you to be seated up here on the family pew, because I'll be right over there behind that screen doing the music and sound system. From this aisle seat you'll be able to see me when I signal you and it's time for you to speak."

Rolf pulls his mouth into a tight line and shakes his head no.

The director persists, "I really need you in the first seat, but you might still be able to see me from this second row. It has also been reserved for family."

"No, no. I ain't gonna sit there either. I'll just go on to the back and sit with the pall-bearers."

Rolf turns and hobbles the full length of the chapel aisle past a hundred or so friends who have come to honor Mother. He pauses at the pew where the pall-bearers are seated, all of them large men who pretty well fill up all the space on the bench. They squeeze close together and Rolf seats himself on the aisle, leaving the funeral director standing at the front waiting to see if he will fit there and to figure out how he will signal him.

Strains of a recording of "The Old Rugged Cross" do little to soothe my silent stinging hurt from Rolf's snub. Pastor Jim Whitman takes the podium. He's not the same pastor as for Dad's funeral, but he is another beloved minister from Malfaits' latter years of church attendance.

Pastor Jim tells us, "Francine loved that old hymn. She loved that old cross. She believed and lived by the message of that song."

He reads the 23rd Psalm and offers a prayer, then proceeds by recalling his own experiences and appreciation of both Malfaits' efforts in his behalf--the yard work and lawn-mowing at the church and parsonage--gardens and window boxes planted for him and his wife to enjoy--various fresh fruits and vegetables from their yard appearing as surprises on their back door step--and preserves and jellies--and wonderful trips to The Oak Tree Restaurant for top-of-the-line prime rib dinners. All these things totally unsolicited expressions of caring and love for their pastor and his wife.

"Both Malfaits always offered the best in all they did for the church, for me and my wife--and for others in need, as well. My family moved, and we've been away from Ridgeview these past ten years, a time of great difficulty for Malfaits. They helped us so often and made our lives so much better when we lived here, and I am sorry we weren't here to assist them in their time of need."

Pastor Jim picks up his Bible from the speaker's stand. "Roger and Francine's son, Rolf, spoke at his father's funeral. He has requested to speak again today. Rolf, would you come forward now?"

Rolf rises from the back pew and hobbles to the front of the chapel, laboring up the two steps, leaning on his cane and pulling with his stronger leg. He wedges his cane between the podium and one of the floral arrangements, lays out a large yellow legal-sized pad on the lectern, and reaches inside his heavy red and black plaid work jacket drawing out his reading glasses. With a wide, dramatic swing of his arm, he forces one of the stubborn bows to open and places the thick, horn-rimmed glasses on his nose. He looks out at the audience for a lengthy, blurry moment, then down to his notes.

I'm thinking, *Deja vu. I'm in a bad movie. I've seen it before--and it may get worse. Is this Rolf's day to cause holy hell?* I shift uneasily on the hard pew.

Dear God, please...

Rolf raises his magnified eyes to the audience. "Mom and Dad were strong, country people. They grew up in West Virginia. Her own mother died when Mom was only thirteen years old. At that very early age, her father expected her to take over running the household and cooking for the family--and whenever necessary for the field hands who came to help on the farm. As the oldest child, she was also left to raise the three younger children: Malcom, Mavis and Maurine. She did all that, and when she graduated from high school, she herself married at age seventeen. She and Dad went their own way, and they took up farming on property Dad owned--that was about 1931. Times were hard for everyone then. She lost her first baby, Franklin. Shortly thereafter Dad came to the Northwest to Randal, Washington, where he worked in the woods. Mom followed him a year later. The next year they moved to Ridgeview, and Dad started working in the lumber mill. I was born that year, and they were a family again. The war was on. Times were still hard. Mom went to work in the mills to help in the war effort. When that was pretty well over, she quit for a while but went back to work a little later."

I mentally replay the time frame he mentions. *I didn't hear it, but I'm pretty sure the time period when she quit was when she was pregnant with me. I was born sometime in that break between the war effort and Mother going back to work. Oh well, I was not mentioned at Dad's funeral, why would I be mentioned today? My birth is a small hurtful omission in this family history.*

Rolf licks his finger and lifts one of the yellow pages, rolls it up and tucks it under the top of the pad. "After the war Mom and Dad purchased the two lots on 20th Street. That's when Mom really went to work, because after workin' all day at their jobs, they'd come to the property and work late into the evening. They built that house at 516 every step of the way themselves. That's the kind of people they were. They did it together, and they knew they could in those hard times after the war. They worked real hard, and they got it built. It was a Malfait goal! That house was most important to Malfaits! There were a lot of times they didn't have the money, but when Dad went into a store and ordered something for the house, they knew the name Malfait was good for the money as soon as he could get it."

Rolf, are you showing the hurt that resulted from my evicting you from something that was most important to Malfaits? Are you saying you are a Malfait, and in some peculiar, twisted way that house is most important to you? I have heard you say about yourself you could walk into a store and order up, and they knew the name Malfait was good for the money as soon as you got it. Are you interweaving yourself as if you are Dad?

Rolf continues building a picture of Malfaits living at 516 happily and productively, which I have to agree they did. His tone of love and appreciation for our parents somewhat eases my hurt at again being omitted from the picture.

"You all know what wonderful gardeners they both were. Mom and Dad had two grapevines at the back of the house--one white and one purple."

Actually they had ten grapevines. There were two whites on a trellis under their bedroom window, four purple Concords on the big arbor in the back yard, two purples on the garden fence, and two pinks on the back alley fence.

"Now, they canned all their grape juice. They had a lot of grapes, and so they had a lot of canned grape juice. They canned that juice in big half gallon jars. They knew what they had, too. They knew exactly how much, and they knew exactly where they stored it. Later in the winter months, Dad, he'd make jelly. He didn't much want Mom in the kitchen at that time. Makin' the jelly was *his* thing.

"Now Mom and Dad really felt strongly about integrity. They sure didn't appreciate nobody who would steal something like grape juice."

Rolf's glare scans the family pew. I glare back.

Rolf, you and I both know of Mother's accusations that Don stole jars of their grape juice from their attic. You're not going to say that now, are you?

Rolf unfurls another yellow page and tucks it under the top of the pad. His magnified glare locks onto the front pew. "Like I said, Mom and Dad both believed strongly in integrity and honesty. If a person would lie in little things, they'd lie about big things, and usually it all just comes back to greed."

I stare up at the blurred orbs.

My God, Rolf, you've just described yourself, but you're inferring it was Don who stole the grape juice--and if he'd steal little things like that, he'd steal bigger things too. It's you, Rolf, you are a thief--not of grape juice--but of oh so much more!

"You know, I recall one time when I was a kid, me and my friend from a couple streets over figured why should we buy comic books when we could just go down to the corner store and *borrow* them. Now when Mom found out what we'd done, she made me go out and cut a cherry tree switch, and then she switched me all the way back to the store with that cherry limb. I paid for the comic books. And when Mom and me got back to the house, she burned the things."

There is appreciative tittering from the audience.

"And I'll tell you what, when it was done, it was done. I never did anything like that again. And it was never mentioned again."

Rolf, you're telling it only as you want it to be told. I remember Mother never let you forget that episode. It was often used as a reminder lesson to you or me or anyone else's child who may have been involved in petty thievery.

"Now, like I said, Mom and Dad both had a high degree of honesty. They never cheated anyone. They hated cheating. They worked hard.

They had a real strong work ethic. Mom's boss out there at Fibex, old Slim Jenkins, he once told me, 'Your mom is a real hard worker---she's one of the best. Most of them women workin' for me don't know how to work. If I could get rid of the lolly-gaggers and just had ten like Francine, Fibex would be a whole lot better run.' I'm sure Slim was right."

Yes, Rolf, Mother was a real hard worker, but are you listening to what you're saying to the friends and fellow workers who are here today to honor her? Many of them were hard workers at Fibex too, regardless of what Slim told you.

Another yellow page is flipped over and tucked under the tablet. "Mom and Dad worked at home just like they worked in the mills. They worked in the garden and canned like there was gonna be another depression. Young people nowadays have got no idea what hard work is. They have everything just handed to 'em. They get everything for nothin'--clothes, allowances, cars, you name it. They don't know the meanin' of hard work!"

I've heard your perspective on this before, Rolf. That's what you said to me about my children and whatever their privileges have been. You said they didn't know the meaning of hard work--you said neither Don nor I knew real hard work either, because we'd only been teachers and counselors and we'd never been out where real work occurred. Teachers were shut up in their plush little classrooms, and they didn't have to work very hard and were overpaid for what little they did. Whatever you're trying to say today it's difficult to accept from someone who has never been married and had children and from some-one who has not held a steady job for the last ten years.

"You all out there know, just like I know, what's wrong with most people nowadays. This whole generation's just got above their upbringing and they forget where they come from."

My eyes close. My brain is churning.

Deja-vu. Deja-vu. Rolf, you preached this sermon at Dad's funeral. You've said these things directly to Don and me that we got above our upbringing. What did you want us to do--get jobs in the mills so we could prove we could do real work? Or should we have driven logging trucks? Isn't there honor to all work? Isn't that what we were taught in our Malfait upbringing?

"Now, me, I've had my fair share of hard work, and I do mean hard work. It definitely was hard work drivin' a log truck a thousand miles a day..."

My brain quickly calculates. *That would be over sixteen hours a day at a constant rate of 60 mph. I don't think so!*

"Back then when I was workin' like that, I'd have to say Malfaits never let me down one time. They drove all over the place bringing me hot meals. Sometimes I was almost too tired to eat them. But, you know, I think they sort of enjoyed all that travel. And, like I said, they never once let me down."

You're right, Rolf, they never ever let you down--but enjoyed that? I remember the griping and moaning that went on about where they had to go to meet you.

"Like I was sayin', Mom and Dad had no respect for thieves and liars. They helped everyone. Mom, she would give you the shirt off her back. As time went on there at the house at 516, they had an abundance of things growing on the property--fruits, vegetables and flowers. There were some less-than-scrupulous neighbors who stole from them, especially flowers. Mom would have just thought, 'Well, they must have needed them more than we did.' She hated having her neighbors steal from her though."

My God, Rolf, what do you get from bringing up hurtful innuendoes about Nosy-bill who happens to be in attendance today? She knew Mom and Dad when they were in good health. Yeah, Mother once flew into a tirade over missing flowers and may have even accused her of stealing--and maybe Nosy-bill did take flowers without asking--but everything Mom and Dad ever touched grew. A few flowers are not important on this day. Besides, Mother accused me, my children, and my husband of theft--and I know none of it was true! Maybe it wasn't true about Nosy-bill either. Why are you doing this?

Another yellow page is tucked under the tablet. "Now, I'll tell you one thing Malfaits always did. They did everything 50/50. That's just how it was. That's how it was expected. That's how it was done! And that's how it is right here today--it's 50/50. *I* made sure they were treated *exactly* alike." Rolf scans the audience from one side of the chapel to the other through his reading glasses and sweeps his hand toward the coffin behind him continuing, "It's the exact same coffin. It's the same service. It's the same music. It's even the same picture inside the coffin lid. You'll notice it's a picture of a little country church much like the one where they lived in

West Virginia, a church like many of you in the audience know well. It's the kind of church a lot of you grew up in and the kind some of you probably still go to."

That's good, Rolf. You're identifying with Mother's cousin and her high school friend whom she grew up with in West Virginia. You know they're both in the audience today, and you're making points with several other Malfait friends who grew up in the South. You're right, there's a little country church like that on just about every hilltop in West Virginia and all over the South.

"Like I was sayin', Mom and Dad did everything 50/50 and that's somethin' they believed in whole heartedly--somethin' they lived by."

Rolf, you're not looking at me, but I know that's for me. I feel your verbal lashes!

"Now, when Mom would go shopping, she'd be gone and gone. Dad, he'd fuss and fume, and when she'd get home, he'd say, 'Francine, what took you so long?' I think it's probably like that now. Dad's been gone four years, and he's probably fussin' and sayin', 'Francine, what took you so long?'"

The audience chuckles.

Rolf continues, "I was just talkin' to Patty, the R.N. who cared for Mom these last few years, and by the things she shared with me..."

She's really an LPN, but that's unimportant. Exaggeration is part of your eulogy. In fact, there's more embellishment in your remembrances than praise.

"I know Mom was well cared for by her, and Mom was comfortable. I know that for a fact." Rolf's voice cracks. He stares at his notes, grips the lectern with one hand, and pulls the other hand several times through his long bushy gray beard.

I concentrate on the beads of sweat on his shiny bald head and the orange glow of sunlight through the stained glass windows behind his bulky figure. I swallow the lump in my own throat. Yes, she was well cared for.

"On that last day, Patty brought the mail in a little after 11:00 AM. The mail had one card in it. It was from Mom's sister, Mavis. Patty read it to Mom, and Mom understood that message. I know she did, and when I talked to Mavis, I assured her that Mom got that card, and that message was the last thing she had understood before she died."

Yeah, Rolf, maybe.... She was fairly incoherent the last couple of weeks, but maybe she did understand it. I'd like to believe that. That's comforting.

"Now today things are ended for Mom. But like Yogi Berra, the great baseball player, said, 'It ain't over 'til it's over!' There are some things that still need to be resolved." Rolf looks up and again scans the audience through his reading glasses, omitting the front pew. The beads of sweat have become trickles moving down the sides of his face disappearing into the coils of his straggly beard. He again pauses and pulls his hand through his beard, staring blankly down the middle aisle of the chapel.

I lean forward and look directly up at him. He looks frozen, despite the profuse sweating. He doesn't look at me nor my family. He unfurls the yellow pages from the top of the large legal-sized pad and smoothes them back flat into the pad.

"Yes, there are still some things that need to be resolved." Rolf grasps both sides of the lectern and turns toward the front pew glaring down at me and my family. With jerking head motions causing the sweat to fly out from himself, he barks, "And they need to be taken care of *FAIRLY*, and *EQUITABLY*, and I intend to see to it that *THEY WILL BE!*" Rolf sucks in a big breath which can be heard in magnified volume through the microphone.

He retrieves his cane, picks up the re-assembled yellow legal pad, and hobbles back to the back of the chapel still wearing the thick reading glasses.

I don't know how he managed to get down the two steps. It was labored, but seemed faster than he had initially gone up them.

Rolf, I think your whole speech was a masterful expression of your creative genius, your guilt, your anger, and your personal vindictiveness. I hear you, Rolf. I don't think this is the right time nor place, but I do hear you. I understand better now your threats to Patty and others that as soon as you win the lottery and fully recuperate from your foot operation, you are going to sue my ass! I don't know if you won the lottery, but maybe you deserve your day in court. Personally, I think your attitude is avaricious and vengeful against people in the audience today, including me and my family, and probably will be in a courtroom, as well. Today you were for sure grandstanding. For the most part, your words were not an honor nor a memorial to our mother nor to our father. Today was the wrong time.

You are so sick!

I sit limp in the pew. I'm sad. I'm angry. I'm seething.

Dear God, where are you now? Why are you allowing this? How can you let him blaspheme our family, our mother, my family--yourself--in this manner on this day? Why? I'll never understand this, but please, oh, God, please don't let me hate him, and if I have hatred in my heart, don't let me speak it today.

Where is my brother?

Thankfully the minister's sermon follows Rolf's preaching. I relax some seeing him stand behind the podium with a Bible instead of a yellow legal pad. His message is based on Biblical insights. He starts by giving a simplistic message of salvation by faith in Jesus Christ. He focuses on Mother's life as an example. "Francine accepted Jesus way long back. She knew the promise and the hope, and she lived her life in that manner. She belonged to Him."

I sense a quiet affirming of my understanding that God holds his children forever, regardless of their straying by choice or mental breakdown. His words move on to describe the resurrection and judgment day.

"All of us must face death, and all arise and face judgment. And God's people, those who have chosen to accept and follow Jesus, will be united. The lost will be lost forever. I refer to I Corinthia*ns 15:12. If* Jesus didn't die on the cross--*if* the resurrection didn't take place--then all of Christ's life was for nothing. It is just a false hope to make us all feel better about the trials of living. It is worthless!"

As Pastor Jim offers a concluding prayer my mind revisits some of the comfort and hope offered in his sermon. I'll never grasp all the Biblical meaning, but I know I'd rather have God's care and attention than the cheap-shot blabbering of a man under a great burden--maybe conviction, maybe guilt, maybe mistreated and cheated, maybe misunderstood--nevertheless, a man who expresses his vindictiveness and his financial desires and greed over his dead Mother's casket! This man's attention I don't need. I guess Dad was right all along: We'll all get to know at Judgment Day.

My cogitation is interrupted by an incredible tenor voice. It's not a recording. Standing near a piano by the curtain on the left side of the stage is a church friend of Malfaits who is sharing the sweet strains of "How Great Thou Art." I feel a chill and then a quietness. I close my eyes.

Dear God, I feel hurt, embarrassed, angry--this is out of my league. It's beyond my expertise. God, I did what I felt I was supposed to do to help my parents, to try to help Rolf, and ultimately to honor and obey my parents. I can continue to do that. The legal stuff--the sale of the property, the 50-50 split--or as Mother's will states "share and share alike"--I'm okay with whatever must be done to bring fair and equitable closure in the formal, legal things. However, in the emotional and psychological aspects of this sibling estrangement, I cannot deal further. Oh, God, I pray for Rolf---I lift him up to you right now--I don't understand him, but I do love him, and I'd rather have the brother. It's as if that person has totally disappeared. I trust you, God, to work with both Rolf and me. I will accept whatever the ultimate outcome of all this is. I know I only have to answer to you for my own actions and behaviors. Up to this point in time I'm okay with all my actions and most of my behaviors. I'm not perfect, I'm sorry for my shortcomings. Right now I feel drained. And yet, in another way, I am at peace with where things are. Please guide me in all things.

The funeral director invites people to file by for a final viewing. After the last of the crowd has left the chapel, he closes the chapel doors and comes back up to the first pew and tells me I may take as long as I like to say my final goodbye to my mother. He will bring the pall-bearers back in whenever I come and tell him.

The rest of my family leaves me. I stand a moment and sense my singleness with the open casket at the front of the chapel. Mother's body was prepared well. She looks peaceful--actually pretty. Even though she lost quite a bit of weight, the navy blue wrap dress is very stylish and makes her look filled out. The white oversized collar with the embroidered piping looks almost like a string of pearls. Mother would like that. The ear rings are imitation pearls, but Mother wouldn't have wanted the real ones to be used on this occasion. I'm glad I asked them to put her wedding band on her finger. She hasn't worn it for years, but I think she would like that, too. I stroke her stiff hands, which are the same temperature of the wedding band.

Dear God, thank you for this special woman who was my mother--all that she was and all that she taught me. Forgive me for my failures and my doubts during any part of my care for her. Thank you for the opportunities to re-unite and to make amends for tragic errors of past years. I know she would never have lied intentionally about me nor my family, and I'm glad you gave us all the opportunity to know those were mistakes and to forgive them. Thank you for the warmth and affection she was able to show us, even as her memory and her health were failing. Thank you for the warm hugs and kisses, letting each of us know she loved us, even when she didn't speak. Thank you for the times her eyes lit up in recognition when we came to visit and she was happy, even if it was only for a short while. Thank you for the joy she showed when Nick visited that last time, and she was so proud that both he and El graduated from university. Thank you for this last Christmas Eve when she giggled aloud until her whole body shook at my Santa Claus impersonation. Thank you for the way she squeezed my hand 'yes' when I asked her if she wanted me to continue singing Christmas carols. Only a mother would have appreciated that singing!

Dear God, there's so much left to do. I have such anger and estrangement with Rolf. It's too big and too much. I can't fix it. But, Dear God, I pray that I have indeed listened carefully to you all along, and I ask you now to help me to keep listening. Please help me to bring final closure to Mother's business affairs justly and fairly according to Mother and Dad's wishes, and more importantly, according to your will.

I commend my mother to you, and I know Dad and their deceased baby, Franklin, are happy at this reunion. I know there are other family and loved ones with you who will joyously welcome Mother. All is so much better today than the arduous tasks that were hers to bear just to exist on this earth these past few months.

For myself and my family I pray for your guidance, strength, and the ability to hear and follow your will in all things.
In Jesus name, Amen.

CHAPTER 34

"Holy Hell" Begins

MOTHER DIED JANUARY 23, 1995. In late March the mail brings notification, "Comes now Rolf V. Malfait, through his attorneys, and respectfully shows and petitions as follows..."

...there is no Last Will and Testament of our deceased mother... objects to the appointment of Betty as Personal Representative of Francine Malfait's estate...requests the Court appoint him as said Personal Representative, or in the alternative, appoint both of us as Co-Personal Representatives...says Betty has claimed more than $30,000 in compensation and reimbursement for her work in the guardianship...believes that he can more fairly and more inexpensively represent the interests of the estate...questions the use of money from the sale of timber on the Whidbey property...objects to the sale of the Whidbey property to Don and Betty...

Dear God, I feel sick. Is this what he meant when he said to family friends and to Aunt Mavis, "When Mom is dead I'm going to raise holy hell?" Oh, God, please see me through this.

Mr. Oats, my Ridgeview attorney, assures me, "Betty, your records are excellent. Your care for your mother has been admirable. There is nothing to worry about. You need to write out explanations to each of the points raised by Rolf and return copies to him and to his lawyer, Mr. Wright. That information will be shared with the judge. Rolf has a right to question. Some time in the near future at a designated court date we will all sit down and discuss the situation."

I follow Mr. Oats' direction and detail each of the issues completely. In summary, I request, "Considering all points raised by the complainant, I beg the court to value my efforts these past several years as guardian for both my parents and to recall through the court process Rolf V. Malfait was deemed unsuitable for sharing in the guardianship process in the best interest of both Roger V. and Francine P. Malfait. He is currently even more unsuitable to participate as a Personal Representative in the final closure of the business of the estate of our deceased mother, Francine P. Malfait. Any such response to the wishes of Rolf Malfait would be in *absolute violation of the wishes as stated in the last will and testament of both deceased parents, wills which were written and witnessed well back in a time when they both were absolutely coherent regarding their business dealings and in making judgments regarding whom to trust to fairly and equitably resolve their affairs after their deaths.*"

Despite the confidence offered by Mr. Oats, I can't help being upset by yet another plunge into an emotional abyss.

Rolf's legal requests are bizarre based on misinformation, lack of information, and lies. He's in his own world and has his own truth. He probably thinks there is no will, because when he *rescued* the insurance policies he probably took other documents, as well. But there's an ironic twist for whomever gymied Malfaits' little black locked metal box--those wills were outdated. Malfaits redid them some twenty years ago. And for safe-keeping Mother tucked both of the more recent wills away in her special private file cabinet upstairs, actually a file cabinet kept in Rolf's bedroom. It was a four-drawer metal cabinet in which Mother stored her treasures: her jewelry, old magazine and newspaper articles, house plans, personal letters, her beloved monumental recipe collection, and anything else she deemed to deserve protection in *her* locked metal file cabinet. None of us knew it also contained hers and Dad's *recipes* for fulfilling their wishes after their deaths, The Last Will and Testament of Francine P. Malfait and The Last Will and Testament of Roger V. Malfait. These documents were discovered when Aunt Mavis, Don and I cleaned up the upstairs *after* the eviction and about half way through our epic garage sale stint. If Rolf is suing me and raising "holy hell" based on a stolen outdated will, he deserves whatever the outcome will be.

I continue to worry about what *holy hell* means, but when the hearing date arrives, I go. Just being in the courthouse waiting for Mr. Oats to arrive is anything but relaxing.

After going through the routine metal detectors, I seat myself on one of the hard wooden benches near the front entryway and watch the bee-hive activity in the courthouse foyer. Several persons accompanied by uniformed police officers pass by in hand-cuffs and orange suits. A man in a dressy business suit, hands behind his back and hand-cuffs barely perceptible under his Fench cuffs, moves slowly between two officers, staring at the floor through tightly squinted eyes. Crying children sit with loved ones--or unloved ones. Pugnacious youthful offenders cluster in boisterous groups building up their bravado. Slicker, more experienced offenders stand less obtrusively singly or in small groups, dressed too well for the occasion and with eyes darting over every occupant in the busy entryway and occasionally over their shoulders behind themselves. I pull my hand-bag up from the bench and clutch it on my lap as I continue to over-hear bits and pieces of other people's happiness or unhappiness, the just reasoning or unjust reasoning of circumstances which bring them to this place on this day. Being here and feeling the conflicts, my own and those of others around me, is disturbing and ominous.

Mr. Oats finally rushes up with an apology for his lateness and a hurried excuse about his earlier meeting with the judge. "Come on, Betty, let me get you into a little more private space and I'll give you the details of the conference Mr. Wright and I had with the judge this morning in his private chambers."

I follow Mr. Oats, weaving through the judicial bee-hive to one of the little private courthouse conference rooms where I vent my complaint, "I hate being here in the middle of all this. I shouldn't have to be here. Rolf's words, behaviors, and now legal actions constitute harassment to me. They are libelous. Isn't there something you can do?"

Mr. Oats mumbles an iota of sympathetic understanding, retrieves one of his oversize yellow legal pads from an enormous over-filled briefcase and scratches a note on a fresh page. Saying nothing about the conference with the judge, he steps into the hallway.

Through the open door I hear Rolf in the next room, "I don't give a damn! I've been fucked over by this guy before. I can't get a fair hearing in front of him. He's prejudiced against me because of the situation before about my logging truck. He didn't treat me fair at that time, and he sure as hell ain't gonna be fair today!"

A calmer voice, probably that of Mr. Wright, whom I have not yet met, assures him, "Well, Rolf, we could file an Affidavit of Prejudice, and ask for a change of judges. We might get it. But if we got someone else today and went into a formal hearing today, we couldn't win. It would be better for you to wait."

There is a quiet lull followed by muffled discussion in the hallway between Mr. Oats and Mr. Wright. Presently Mr. Oats comes back into our conference room and announces, "Mr. Wright has convinced Rolf he can't win today, and he should keep his questions for a later time. Rolf is willing to do that, but for today he would like a key to the gate across the road to your mother's property on Whidbey."

"I don't have a key to that gate, not even for my own use. He should see the realtor or the property owner across whose property the road goes."

"Okay, I'll tell them that. But at the time of any potential sale of that property, Rolf wants a full disclosure. He wants to be sure the final sale is for Fair Market Value, and he wants to be sure you and Don don't buy it."

"Mr. Oats, one of the first phone calls I made after Mother died was to tell you to stop any proceedings regarding Don and me buying that property. Our offer to buy was purely for the purpose of having money to keep Mother in Patty's foster care."

"Yes, I know that."

"Well, we didn't want that land then, and we don't want it now. You did stop the process, didn't you?"

"Oh, yes--yes, of course. I'll tell them that."

The formal exchanges from my little conference room to Rolf's little conference room via legal counsel, to a judge someplace in the building in private chambers, and back to each of us separately carries no shred of familial love. In these moments I am alone in my tiny private court-house space with only four dull yellow walls, a bare scratched up table, and knowledge that Rolf is in a similar room just a thin wall away.

As the morning progresses we do not see each other nor talk to each other. As I stare at the walls, I perceive this is how our future will be--bare and scratched up. By noon a number of legalese huddles have occurred in the hallway following repetitious, meaningless discussions in each of our little yellow-walled cells. Rolf has lost on all six of his objections, or at least he must wait until a later date to question the issues. If I am supposed to feel some kind of sibling victory, it doesn't happen. I am miserable.

In the next weeks and months Rolf often raises questions via his at-torney regarding potential sale of the Whidbey property. I don't mind the potential buyers and all their questions--ones who want to buy, but can't get financing--or ones who want to buy but offer ridiculously low prices. I do mind Rolf's continual questioning of everything.

I plead with Mr. Oats, "Do I have to run every potential sale and all the negotiations past Rolf?"

"No, but you have to send his attorney notice of any potential sale. And if Rolf objects, he will have to go to court and state the objection."

"But, Mr. Oats, I want this settled as soon as possible. I want her prop-erty to sell. Isn't that what they want? I want this whole business to end--all of it. It's tough to try to work a real estate deal and have to notify Rolf of everything. He has objections to objections! I am concerned about the legal bills, as well. Yours is now over $5,000. Is all of this legal procedure and expense necessary?"

"Yes, but Rolf's legal debt is already more than yours. His bill to Mr. Wright is right now over $6,000. The estate will not be paying that either. He will have to pay his legal bills out of his share at the end--and Mr. Wright can't be paid until Rolf gets his."

"Well, I told you before if he keeps hassling and objecting to every-thing, maybe you should give him notice of his debt to his parents and try to collect that in behalf of the estate. Can you do anything with that at final settlement time?"

"Well, yes--but that's not too likely. You have to understand they do have a right to ask for the things they've asked for. We have to send them the notices. And if they want to object, they have to go to court on the issue. We can hang that $67,500 debt out as a red herring, but that's all it probably is.

"Yes, I know that when I stop to think about it, but I am so angry over Rolf's accusations--and the fact that he did almost nothing in the care-giving years but seems to be passing himself off as having been a live-in care-giver all those years.

"And, I get angry with me! I thought I had settled the big debt issue in my mind a long time back. Now here I am asking about it again. I repeatedly tell myself that was business between Mom and Dad and Rolf. It didn't involve me, but it's hard to think about all the guardianship years without dredging that up again."

"You do have to understand Mr. Wright is going to represent Rolf just as vigorously as I am prepared to argue in your behalf--but, sure, Mr. Wright and Rolf should be reminded of that outstanding debt against the estate."

I leave Mr. Oats' office floundering in angry frustration. My job as executor is to carry out my parents' wishes, but at this point I'm angry at everyone--Rolf, Mr. Wright, and Mr. Oats--they're all slime-balls! I feel slimy too even thinking about taking issue over the family debt. It's none of my business. Lawyers in general are annoying in their double-breasted pinstripes, carrying their oversize brief-cases and those infernal oversize yellow legal pads. That was one of Rolf's props for his oration at Mother's funeral. I suppose next, *he'll* show up at one of these hearings, having traded in his blue jeans, wide red suspenders, and hickory striped shirt for a double-breasted pin-striped suit and French cuffs!

Dear God, I'm so irrational. I hate myself. I don't want to be a greedy slime-ball, too. I'm pissed at everyone, even my deceased parents. God, why didn't they ever do any of their legal business? It's in as much a mess as their house was! Dear God, I hate my family! I hate lawyers and the whole court system! I hate this whole mess!

Oh, God, forgive me. Please help me be rational. Please guide me.

Later in the week I seek a second opinion from my own family attorney in my community. He tells me the procedure is typical. Mr. Oats seems to be up to the task. In regard to seeking payment of the family debt, he probably wouldn't advise it. The usual situation when these cases go to trial is that the judge decides such debts are to be forgiven.

I don't like this second opinion very much, but I feel better. I tell myself to be more attentive to the legal advice I'm being given and work on my own attitude.

CHAPTER 35

⎯⎯◦◦◦⎯⎯

Preparing For The Deposition

IN AUGUST, MR. Wright, Rolf's attorney, expresses to Mr. Oats that he has a few questions concerning the guardianship. He wants me to come to Ridgeview and give a deposition. After that, he says all parties should be ready to sit down together and work out a reasonable settlement.

I complain to Mr. Oats, "I don't even know what a deposition is, nor can I imagine how anything reasonable could happen with my unreasonable brother. Rolf has been telling everyone who will listen that I am a liar and a thief, and recently several different family friends and relatives have asked almost verbatim, 'What's all this Rolf's talking about? He says you and Don will do anything to get your hands on your Mom's Whidbey property. He says you all got plans to develop the whole mountain top and you don't much care how you do it'.

I continue my lamentations, "Mr. Oats, this is ludicrous. I'm trying harder than ever to maintain self-control, but I can't help reacting to these assaults. Based on all the havoc he is causing with family and friends, and because of his threats, his rage, and his vindictiveness, I don't really feel safe sitting down with him in the same room to give some deposition nor to try to work out a reasonable settlement. The presence of you and Mr. Wright in the room, and some almighty powerful judge someplace else in the building, doesn't make me feel any better."

"Betty, Rolf doesn't have to be there in person when you give the deposition and for our discussions. We can ask specifically that he not be present. Mr. Wright just needs to get some clarifications on a few things about the books. He has his own perceptions of Rolf's irrational, suspicious nature, but it's still his job to protect Rolf's interests."

"But, Mr. Oats, how many times do I have to answer and explain the books? I've presented to you, to the *ad litem* lawyer, and to the judge. I've reported on the finances several times over the years. All my actions are a matter of record."

"But Rolf has a right to ask *now.*"

"Much of the detail regarding records are in my personal journals. Do I have to share them with Mr. Wright or present them to the court?"

"No, don't bring your journals. Bring all the formal documents. One of the things Mr. Wright will question you about is the way in which the $100 per month allowance for your mother was used. He will want you to verify how that money was spent for your Mother's benefit, or he will want to know if you just put it in your bank account."

"My God, Mr. Oats, it was over three years ago the court allowed me to spend that amount of money on Mother without having to show every receipt. In the guardianship it was overwhelming to keep track of every little popsicle stick or restaurant tab. I did do that initially, and I kept all that stuff scotch-taped into my personal journals; but the court agreed that was being pretty fussy. It was determined, based on how I had spent money for her in the first two years, a hundred dollars per month was the usual miscellaneous amount and didn't need to be accounted for specifically. I can tell Mr. Wright the things I spent money on, but I can't verify specific purchases with receipts."

"You don't have to. Yes, the court did give you permission to use that designated amount to spend on your mother and receipts were not required. Don't be worrying about receipts. Just be able to tell how you spent the money."

"I do worry about all the questioning. Rolf's attorney's letter to me expresses the same kind of intimidation Rolf uses--"If your client feels that she only needs to bring what is specified, then I will take her deposition and I will issue a detailed *Subpoena Duces Tecum*, and we can proceed to do this the hard way."

"Betty, he's just doing his job. That's just legal talk. Just bring the required formal paperwork."

I am oblivious to people in the hallway and in the parking lot as I leave the attorney's office muttering to myself, "Damn--another huge copying job for me. The court has demanded this information before. Doesn't anyone ever save papers? Mr. Oats has copies of all this stuff. He acts as if it's too much of an imposition for him to dig it out. Maybe that would be expensive for his time, but isn't my time worth something? I have hundreds of business letters related to the guardianship--files upon files. This whole process is an imposition upon me, my family, my house and my storage space. I have boxes of paperwork, furniture, and commercial storage boxes in my basement. They stink like the Ridgeview house. I have boxes of personal items from the Ridgeview house which I have saved to give to Rolf. How naive I was when I started this guardianship with one big old briefcase which I thought would more than hold all of Mom and Dad's paperwork and whatever else I might accumulate to carry out their business."

Dear God, what's the use? I want to burn all this paper-work and stored junk and run away! Why don't you help me do that?

CHAPTER 36

———

Deposition Reality

IN LATE AUGUST I go to Ridgeview to give my deposition. I sit in yet another stark little courthouse conference room with the two attorneys and a court recorder. Mr. Wright asks me to start at the very beginning and give a narrative of family events that caused me to seek a guardianship. I relate the family feud and Malfaits' general mental and physical condition. He is not very familiar with this aspect of the story. It's grueling and intense for me to recall this beginning that was so long ago—it's twelve years or more. It is even more painful describing the deteriorating years of my parents, their house, the evidence of their incompetence, and eventually Rolf's physical and emotional abuse to them. My face burns. The tears spill.

Mr. Wright ignores my reactions and changes the subject, "Tell me about this $67,500 debt."

I retrieve a crumpled restaurant napkin from my pocket and labor through the details. My tears dry up and my pain turns to anger.

Mr. Wright interrupts my summary, "Wouldn't you say your Mom and Dad probably gifted him that amount?"

Before I can even respond, he flips over a page of his yellow legal pad, and continues, "Now tell me about Rolf's cooperation in the care of your parents while he was living in their house."

I suck in a breath, swallow my unvented anger, and snort out a nasal sigh. "Maybe Rolf has convinced you that he was a live-in care-taker, but that just wasn't so. He was in and out of their home through the years, but he definitely didn't live there, and he was less than cooperative in anything to do with their care. There's a pile of documentation with Adult Protective Service, Senior Community Services, and police reports indicating his unsatisfactory efforts in care-taking. These are not my opinions. These come from..."

Mr. Wright interrupts, "Tell me about the garage sales. How much money did you make? What did you do with that money? How did you compensate Rolf for his help in cleaning up the place and for his things which you sold?"

I feel like I'm being peppered by the class bully with nasty spit-wads and the teacher is out of the classroom. Mr. Oats may as well be out of the room. He is a useless, mute piece of legality, alternately studying the stains on the yellow conference walls and his folded hands in his lap.

I heave a sigh and face Mr. Wright. "My Aunt Mavis was in charge of the garage sales. This is the book she kept." I push a beat-up, water-stained red spiraled notebook across the table. "You can see which days we were open and when we all worked and what our total intake of money was. Here's Mother's checkbook, as well, showing the deposits after each sale."

It's obvious Mr. Wright's perspective on Rolf's contributions to the guardianship is the antithesis of mine. He rakes the books across the table and begins thumbing through Mother's check book matching garage sale receipts with checkbook entries. "If Aunt Mavis sold anything of Rolf's, she personally paid him and noted it in this book. I had no communication with Rolf during this time other than letters telling him of the deadline dates he had missed for removal of his personal things. My aunt delivered those letters to him. I personally sold nothing of his."

Mr. Wright leans close over the checkbook. "Oh, yes, Mrs. Alder, now here's a point I want some detailed clarification on. Why did you pay money to Don Alder and Nick Alder. That's your husband, right? And your son?"

"Yes, that's my husband and my son, both of whom have been far more helpful than any amount of money could ever compensate them for. We did almost four months of house clean-up and garage sales, and Don accumulated over two hundred and fifty hours of nasty physical labor. Sir, I probably couldn't have hired anyone to do the kinds of things that man did. Our work was mostly on weekends, and the routine usually started at 6 PM on Friday and lasted until midnight--up again at 6 AM and work until midnight Saturday. Sundays we usually worked until late afternoon, maybe 4 or 5 PM, and then we drove the three hours back to our home. Don had not been in Malfaits' home at any time during all the years of the guardianship, and my aunt and I could not do all that needed to be done. We needed the manpower, and I didn't feel I could have him work like that for nothing, but I couldn't pay the going wage for laborers either. There just wasn't money for that, and I didn't pay Don at all until I was taking care of the final settlement of Mother's bills. At that time I paid Don $1,500.00--that's less than $6.00 per hour--that's less than the minimum wage. What should I have paid someone to scrape frozen rotten blood out of old freezers, sweep up boxes full of cat and dog feces and haul away truckloads of urine-soaked newspapers and clothing?

"The work that Nick did was relevant to the two old cars, which remained on the driveway and in the front yard because DSHS suspected they were classic cars and being held back by me for their value. They were actually rusted out rotten junkers. I hired Nick to jerry-rig them and get them out of there. They had to be moved in order to even be able to open the garage door! I called several companies who dealt with junked automobiles, and each of them wanted $50 apiece to haul them away. I couldn't take care of that problem by myself; and based on what I learned from the junk yard people, I paid Nick that amount to come down and get them running and move them to the junkyard. That is the *only* time Nick was on the Malfait property during the entire guardianship period, and that was the only time he worked on the premises or was compensated for anything at all."

Mr. Wright ignores my defensive lamentations and continues scrutinizing the checkbook. "So, your logging contract was for a 50/50 split. That's not a very good deal, is it? You should have been able to get at least a 60/40 split on a logging deal, right?"

"Sir, those words sound like Rolf's words from his self-perceived expertise as a logger and a log-truck driver. In all of his working years Rolf has never managed a logging project start to finish. You need to know that Whidbey Island was totally logged in the 30's and timber nowadays on the island is not as large and it's more of a mix of fir, cedar and heavy broadleaf trees. I had the property cruised by an independent timber management consultant prior to contracting with the logger. He was a professional with thirty years experience as a timber cruiser with several major timber companies in this state. That was one of the reasons I chose the logger that I did--even though he turned out later to be a disastrous choice--his cruise was very close to the professional consultant's in board feet, and he had not known that I had anyone else do a timber cruise.

"Also, Whidbey logs have to be ferried off the west side of the island to Port Townsend, taken on a long truck haul off the north end to Port Angeles, or ferried off the south end to Everett. Any one of these options makes it more expensive to do logging on Whidbey. Considering all these things a 50/50 split at the mill was reasonable.

"I think you also have to remember the property in question had no legal access. This particular logger was able to get started by taking some of the timber out through the gravel pit. Because he had built some roads for the owners of that pit, they allowed him temporary road use, but they didn't want him to use their roads forever. I doubt any other logger could have accomplished that negotiation, considering Mother's property was otherwise land-locked.

"How many timber jobs had *you* done, Mr. Wright?"

There is an embarrassing pause before he says, "None."

"Well, where do you get those kinds of figures? I admit I didn't know jack about this type of project, but I studied carefully and sought help. I feel I did the best possible job I could, and I don't think I could have gotten 60/40."

"Tell me about the lawsuit against the logger?"

"The lawsuit doesn't have so much to do with the volume of board feet as with a particular cheating incident and questionable reforestation of the land."

"How did the logger cheat?"

"He sold logs to a place and didn't tell me. I found out and confronted him--that was for about $18,000. He admitted the deed and said he felt like a rotten heel for having done that. He had used the money for doing some equipment repair. He paid for the *misplaced* loads, and I watched very closely after that. I feel he stole six loads at the end anyway, when the price was very high on the export market. He probably got his money back, but I couldn't prove it. On the reforestation aspect, he charged $5,000 for reseeding but he didn't plant as many trees as required by state guidelines."

"What is this expense for roads? Your mother paid some $9,000 for a road. Doesn't that road benefit land which you and your husband own to the north?"

"Yes, but we paid our own road expenses separately. Our share of the cost for the road was $5,000. The determination of each party's amount was based on road uses. Mother got four road uses because she had always paid highest and best-use taxation, and her property is described as four five-acre salable parcels. We got only two road uses, even though our parcel is forty acres, because our property has been in a forest plan and by current zoning can only be sold in two salable pieces.

"When the project was completed, we each settled up on the road compensation, but I sued the logger in Mother's behalf for the unshared loads of logs and the poor reseeding of the land. I sued for $22,000, and I was awarded $17,500 of which I paid $4,500 in legal fees and collected $13,000 for Mother. I doubt that covered the total amount she should have gotten, but it was reasonable.

"This is all the related paperwork for the logging project." I shove a wobbly stack of various-sized papers across the table. "There's verification for all the things I've told you about here--receipts for logs, tickets from the mills, and copies of Mother's checkbook ledger showing deposits of timber checks."

Mr. Wright adds the papers to the accumulation of stacks on his side of the table. "Were you satisfied generally with the outcome of the timber project on your Mother's land?"

"Yes, I think I did a good job under the circumstances."

"I probably couldn't have done any better," Mr. Wright admitted quietly.

"Now tell me what this $100 per month Guardianship Reimbursement is? What was that for?"

"At the suggestion of a court-recommended counselor on guardianships, I requested this amount per month to help me with small personal expenses for Mother and to cover some legal type expenses for things like this event today." I point across the table at the paper wall between us. "I have had considerable travel expenses and as you can see, that's a lot of paper copying."

Mr. Wright glances at his paper barricade just in time to lurch sideways and catch the stack from the timber project and keep them from sliding over the edge of the table.

I ignore my secret desire for the papers. "I've written literally hundreds of letters. I've had previous presentations to the court. I've had a considerable amount of travel to Whidbey, to Everett, to Ridgeview and other places. I've had a lot of mailing, faxes, long distance calls--just the stuff for today took seven and a half hours at a copy machine, and I don't have a secretary. The Guardianship Reimbursement of $100 per month was still not enough to cover my own expenses inherent in this guardianship."

"What about the $100 per month--did you just put that in your bank account?"

"No, I did not just put that in my bank account. I had done so much nit-pick documentation of every restaurant ticket, mileage record, treats, gas, hair cuts, stamps, etc. that I asked the court to allow me that amount to spend on her per month without documentation."

"What did you do with the money?"

I did the kinds of things I just mentioned. I also bought her personal things--night gowns, tee-shirts, snow boots, a coat, hand lotion, cards, body cream, bed-pads and Depends in smaller packets for when we traveled or she came to my house, a toilet seat for our bathroom to elevate her when she visited our house, stamps, restaurant treats--a fresh-caught salmon from the Skokomish River--I don't know all the things, but I spent it for her!"

"And did anything like that salmon end up at your house?"

"Absolutely not. We bought that salmon one day on an outing when we had been watching the Indians fish, and we took it back to Patty's, and she used it there. Whenever I'd take Mother on a trip such as to Potlatch for lunch to watch the fishing or shrimping, I used her cash to buy us lunch and to refill my gas-tank, but I never took Don or my children on these jaunts. It was just Mother and me, and we usually went in the truck. She loved to ride in the truck and be up high to see."

"Where did you keep her money when you got it in cash?"

"In the pocket in the back of her checkbook and in her little change purse. When she was more able, she liked to pay for treats or flowers or things like that herself. She enjoyed that, and just carrying small amounts of money allowed her to maintain a small shred of independence."

"Did you ever feel you worked hard and a little extra would be okay for you?"

"No. My whole argument with Rolf is that Mother's assets should be used completely for *her*! They don't belong to anyone else until she is gone."

Mr. Wright begins to gather the multiple stacks of paper, more than could possibly fit in his mega-sized briefcase. "Well, I'll be going over all this material. I might have further questions later, but that's all for today."

I lean back on the hard wooden chair. I am drained. My armpits feel sticky. The room is stuffy. The phrase *further questions later* throbs in my head. Mr. Oats has been about as useful and comforting as this chair. I think both Mr. Oats and Mr. Wright are stretching this legal process out unnecessarily. I hope I have enough energy to pack up my own papers and get out of here.

A brief breath of fresh air wafts into the room as Mr. Wright departs with his giant briefcase and an unwieldy sheaf of papers clutched precariously in his free arm. All that paper work is bound to rack up more hours of attorney study time--and more questions.

Mr. Oats drops his single yellow legal pad into his own briefcase. "Well, Betty, let's get out of here. Mr. Wright will now go over all of this with Rolf in the room next door."

I force myself to pick up my own remaining stacks of papers, useless papers verifying useless things that were not asked about.

Dear God, I hate this day. I hate what Rolf is doing. He has such a know-it-all-I-could-do-it-better perspective and a lawyer who believes him, I guess. God, please help me to continue to the very end. Oh, God, I hope that doesn't mean the VERY end!

God, today's session confirmed for me that I want no further direct confrontations with Rolf. Please, God, keep us away from each other. I don't want him hollering and shouting in my face. Today I felt like his lawyer was in my face in a quieter manner but with Rolf's words--with demeaning suggestions of my inabilities and innuendos that I may have been dishonest. Why is this necessary?

Help me, oh God, to do your will!

⸺◦⟡◦⸺

CHAPTER 37

Rolf, A Frivolous Objector

In early November Mr. Oats tells me, "Rolf is still being difficult. He's off the wall. He insists you got taken in the logging contract, even after Mr. Wright shared the information from your deposition. He just feels you didn't know what you were doing."

"So what's new? He's said that all along. What does that mean now?"

"It means if we cannot sit down together and reach a fair settlement, we will have to go to trial. We will all have a court date later this month, and the judge will decide when and if there is to be a trial. At that time I'm going to try to limit them to just questions on the logging issue."

"What do I need to do to prepare for that?"

"You need to have copies of the cruise and all the papers related to the forestry project handy. We really need the forest consultant to be here in person, or at least to agree to a telephone deposition. You need copies of scale tickets, timber tax, and such."

"Mr. Oats, you know some of that is impossible, because the logger either couldn't, or wouldn't, give that stuff to us. That's how he stole loads at the end, but we weren't able to force him to give us that paperwork. His lack of paperwork was part of the lawsuit against him."

"Just bring everything you have."

Two weeks later I make the trip to Ridgeview with everything I have, including my fear, nausea, lack of confidence, and paranoia. Mr. Oats said the hearing may take two days, and as I unpack my two-day travel necessities in my motel room the phone rings. Mr. Oats' secretary tells me Rolf cannot make it to the hearing tomorrow morning, but I should meet Mr. Oats at the courthouse.

God, is this your work? Dear God, I pray your blessings for Rolf, too. I'm not sure what that means--what blessings am I asking for him? I trust you are working a bigger plan. I'm just a tiny part, and so is he. I gave up trying to reason with him personally a long time ago. I think I've even given up trying to reason with him through the system--legal, paperwork or whatever. God, I don't wish him any ill will though. I know you can still work with him; and if his not showing up tomorrow is of your doing, then I thank you that I don't have to listen to his angry vindictiveness and false accusations. If this is not your doing, then please be with Rolf. Please help us all to proceed to bring closure to the business at hand.

Thank you for purple tulips.

The next morning when I meet Mr. Oats at the courthouse, he tells me, "The good news is Judge McVey now perceives Rolf to be a frivolous objector. A late cancellation or failure to show for a court date like this is a serious error on Rolf's part. I met with the judge and Mr. Wright earlier this morning. Mr. Wright told him Rolf couldn't make it to Ridgeview because he didn't have a ride. The judge didn't think that was a very good reason. Mr. Wright told him Rolf wasn't a very reliable person. The judge's response was, "Well, send his sister down to his place to pick him up." I, of course, wasn't about to have him direct you to do that. Then the judge told Mr. Wright to drive down to New Castle and pick him up. Mr. Wright said he didn't have time to provide that kind of personal service for his clients."

"Mr. Oats, I understand his not having that kind of time, but neither do I. I've already traveled over three hours and stayed overnight in a motel to do this hearing. So what do we do now?"

"Well, it probably turned out just as well for you. The judge said he had heard enough of the situation to decide today there are to be no other questions raised by Rolf regarding the guardianship accounting at this time. And, in the future Rolf will no longer be able to object or question the sale of your mother's property. However, he still should have opportunity to have his questions answered regarding the timber project. And he should have a right to seek the answers to those questions in person in court with his counsel present. The judge said he can exercise this right at the time of a final estate accounting."

"That means when Mother's Whidbey land is sold--when everything is finished, right? That means another hearing or a trial, right?"

"Yes. Rolf will raise no further questions until a final trial day in court."

"But, Mr. Oats, that could be tomorrow--that could be next summer--or that could be years from now."

"Yes, that is correct. Rolf has a right to question, but he will have to wait until the day or days of the estate settlement in court."

"But Mother's will said I have a right to settle her business without obstruction."

"Yes, you have a right to settle her business, but Rolf has a right to question. It's your obligation to answer."

"Is all of this at my time and expense?"

"Legal expenses of the guardianship are expenses of the estate. Expenses of probate come from the estate. So, in fact, Rolf will pay half of my expenses, as they come off the top of the settlement. Then Rolf will pay Mr. Wright from his half of the estate settlement. The actual check will be made out to Mr. Wright *and* Rolf jointly. So far Mr. Wright has received nothing from Rolf. The best possible force to bring this estate to closure would be for her land to sell today and for there to be money in the bank. Mr. Wright would really be antsy then."

I'm not totally stupid. These two pin-stripers have obviously been talking about their billings and payments, or lack of payment. I don't care if they ever get paid. I've accomplished what I felt obligated to do in the care of Mom and Dad, and I wasn't expecting to be paid for it. But I am so tired, and I had not anticipated this extended time and these additional tasks! I don't know if there's enough of me left to do this!

"Mr. Oats, what if I just walk away?"

"You mean now--today?"

"Yes."

"The court will have to appoint another executor in order to conclude business."

"Isn't there some point at which someone besides me realizes Rolf is mentally unstable and this kind of action is ludicrous?"

"Yes, *I* realize that. Part of today was to get the judge to understand that. I personally think Rolf is mentally unbalanced. He's mean and vindictive. And he may even be dangerous."

"Did you express that today when you were with the judge?"

"No, that couldn't be part of today because Rolf was not present *with* Mr. Wright. I can't talk in that manner, even though those points are fairly evident in the recorded deposition. I can't influence the judge when the other party is not present. He would have just waved me off."

"So what is your advice?"

"Annotate all your time and expense. Keep me informed of the progress you make with any potential buyers for the Whidbey property. You will not be called here again until a final accounting and settlement of this estate. Today was an important step to establishing Rolf as an obstructive, frivolous objector. You must keep proceeding and you must give Rolf all his chances. But for now any questions Rolf may have are deferred until the time of a trial. He may not ask anything else until then."

Dear God, I hope so. This stuff of today is evil from someone I don't know! I don't even know if it's all Rolf's doing. Do I have "pinstripe paranoia" too? Please help me, God. Help me get this completely over with!

CHAPTER 38

The Trial

It's June, 1997, when Don and I make the trip to Ridgeview for the final Malfait estate trial. It's been two and a half years since Mother died. It's been fourteen years since this family saga began. I hope these time frames are not an omen for the length of the trial. I am nervous and nauseous, but I steady myself with the belief that this *has* to be the end of this family mess.

Don and I arrive at the courthouse, get ourselves and our briefcases and boxes of paperwork through the scanner without incident. We meet Mr. Oats in the lobby. I feel numb, immune to the surrounding aura of other people's personal troubles. I am weighted down by my own concerns. The three of us make our way to the appropriate courtroom. Rolf and his lawyer are huddled at one end of a long dark mahogany table that spans the width of the room, each of them with their oversize legal pads spread out on the table. Mr. Oats and I take the obvious place at the other end of the table, deposit our briefcases and boxes of papers. Don seats himself on a bench behind us. Rolf's truck-driving friend Mike is seated in the last row near the door. A court recorder slips in from a side door at the front of the room and takes her place at a prominent desk on a raised platform slightly higher than our table.

Shortly a be-speckled, black-robed judge, whom I assume from previous paperwork to be Judge McVey, enters from a side door. We all rise at a command from the uniformed bailiff who entered the court room behind the judge. The judge seats himself at a huge dominating desk on a level considerably higher than the desk of the court recorder.

I am asked to testify first, and I take my seat in the witness chair, boxed in securely on the platform at the same level with the court recorder. The swearing in procedure occurs as I expected, though my only experience is television-based. In the same monotonous voice used at the deposition, Mr. Wright asks me to again explain the family events which caused me to seek a guardianship.

I barely begin my narrative when Rolf starts coughing--loud, chunky, distracting hacks. When the coughing stops, I resume my story for another few sentences. Rolf has another coughing siege. Momentarily I think he's faking, but the color of his face, and the wheezing efforts after each episode are scary. He looks especially haggard, eerie, unkempt.

When the coughing occurs a third time, the judge decides Rolf is unwell, and he should take the stand and get his story over with.

The necessary changes are made, but I'm thinking if he is as unwell as he sounds, he should leave and go get medical attention.

Between labored wheezing and coughing, Rolf, led by Mr. Wright, creates a long rambling dissertation of his own background, complete with his usual "poor-me-persona" and his turns of bad luck because of the Mt. St. Helens eruption, loss of his logging truck, lack of jobs, and subsequent financial stress. The coughing subsides as Rolf speaks authoritatively about his logging experience and expertise, his informal timber cruise of the Malfait property, and a highly embellished description of the potential timber harvest that should have happened on that property.

Rolf is dressed as if he came directly from the woods after doing his timber cruise, complete with black and white striped hickory shirt, cut-off dirty blue jeans and the well-worn Romeos with heavy gray wool socks sagging down into them. If I didn't know him, I would be inclined to accept his expertise.

My silent angry mental muttering is shattered by another coughing and wheezing spree. Judge Mcvey dismisses court for a ten minute break and expresses his hope this will allow Rolf to calm his coughing.

Court proceedings resume, but Rolf does not return. We can all hear him in the hallway area. There is no letup in the uncontrollable deep, throaty hacking.

I am asked to resume the witness stand and continue my narrative. I try to do that, but I am abruptly interrupted by Rolf's attorney.

"Your Honor, I'd like to have the witness move to more specific things. My client is very ill this morning. The courthouse attendant monitoring the metal detector gate has called for emergency help to check him out. His friend Mike is going to drive him to the hospital. It's pretty obvious there was, and is, a substantial lack of communication between Rolf and his sister. Betty is the Personal Representative of their mother's estate, and Rolf has a number of questions relevant to that. I would offer that the personal representative of this estate made some financial mistakes, and I'd like to get right to those issues."

My brow wrinkles and I squint toward Mr. Oats, but I am silent. *Rolf got to tell his whole story. Don't I get to tell mine? What mistakes? Mr. Oats, you said my budget book and checking/savings were all in order. The court has validated them repeatedly.*

The judge nods approval to Mr. Wright, who walks over near me in my secured witness chair and waves a sheaf of papers. "According to Court File 43, you should have had a blocked bank account. You did pay a bill of $1500 to yourself, did you not?"

"Yes, but that was to pay Patty, because Mother had no more money of her..."

"That's all we need to know, because we already know it should have been a blocked account."

My brain is silently churning. *What's a blocked account? Didn't I do that? I'm the only one who can use those accounts. Mr. Oats told me to pay all the outstanding bills before coming to trial, and that $1500 was the $500/month Don and I paid for three months to make up the difference when Mother's bank funds ran out in November before she died in January. We needed to supplement her income in order to keep her in foster care, and she had no other money. It was a bill to the estate just like any other bill. I didn't take anything. I paid a bill. Mr. Wright, you made it sound as if I am a thief.*

I look at the judge, "May I respond to that further?"

Mr. Wright barks at me, "No, you've already said you paid $1500 dollars to yourself, and the court record shows it should have been a blocked account. Now, let's go on to your Mother's budget book."

I look helplessly at the judge, but he doesn't look at me. Mr. Oats shuffles his legal pad pages on the table and says nothing.

Mr. Wright pounds on with questions to me on the budget book, the bank account, the timber project, then back to the $100/month spent for Mother. "When you bought tee shirts for your Mother, did you pay cash? Did you also buy tee shirts and pay by check?"

"Sometimes if we went shopping, we..."

"Did you buy Depends with her cash? Were those the same Depends as those indicated in the checkbook? Were you paying by cash and by check for the same items?"

"No, they were different, but..."

"What was the $100/month Guardianship Reimbursement for?"

The pace and tone of his questions don't give me opportunity to explain there were different tee shirts--or Depends by check were the ones we purchased by the case at Costco, huge boxes three feet by three feet with several hundred pads. Depends by cash were small packets for a visit to our house or ones to stow in the truck for our short afternoon trips. The court approved the $100/month Guardianship Reimbursement. Before I can answer anything on either subject, Mr. Wright is on to something else.

Judge McVey commands me, "Answer the question, please."

"I don't know which question you mean..."

Without waiting to clarify which question and ignoring the judge's command to me to answer *the* question, Mr. Wright proceeds, "I see you have a charge here for copying expenses. Did you have a secretary do this, or did you pay yourself? It appears you paid yourself."

"No I don't have a secretary. No, I didn't pay myself."

The tears well up. I face the judge and burst forth sobbing, "Your Honor, I don't know who I'm supposed to be answering, Mr. Wright, Mr. Oats, or you. Everyone is asking questions all at once or barking commands. I can't even think straight, and no one is letting me explain."

Mr. Wright speaks up immediately, "Your Honor, I move for a break. That will give me a chance to copy this checkbook ledger. I've not been provided with this before."

I want to scream. Yes, you have--at the deposition--and I would have copied the whole thing for you again if you had asked. It wouldn't have added that much more to my seven and a half hours of copying. Now, you're

going to run out and do it at $150 per hour, but you have already embar-
rassed and belittled me for wanting to account for my time at a copy machine
based on a school secretary's wage. I sit frozen, inept--in silent, frustrated
rage.

The judge calls for a lunch break. Don and I escape to a cramped little cafeteria in the basement of the courthouse. I don't know what we ate.

Rolf does not return for the afternoon session, and we learn he is at the hospital. The judge asks us to re-convene in his chambers.

We gather our papers and follow his request.

As everyone settles into this smaller, more private setting, Mr. Oats immediately completes a conference phone call to the forest management consultant I employed for Mother's timber project.

After appropriate introductions are made, Mr. Wright gives the forest consultant a summary of Rolf's morning testimony describing Mother's property and Rolf's perception of the potential timber on it. He then asks, "Is that pretty much the kind of timber stand which you found to be on the Malfait property?"

The forest expert responds immediately, "There are no stands of timber on all of Whidbey Island as large as you just described. The property in question is in the middle of the island, and there have never been trees that size on that part of the island. Even when the property was first logged in the thirties, the timber wasn't that large."

Mr. Wright continues, "Considering the timber that was harvested, was a 50/50 split a reasonable deal?"

"Yes, a 50/50 split is reasonable for timber harvest on all of Whidbey, based on the less desirable timber mixes and restricted growth due to climate and soil conditions. If you looked at records for logging on the whole island, 50/50 splits have been the historical norm. There can be variation, of course, based on transportation expenses, site preparation, difficulties in falling trees, yarding, bucking, roads, and such."

"Would you say the timber cruises for this land were accurate?"

"Yes, those cruises are probably pretty accurate, but they were walk-throughs, so they were conservative."

"The paper I have before me is your cruise. It indicates there should have been 202,000 board feet on the Malfait property. The actual harvest was 303,000 board feet. Is that difference normal?"

"That is not unusual. As I told you, walk-through cruises are conservative. If my cruise said 202,000 board feet, and the project actually resulted in 303,000 board feet, that was an excellent harvest. That would have been a very thorough harvest."

"Could that harvest have netted $50,000 to the owner?"

"From that harvest on that particular piece of land, and based on the rates at that time, to have gotten $50,000 net to the owner was not possible. You would have done very well to have netted $50,000 to <u>both</u> the logger and the owner. Anything more than that you would have had to sweep the forest floor with a broom and get every possible penny you could get off of the timber <u>and</u> the chips."

I feel a small sense of quiet confidence. *I know I did a good job, whether Rolf is in this room to hear this or not. Mother's half of the split was $28,718.83, and that doesn't include the amount from suing the logger. Rolf couldn't have done any better on this project--and neither could Mr. Wright1!*

The timber consultant call ends, and another conference call is immediately placed to the lawyer who handled the road access settlement and the suit against the logger.

"Yes, Malfaits and Alders each absolutely paid for their own road and legal expenses. In fact, the Alders, who own the north forty acres also granted, without any reimbursement to themselves, a strip of property thirty feet wide and six hundred and fifty feet long in order to secure the legal access to the Malfait property, which was otherwise land-locked. That was completely voluntary on their part. The cost of the road was a cost to both parties and was based on tax records. Malfaits had always paid highest and best use taxes on their twenty acres, so they got four road uses. The Alders' forty acre parcel had been in a forest program with reduced taxes, so they got only two road uses. Expenses for the access and legal expenses were based on this same formula--the cost to Malfait was $9,000 and to Alder was $4,700."

Mr. Wright asks, "Was the Malfait property accessible for logging without having to build a road?"

"No, sir, it was not. The gravel pit owners allowed some loads to be removed over a piece of their road on the south end because a ravine separated that part of the property, but they didn't want log trucks running in and out over their property for the whole logging job. In fact, they constructed a berm across the property at that point, and no other trucks were allowed to cross their land. By that time the logger and Mrs. Alder had worked out a deal with land owners on the west side of the property to complete the logging operation, and in that process Mrs. Alder negotiated further for a permanent legal access to both Alder and Malfait properties."

"Was the logger professional and honest in his dealings?"

"The logger for the Malfait project appears to have been less than perfect with records--and less than honest. It was evident that he did co-mingle loads. He was very difficult to work with and hard to collect from. It was cost effective to settle rather than litigate. Your client wanted $22,000--the logger offered $11,850. We settled for $17,500. In my estimation that was a fair settlement."

I feel some sense of success. I did give the correct details. Both Mr. Oats and Mr. Wright are jotting notes furiously on their infamous legal pads. Mr. Oats expresses a brief thank you to the attorney for his cooperation in the telephone conference, but no one makes any comments about previous courtroom testimony.

Judge McVey, seated behind his huge immaculate desk made no notes nor asked any questions. He is no longer dressed in his official black robe, but even in a soft Mr. Rogers cardigan, he is still in command. He leans toward Mr. Oats, "Thank you for arranging these informative calls. Court will resume in the same courtroom tomorrow morning at 9:00 AM." He stands and leaves. We all exit his chambers without any communication.

CHAPTER 39

The Trial, Day 2

THE SECOND DAY of the trial, everyone arrives about the same time and seats themselves in the same positions as the previous day. Rolf is present and looks somewhat better. I am asked to resume the stand. Mr. Wright waves an official document with a grandiose flourish and approaches the witness stand. "I would like to start today with questions about Court File 43. The Personal Representative seemed to have been confused by this document yesterday."

He hands me the three page stapled packet. "Would you look over this file and tell us if you have read it before."

"Yes, I've read this before, but I didn't recognize it when you just referred to it as Court File 43. It's longer than I thought."

"You seemed to have not recognized it yesterday. This is the court order requiring a blind trust. Please read it."

The loose pages rattle in my shaking hands as I try to read. *Oh God, is this the financial mistake? Where did this come from? Could I have really missed this? I feel like a fool--years of integrity and careful matching and balancing doesn't matter. Having spent Mother's money only for Mother is meaningless. Having every penny accounted for and in the bank account without ever touching it for myself for any purpose except to pay a debt which I thought I was paying legitimately. None of that matters.*

I answer, "Yes, I have read this before, but I don't see where I made a mistake. I'm not sure about this third page."

"What does page three say? Read it."

"It's a single sentence requiring a blind trust. I don't know for sure what a blind trust is. Yesterday you said a blocked checking account, and I thought I had..."

Mr. Wright's voice is quietly victorious. "Thank you. That will be all."

Rolf is called to the witness stand and swears to tell the truth, the whole truth and nothing but the truth. He immediately turns toward the judge. "I beg Your Honor's forgiveness for yesterday. I been pretty stressed lately, and you know how a person can catch any number of kinds of viruses when they're under stress. I guess I pretty well scared everyone yesterday, including all the folks out in the waiting area. I was a very sick man, but my friend Mike, there, got me to the hospital and they pumped fluid out of my lungs and filled me up pretty good with antibiotics--and, well--here I am."

Even Mr. Wright looks slightly embarrassed at the ingratiating emoting as he begins to address Rolf. "Now, Mr. Malfait, you've got some things you want to say about the alleged family debt in question today. Tell us about that debt."

"Yeah, well, I've worked a lot of years, and I've worked hard as a logger and as a log truck driver, and then a long-haul trucker. It wasn't always easy, and I got into a little difficulty when old Mt. St. Helens blew. That pretty well wiped out all of us who were working in logging."

Mr. Wright guides the narration, "Tell us the purpose of the family debt."

"Yeah, well like I was sayin', I got pretty well wiped out financially. That debt was incurred by me and my folks in order for me to consolidate my debts and help me get back on my feet."

"Did you make payments on this loan?"

"Yes, when I could."

"How much was the amount?"

"It was $468 per month, as I recall."

"How did you make payments?"

"Cash--I always pay in cash."

"Do you have a bank account?"

"No. No, I don't. I don't trust banks after a bad experience a few years back."

"Now, Mr. Malfait, the loan started in 1980. You said in your deposition that the amount was $25,000. Is that correct?"

"That's the amount—it's whatever the paperwork says it is."

"Tell us about your financial difficulties."

"Yeah, well, to put it bluntly I went broke in '84. Times was really hard. My friend Mike, there, he taught me to do long-haul driving. I drove until August of '88 pretty regular. As a matter of fact, along about that time in a conversation with my folks--in front of Mike, I might add--they said they would buy me a truck. In fact, the folks said they would sell the Whidbey Island property and buy me a truck. Mike, over there, could testify to that."

"Now, Rolf, after 1988 did you make any payments on the loan?"

The question was simple enough, but Rolf's answer was, "Well, since that time I've worked at jobs here and there. There's some guys around this community who still owe me for work I've done for them."

Mr. Wright ignores the lack of an answer to his question and moves to another subject. "Now, Mr. Malfait, you have a suspicion that the logging project on the Malfait property was not very well done. Tell us about that."

"Well now, I've got more than a suspicion--it was very poorly done! I myself have worked in the woods for thirty-five years. I hauled for seven years. I know what I'm talkin' about. The paperwork for Mom's timber job says they got over 303,000 board feet of timber off that land. That's questionable. I walked through that stand myself in 1979--no, that was '76--or '74. They say eighty-seven loads come off there. Well, I talked to a guy by the name of Norville Buetner up there on the island in the County Assessor's Office, and he said--and I quote, "We have *records* of eighty-seven loads, but just between you and me, there was probably twelve or so loads that went off and were not counted."

Judge McVey lifted his sagging chin, unlaced his idle fingers, and straightened up on his bench. Peering down at Rolf he asks, "Mr. Malfait, was this information from a formal timber cruise?"

"Well, I got a friend who's pretty astute at timber cruising, and he said they should have grossed $75,000--that should'a been easily possible from that particular twenty acre stand of timber."

Mr. Oats finally seems to awaken and offers weakly, "Objection."

Judge McVey looks steadily at Rolf, "Your friend's word cannot be part of this record, Mr. Malfait."

Mr. Wright resumes, "Did your sister ever ask you for your expertise in this logging operation?"

"No."

"Do you have anything else you would like to question today, Mr. Malfait?"

"Yes, I have some real reservation about the real estate property values as stated in the court records."

"Were the property values wrong?"

"Yes."

"Tell us in your opinion what is wrong with the values?"

Rolf launches into a continuation of his narrative on the timber project rather than speaking about real estate values. "A lot of the timber come right out through the gravel pit. There was no road required for that. The logging operation fell flat on its face. Then, as I've been told, there was a payment of $9,000 for a road. That don't make no sense when they already had a road to use. I don't see why Mom should be paying for Don and Betty's road."

I sit tight-lipped wondering, *Who's going to correct his unrelated answer to real estate values? If they're going to let you keep rattling on, who's going to correct your misperception about the amounts of money for the road? You missed the conference yesterday in the judge's chambers when the attorney revealed that the $9,000 was payment for the access over private property other than the gravel pit, as the gravel pit road was only for temporary use. You missed knowing Don and I paid our share of the road in cash and separately from Mother's share, and we gave her free of charge access over our land. Why isn't anyone stopping you with all this misinformation?*

"Now on top of that Don and Betty paid themselves $1500. They shouldn't be getting nothin'."

Rolf, that money has nothing to do with logging, the road, or real estate values. I guess no one is going to stop you or correct you about the $1500 reimbursement for Mother's foster care for the months after her funds ran out. Maybe Mr. Oats will clarify these points later when we have our turn--if we ever have a turn.

Finally Mr. Wright urges Rolf back to the subject of property value, "Rolf, how was the property value in error?"

"It seems to me that after the property was logged, the appraisal was pretty low."

Mr. Wright guides him again, "Was there another access to the Malfait property?"

"Yes."

"And what was that?"

"The other access was via the Greenwich Sand and Gravel Pit. The logger could have just pulled in to Mom's property over the gravel pit property, backed a truck up to the loading dock and loaded up and taken it right back out over gravel pit property. All logs could have gone out through that pit. Those neighbors next to Mom's property obviously got their pockets cleaned by the same logger. I seen this set-up many a time. I know what them guys do."

Why doesn't Mr. Oats or the judge stop this foolishness? Why doesn't someone tell him about the phone calls in the judge's chambers yesterday?

Rolf drones on, "Now, on this land deal--these appraisals--the low appraisal was $70,000, but the high appraisal was $110,000. Don and Betty, there--they offered $77,000. That was no good at all. They were just tryin' to get some cheap land."

Here we go again. The appraisals were well documented in letters to the attorney in Ridgeview and the court. The confusion in the appraisals was because the one for $110,000 was done while the timber was on the land, and the one for $70,000 assumed there was no timber on the land. When Don and I made an offer on the land, we petitioned the court and ask them to make a fair determination between these two prices. The "Fair Market Value" was decided by simply dividing the $40,000 difference between the two appraisals. That made the value around $90,000. Our offer for $77,000 was a bit low but in the ballpark. Technically, we should have offered 90% of the FMV, or $81,000. We didn't know how much longer we would be paying the $500.00 per month to keep Mother in Patty's foster care before a sale of the land to us might be finalized. Our offer had seemed reasonable.

Rolf shifts to a new topic. "Then, you know, Mom, she died, and there wasn't any will. Then, all of a sudden when I apply for a shared executorship--then suddenly a new will appears."

Dear God, how much longer can this go on? At least you know it wasn't suddenly--and it wasn't new. There was always a will. It just wasn't the missing one from the metal box. Oh, God, what is happening here?

"Then the next thing I know Betty has listed the property on the open market for $120,000. If that's the appraised value, that's what they should'a been offering if they wanted to buy it."

Why doesn't someone explain it was listed high on the open market to allow some possible negotiating room. Anticipating a realtor fee of about $12,000 might net an amount pretty close to the high appraisal originally. No one mentions that was a great price to get since it was sold without the timber.

Mr. Oats asks for no clarification. He makes no objections.

I have a thousand questions and even more objections, but I am not asked to speak.

Mr. Wright's voice breaks in, "Do you have any other objections to personal property assets of the Malfait estate?"

"Yeah, as a matter of fact, I do. I got some objections about jewelry and personal items. I went through the house in November, 1991--and I mean drawer by drawer. I know what was there. It was at that time I rescued a plastic sack and took it with me--a sack that held insurance policies. There was also four or five sacks of mint coins--you know, brand new uncirculated coins--four or five bags of 'em."

I lean over and whisper to Mr. Oats, "In his deposition he said four or five transparent recipe boxes--but actually there weren't *any* uncirculated minted coins--sacks or recipe boxes. Such items just weren't there."

Mr. Oats scribbles a note but says nothing. He seems to be concentrating on Rolf's rambling.

"Another thing--I had an Alaskan jade and pearl necklace in one of those drawers at that time. It's a very valuable piece. And there was a small baggie with one diamond ear ring--a nice half carat diamond."

I lean over and whisper again. "The jade and pearl necklace is his--it was a gift to Mother. It wasn't in any of the drawers as he is describing, but it was in her file cabinet upstairs. I put it in a box of personal items that belonged to Mom and Dad and which I held out from garage sales for Rolf--things like family pictures, dishes, books, saws, cameras, tools, ceramics made by Mother. I told you about the box. The stuff is already boxed up for him. His necklace is there."

Rolf glares at me as if my whispering is bothering his testimony.

"I'd guess my sister Betty, there, is in possession of that necklace *and* the diamond ear ring."

I stare blankly at Rolf without comment. *Yes, I know about the necklace, but there was no plastic baggie with a diamond ear ring. I do know the story though. Mother told of Rolf getting angry with her for wearing only one ear ring after losing the other one. He made her give him the one because he said she looked like a damned hippie wearing only one. Who knows where that ear-ring might be? In all these years I've never touched it.*

"Yeah, my sister Betty, there, she'd best know where that stuff is. She *has* the stuff, I'm sure--and the reason I know that is that I gave that plastic bag with all those items in it directly to her. No one else was there at the time I gave them to her, but she knows I gave it to her."

I am barely able to breathe. *Liar, liar! The only plastic bag you've ever handed to me was in front of Aunt Mavis, and it contained Dad's life insurance policies. I had to beg and plead for them, and I suspect you only did it because Mavis was there and she also begged you to return the policies. Besides, the day of your deposition you said you returned them to me in the presence of Aunt Mavis and your friend Mike. That wasn't truthful then, and it isn't truthful today. You also said it included four or five recipe boxes full of minted coins. What is your story? Do you invent these tales as you go along?*

I whisper desperately to Mr. Oats, "Do we have to let him tell such lies? You know none of this is true. That's not even what he said in his deposition."

Mr. Oats answers back, "It's not our turn to ask questions at this time. Were those bags or boxes of coins?"

"In his deposition he said four or five transparent plastic recipe boxes of coins, but those things were not in those closets and drawers when we cleaned out the house. Now he's saying bagsful of coins. Mr. Oats, none of what he is saying is true! Don't you hear what he's saying?"

Oh, God, I don't believe this. I don't think anyone is listening. Don't I get a turn? Do Mr. Wright and Rolf both get to smear me like this and my own counsel is going to make no response. God, you know I didn't take those things. Are you here in all of this somewhere? This is all wrong. I feel as if I'm in the same demented Malfait blender of years past. This is crazy!

There is a lull and a shuffling of paper. In a quiet voice, Mr. Wright questions, "Let's go back to the timber deal, Mr. Malfait. According to my notes there were possibly five loads of alder left on the property. What do you think of that?"

Rolf clears his throat, straightens up in the witness chair and crosses his arms over his chest glaring angrily in my direction. "Well, if you ask me, it shows gullibility, naiveness, and incompetence."

"Thank you, Mr. Malfait. Your witness."

Mr. Oats grabs his yellow pad, pages fluttering. He leans over and mutters in my direction, "Don't worry about all this. That was the appropriate time for him to ask Rolf things like that. Now it's our turn."

Rolf is still sitting in the witness stand with his arms crossed and a smirk playing at his lips gloating over his testimony. I sit at the lawyer's table, feeling limp, beaten. Mr. Oats is striding toward the witness stand, thumbing the pages of the big yellow pad. Maybe this is where he makes the picture come into focus. Maybe this is where truth comes out.

"Mr. Malfait, what year did you walk the property?"

"I walked it in 1979. Dick Vetter, a friend of mine and a reputable timber consultant here in town, he walked it again in 1980."

"Mr. Malfait, the guardianship was established in 1990. Where were you at that time?"

"I was basically at the house--at 516."

"It was evident at that time that your folks were displaying symptoms of Alzheimer's. What kinds of signs did *you* note?"

"Well, there was incontinence--Mom, she was pretty bad about that--and they both had problems with feces drippings on the floor and on themselves."

"What did you do to help with that situation?"

"Well, I figured Betty was the guardian--she should take care of that!"

"Please tell us what did *you* do to help?"

"I mowed lawns. I trimmed brush. I moved the junk cars on the front drive."

"Were you paid?"

"No."

"At the time your father had the stroke, what did you *do*?"

"Well, Dad had that stroke, and he was layin' in the floor. Mom, she finally got him up into bed, but then she waited for me to get home from a trucking job and take him to the hospital. In '90 Dad was in the nursing home. At that time I drove log truck. I took local jobs. That was about the time I started to drive for old Curtie Leffer."

"During that time what services did you provide for your parents?"

"Like I said, I mowed lawns. I cleaned out that back shop by the ally. I cleaned that out completely--and I completely cleaned out the garage, too."

"Mr. Malfait, after February, 1991, and your father's death, what services did you provide to your mother?"

"Well..."

"Did you provide any services?"

Well, Betty was in charge."

"Did you visit?"

"Yeah, I visited Mom three or four times when she was on Whidbey."

"Did you visit your mom when she was on the mainland later?"

"Oh, yeah--I visited her two or three times at Patty's, but then from May, 1992, to December, 1993, I was in Bristol Bay, Alaska. I couldn't very well visit from there. I called frequently though."

Dear God, you know these are lies, too. He took double and triple pay for any work he ever did. He didn't do all that cleaning--Don did it. He didn't move those old junker cars. I hired Nick to do it. He called once, and he visited once on Whidbey when Mother was at Janice's. And he visited once on the mainland when Mother was at Patty's.

God, help. This is not fair! This is not justice! God, where are you?

"During the time you were in the home at 516, did you get paid for your work?"

"Like I said, I didn't get no pay."

"Did you pay rent?"

"No, Mom said that was not required."

Mr. Oats closed the flapping pages of his yellow legal pad and turned to the judge, "Your Honor, I'm going to consider at the time of the sale of the Malfait house in Ridgeview that the remainder of Mr. Malfait's debt was $7,737.26. That outstanding debt should be collectible to the estate."

Judge McVey suddenly sits upright as if he has been jolted by an invisible lightning bolt. He pushes his own papers around and begins to scribble and call out a mumble-jumble of numbers--amounts that have a vague semblance to parts of the testimony of the past two days. The numbers are juggled faster than I can possibly keep up. Both lawyers are adding columns of figures furiously. The judge is intent on his own figuring, muttering as he continues scrawling. Suddenly he announces, "There!"

Both lawyers are seated at their respective tables, figuring and scratching wildly on the yellow legal pads.

Mr. Wright glances up. "Do I have time for rebuttal?"

The judge's voice is decisive, "No, there will be no rebuttals."

The judge turns toward our table, "Does the Personal Representative of the estate have her checkbook here in the courtroom?"

I scramble through my tattered straw bag and lay the checkbook on the table.

"Fine. I direct you to write a check to the relative specifically named in the will as Mavis Clarke, the deceased's sister, for $1,000. I further instruct you to keep out $2,000 for the purpose of filing estate taxes--then simply divide the remaining amount in two checks. The most recent will of Francine Pauline Malfait says *share and share alike*, and in my estimation that will fulfill the wishes of the deceased. I will not expect either party to appeal this decision, because if you do, I will simply arrive at the same finding. Make the one check payable to Mr. Malfait *and* his attorney, Mr. Wright. Make the other check payable to yourself. Do this right now while you are in the court room and leave the checks with the Court Recorder. She will get them to the correct parties.

"Case dismissed!"

The judge rises and steps back. Looking at Mr. Oats he mumbles, "Oops."

I look at the judge. He quickly looks away. I look at Mr. Oats, but his head remains bent over his yellow pad.

Oops?" I wonder. *"Oops?"*

Mr. Wright is grumbling aloud, "That's not right for Rolf to have to pay half of his sister's legal expenses and all of his own."

Mr. Oats continues to add and re-add a column of numbers. "Let me be sure this is correct."

The judge approaches our table, glares at both mumbling lawyers, silencing them temporarily. He hands Mr. Oats his hand-scribbled order, speaks to neither one of them, and certainly not to me. He turns and quickly walks back across the courtroom, his black robe swirling about him with each hurried step. The baliff opens the door for him, and he disappears into his chambers, the baliff following him..

I sit frozen in disbelief.

Is it over? Is that it?

Dear God, is it really over? Thank you--I think?

I write the checks as the judge ordered, watching my trembling hand perform the task as if it is not connected to my body. I walk numbly to the Court Recorder's desk and reach upward to place the checks in her extended hand.

CHAPTER 40

⸎

Debriefing With Mr. Oats

In Other Words, "The Justice System Sucks!

MR. OATS GATHERS all of our huge stacks of futile documents and notes and dumps them haphazardly into two large cardboard boxes. He and Don each take one box, and I follow carrying Mother's tattered, straw briefcase as our awkward caravan edges sidewise around Rolf, who is still slouched in his chair with his back to us even though his attorney has left the courtroom. We exit the courtroom, follow a hallway a short distance and then proceed through a doorway into a back hallway and duck into a small conference room.

Mr. Oats drops the heavy box and his briefcase on the table. "Betty, we need to debrief a bit." He turns and shakes my hand, "We made it. I want you to know what a wonderful job I think you have done over all these years. It's been over ten years, as I recall. You need to know I understand how you felt today, but Rolf had to have his chance to speak. You know I believe *your* story, and I think you did a wonderful job the whole way along."

Mr. Oats' comfort and compliments ring hollow. I don't need affirmation from someone whom I considered let me down at the most crucial time. Mr. Oat's contribution to the last two days was almost nil.

My own words are about as meaningless as his, "There were no winners here today. Justice wasn't served. Rolf lied and lied. No one stopped him. This whole trial thing was a sham--an exercise in futility!"

"Betty, Judge McVey had unwavering confidence in your work and your integrity. Even though you made a couple of little mistakes in accounting methods, he knew you were honest and truthful."

307

I feel my shoulders slump. "It didn't feel as if he knew."

My inner-voice is screaming, *Bullshit! I don't need confidence in my integrity from the judge, nor from you, Mr. Oats! I know what I've been through. I know who did what. I might feel better if you, Mr. Oats, would at least admit that you may have made a mistake regarding the third page to Court File 43. You never defined a blocked account or a blind trust or whatever it was that was required. You told me I had the bank account and the checkbook set up right. The court approved that setup for years. I still don't even know what the error was. I might feel better if you had at least tried to object more than one feeble time during this whole two-day circus. I might feel better if I had gotten to express my story.*

"Mr. Oats, it wasn't fair—it wasn't right--that I had to sit there and listen to Rolf's lies over and over--to allow him to publicly degrade me and all my efforts. His words became the public record. I never had a chance to tell how I felt or to dispute his assertions. I didn't get to tell the judge my story."

"You did have opportunity to express your story. You told your story."

"No, I didn't. I for sure did not have equal time, and what I did get to tell was in incoherent bits and pieces. I was constantly interrupted by coughing, concern for emergency treatment for Rolf, concern for Rolf's financial instability, and Mr. Wright skipping from one topic to another faster than I could mentally shift gears. It just wasn't right--it wasn't fair."

"It didn't matter if your story was disjointed and in untimely bits and pieces. The judge got it. He knew what was going on. Rolf's mental, social or psychological condition was really not relevant to the settling of the will, which stated "share and share alike." Yes, Mr. Wright emphasized Rolf's financial stresses and the situation of him about to lose all his personal things in storage--and, yes, he stressed Rolf's health issues--and, yes, Rolf's poor health was an interruption to the hearing process--but none of that really had any bearing on the final outcome."

"And, Mr. Oats, what was the final outcome? What about the judge's last word in the courtroom--the big *Oops* as he looked at you? What did that mean?"

Mr. Oats looks at me blankly. "I didn't hear any *Oops*."

"He looked right at you and said, "Oops!"

"I didn't hear anything like that. The judge didn't say *anything* to me."
My mouth is agape. My shoulders sag even further.

Yeah, right--Mr. Oats, you didn't hear it. So much for integrity--yours, Rolf's, Mr. Wright's, and Judge McVey's! I'm losing my rational senses, too. The "Oops" must be another item for you all to discuss in private chambers. You people are all bonded so firmly in your arrogant judicial sanctity. There is no such thing as justice. Truth doesn't matter.

My head sinks onto my arms. The tears spill over. The sobs rack forth. I feel Don's fingers gently kneading my neck and back. I raise my head and scream, "THE JUSTICE---SYSTEM---SUCKS!"

As the words echo off the drab yellow walls of the conference room, I manage a chuckle and blow my nose, "At least the vocabulary I learned over my years spent with high school kids was worth something today when all other words fail me!"

Don's words are gentle for me, "Come on, Betty. It really is finally over."

Don rises, shakes Mr. Oats' hand, and hefts our box of papers. Mr. Oats shakes my hand, too. His hand is cold. Mine is numb. Whatever goodbye words we exchange are equally cold, numb, meaningless.

CHAPTER 41

~oxo~

My Personal Debriefing

DON AND I make our departure from Mr. Oats, from the courthouse, from Ridgeview. During the three-hour ride home, my body and my brain revel in surrealism.

My mouth blabs incessantly as if it is disconnected from my body. "It's over, isn't it? I hate the legal system. I hate lawyers. They are a step below used car salesmen. They're even lower than gypo loggers! There is no such thing as right. I'm not even sure there is truth. Mr. Oats said he hadn't heard the word *Oops*, but you and I heard it. He said the judge's final ruling might not have been completely fair, but it was the judge's ruling and it was final. He said I should be pleased with the fact that half of his fees and all of Mr. Wright's fees were Rolf's responsibility out of Rolf's half of the settlement, and right now they amount to about $13,000. Who the hell cares? Those numbers don't mean anything to me."

Don drives on silently. The countryside passes.

"Don, you know the will stated I would be allowed to settle Mother's estate in an unobstructed fashion. That did not occur. Rolf was an obstructionist throughout the guardianship, and for sure after Mother's death right up through this final court day today.. It strikes me as wrong I had to endure his ranting and raving, his lies and personal attacks, his personal venom spewed all over all parties in the court room and out of the courtroom whether he was speaking, hyperventilating, coughing yucky hunks of lung junk or just sitting giving off his own brand of despicable stench!

Furthermore, I find it offensive I have to be responsible for *any* attorney fees that allow him to do this--and especially fees to an attorney who turned out at my most strategic time of need to be ineffective in defending or staving off the attacks to me personally these last two days.

311

"Lawyers generally belong to a sleazy, closed fraternity that establishes its own discretionary form of justice. The laws of our land through precedence have perpetrated this judicial arrogance. And small people, for all of their altruistic or noble callings founded in Biblical teachings and convictions internalized from childhood on, cannot fairly compete on the legal turf. The turf is tipped in favor of the judicial hierarchy, and over years of history the slant of the turf has become more acute as the judicial side attracts greater numbers of sharp but greedy, overpaid, holier-than-thou judicial zealots.

"In this particular court case the numbers are small, but the percentages are significant. The total of the legal fees for the estate, including all attorney services--property access, cheating logger, and all--was $17,702.68 up to the time of the final estate hearing. At the time of settlement Mr. Oat's bill was $10,873, plus the $2,000 for filing estate taxes, plus maybe $13,000 to Mr. Wright. The grand total equals $43,575.68. All of this to settle the earthly legal affairs of two people who worked very hard, who loved both of their children, who did not have their legal affairs in order and whose total earthly possessions amounted to the sale of their home netting $45,000, sale of timber netting $28,718.83, income from logging lawsuit bringing $13,500, sale of Whidbey property netting $98,582.28. The grand total of this whole estate was $185,801. The legal fees required a bit more than 23.5%. This is just and fair?"

Don drives on. The countryside passes.

It's a month before I am able to quell the anger and bitterness of the two day trial to even ask what am I left with that's positive? My greatest sense of relief comes because IT IS OVER! Flawed as it may be, the only means by which there could have been some semblance of a conclusion to the Malfait tragedy had to be through the court system. The public documentation was momentous. It's written history. It's over!

Did justice occur? No! Was what was morally right recognized and rewarded? No! Were there any winners as a result of the legal process? No!

Guardianships are thankless, painful assignments designated by our social and judicial system to put controls on unsavory and immoral human conditions until death can be a rescuer.

Doing what is right has no monetary value, and it will not be rewarded in the judicial system. There is a satisfaction in knowing I did an impossible task and I did it right to the best of my ability over extended time periods and against great odds--when no one was watching--and when everyone was watching.

Adversity gave me recognition and use of my faith in traveling through uncharted waters and being solely dependent upon God.

I have an appreciation for *purple tulips* that exceeds any other feelings or emotions of my life. Does that make up for the years of emotional and physical expenditure? Does that make up for the episodes of humiliation and degradation perpetrated by the persons whom I loved most in all the world? None of the old hurts matter at this point.

I have had a walk in this life with God who really does know me--who heard my anguished cries from the six billion of his other children who inhabit the earth, and who enveloped me mercifully in his care. This God gave me strength and wisdom far beyond my own abilities. This God comforted me, renewed me, forgave me and sent me back again and again until the task was completed.

I know I made mistakes, but I have an enormous sense of satisfaction in having answered my Mother's initial call for help, in having persisted for years to do the tasks which I saw to be needed and to be morally right. I know I started from a self-centered base of using my intellect shored up with a shallow smattering of past-learned Sunday school lessons and noble platitudes. I know that in my anguish and frustration I cried out, maybe sometimes disrespectfully, but I know God heard me.

Dear God, in these last years I have had an abundance of purple tulips. They're usually not in the cracks of the side-walk and not always in December, and most certainly not because I commanded you to send them--but they are constant--they are there when I ask--and best of all, they are there often when I don't ask.

Purple tulips have allowed me to develop faith and compassion far beyond the thin insecurities of my intellectual searching.

Dear God, I truly do thank you for Alzheimer's and purple tulips.

As life progresses, may I someday thank you for Alzheimer's, purple tulips--and Rolf!

Afterword

IT'S BEEN A long time since summer, 1980, and the crisis which caused permanent splintering of our family. Dad died February 2, 1991, and Mother died January 23, 1996. There was no further communication between myself and my brother Rolf—until he sued me! That event resulted in a two- day trial, which ended the Malfait saga in June, 1997.

I lost both my parents. I lost my brother. I lost a significant part of myself.

But on a cold, dark blustery late afternoon in September, 2001, the ringing of the telephone shatters the quiet of our evening. A very official female voice identifies herself as the Chief Deputy Coroner of a nearby county west of the City of Ridgeview. After a sequence of questions which satisfies her obligation that she is speaking to the correct party, she says, "I'm sorry to inform you that your brother, Rolf Malfait, suffered a cardiac arrest in front of the Quick-Stop Market and Video Store, a business in the community of Columbia Park, just west of Astoria, Oregon, early this morning. He was taken to the local hospital in Astoria, where he was pronounced dead on arrival.

"He was carrying an envelope in his shirt pocket with a local person's name on it. The content of the letter indicated the woman to be a friend of Rolf's. A call to her gave us your name and a city where you lived a few years back. I apologize for the extended time having elapsed from the time of Rolf's death until now, but because you had moved it took me a while to find your current address and phone number.

"Records show Rolf had been seen at that same hospital previously. He was taking meds for high chloresterol, diabetes, and heart failure. According to the doctors who attended him at the ER, he died of ventricular arrhythmia, which was confirmed by the County Coroner who examined him later. The Coroner's report says the interval between the onset of his attack and his death was less than a minute. He was wearing a heart monitor which identified this detail precisely.

"There appeared to be no foul play in the circumstances of his death.

"The body currently is at Peace Haven Chapel By The River in Columbia Park.

"Rolf did have two guns on him at the time of his attack. Therefore a Sheriff was called to the scene, and the guns were taken by the officer, Sergeant Boyd Hinton. The sergeant also took any other personal items that were on the body. As next of kin, you may retrieve those guns from the Sheriff and any other personal items.

"The Coroner placed a hold on the body until Monday, October first, until our people could locate you as next of kin. You may want to call the mortician, Mr. Ross Hanson. I will give you his name and number before we end this conversation.

"Do you have any questions?"

"If I don't call Mr. Hanson, what happens to the body?"

"You have a right to refuse to claim the body. As next of kin, you are under no obligation to deal with your deceased brother any further. It is only my obligation to identify next of kin and to apprise you of the circumstances. I'll give you the appropriate names and phone numbers, and whatever your decision is will be acceptable to county officials. That decision is purely up to you. Again, you are under no legal obligation in regard to the body or closure of any other business of the deceased."

Over the next three weekends, Don and I work together to clean up another Malfait mess. It had its own complicated twists and turns, as much of life does—but as mysterious as some of it was, it is not going to be another book for me to write. Rolf was indeed an intriguing character, but he should have written his own memoir. The parts of the family story which I feel are worthy of print offering lessons and learnings for a reading audience have been expressed in my first book, *OLD PARENTS AND PURPLE TULIPS* and its sequel, *GUIDING MOTHER HOME.*

Appendix 1

RESOURCES FOR CAREGIVERS:

In Washington State, Kitsap County and nearby areas around Hood Canal, the most detailed list of resources for caregivers is found in the very well done and concise booklet entitled

KITSAP PENINSULA SENIOR RESOURCES
Authors: Elaine Phillips, RN, WHUP and Stephen Boyd
e-mail at guide@olypen.com
toll-free phone at 1-866-379-3710
FAX at (360) 379-3710
P.O. Box 1717, Port Townsend, WA 98368-0160

In other communities general places for seeking caregiving support and/or assistance might be

1) Alzheimer's Association Support Groups
2) Alois Association publicatons
3) Mayo Clinic Research Papers
4) Recommendations from doctors, nurses and other hospital staff, attorneys specializing in senior services or estate planning
5) Elder Abuse Service also called Adult Protective Service (APS)
6) Local Sheriff's Office or Police Department
7) Food Assistance Programs
8) Home Health Care

9) Adult Family Homes/Adult Foster Care
10) Nursing Homes and Dementia Care Facilities
11) Assisted Living Facilities
12) Respite Care Services
13) Senior Centers
14) Long Term Care Ombudsman (County Position)
15) Church Referrals such as Catholic Community Services, Lutheran Community Services, Elder Volunteers, and Comfort Keepers
16) Hospice
17) Adult Day Care Programs
18) General Hospitals and Clinics

Appendix 2

QUESTIONS TO THINK ABOUT / WHAT WOULD YOU DO?

Having been a career teacher, one of the author's goals in telling her story and publishing it was to be helpful to others who may face similar situations in becoming the parents of their parents. The following questions are added to the story to give readers opportunity for thought to prepare for this part in their life, hopefully to stimulate conversation in families, book clubs, church groups, or around the office water cooler.

1) Did you learn anything from this story which you could apply to your own life? If I were the author, what would I have done differently?

2) If you were part of this family what would you have done differently?

3) Do you have a will? Has it been updated in the last 5 years? Is it filed with someone?

4) Do you have a Health Directive / Living Will? Is it filed with your doctor? Is it in an identifiable place in your home?

5) Do you know the difference in a Power of Attorney for another person and a Durable Power of Attorney? Do you know what rights the person gives up when they give a Durable Power of Attorney to

another person? Do you know when a Durable Power of Attorney goes into affect?

6) Do you know what a Guardianship is? Do you know when one needs to apply for a Guardianship?

7) Do you understand "transfer of assets?"

8) Do you know the difference between Medicare and Medicaid?

9) Do you know what an "ad litem" figure is?

10) If you buy or own acreage or a home property, do you have a legal access to it? Who holds the deed to the property? Is the deed registered?

11) Have I done my own legal paperwork and directives in preparation for the end of my life?

12) What decisions, directives, and legal paperwork do I need to do?

13) Have I talked with my spouse, significant other, family members regarding my wishes? Have I written it down and had it notarized or made as codicil to my will? Do I know what a codicil is?

14) Have I named an executor of my will? Did I ask that person's permission to do that task for me?

15) Have I appointed a Durable Power of Attorney?

16) Have I gathered all my important paperwork and secured it in a safe place or a safety deposit box?

17) Likewise, have I secured all insurance policies? Have I updated beneficiaries for life insurance policies, IRAs, and other investment assets and household and personal gifts? Are these directions clear, labeled or directions in writing?

18) Do I have a burial plot? Do I wish to have a funeral? Do I wish to be cremated? Do I want my ashes to be placed in a vault or shared with loved ones in urns or scattered in some manner? If the latter, where? Do I wish to have a memorial service? Have I written out elements I would like to have in any kind of service, such as favorite Bible verses, poems, memories, pictures ?

19) Have I written an obituary?